Literature and Censorship in Renaissance England

Also by Andrew Hadfield

A VIEW OF THE PRESENT STATE OF IRELAND (*co-editor with Willy Maley and Edmund Spenser*)

EDMUND SPENSER (*editor*)

LITERATURE, POLITICS AND NATIONAL IDENTITY: Reformation to Renaissance

LITERATURE, TRAVEL AND COLONIALISM IN THE ENGLISH RENAISSANCE, 1540–1625

REPRESENTING IRELAND: Literature and the Origins of Conflict, 1534–1660 (*co-editor with Brendan Bradshaw and Willy Maley*)

SPENSER'S IRISH EXPERIENCE: Wilde Fruyt and Salvage Soyl

STRANGERS TO THAT LAND: British Perspectives of Ireland from the Reformation to the Famine (*co-editor with John McVeagh*)

THE ENGLISH RENAISSANCE, 1500–1620

THE ETHICS IN LITERATURE (*co-editor with Dominic Rainsford and Tim Woods*)

Literature and Censorship in Renaissance England

Edited by

Andrew Hadfield
Professor of English
University of Wales
Aberystwyth

First published 2001 by
PALGRAVE
Houndmills, Basingstoke, Hampshire RG21 6XS and
175 Fifth Avenue, New York, N. Y. 10010
Companies and representatives throughout the world

PALGRAVE is the new global academic imprint of
St. Martin's Press LLC Scholarly and Reference Division and
Palgrave Publishers Ltd (formerly Macmillan Press Ltd).

ISBN 0–333–79410–9

This book is printed on paper suitable for recycling and
made from fully managed and sustained forest sources.

A catalogue record for this book is available
from the British Library.

Library of Congress Cataloging-in-Publication Data
Literature and censorship in Renaissance England / edited by
Andrew Hadfield.
        p. cm.
    Includes bibliographical references and index.
    ISBN 0–333–79410–9
    1. English literature—Early modern, 1500–1700—History
and criticism. 2. Censorship—England—History—16th century.
3. Censorship—England—History—17th century. 4. English
Literature—Censorship. 5. Renaissance—England. I. Hadfield,
Andrew. II. Title.
PR423 .L58 2001
363.3'1'094109031—dc21
                                                    00–054208

10   9   8   7   6   5   4   3   2   1
10 09 08 07 06 05 04 03 02 01

Printed and bound in Great Britain by
Antony Rowe Ltd, Chippenham, Wiltshire

Contents

Afterword

Notes on Contributors

Richard Burt is Professor of English at the University of Massachusetts, Amherst and the author of *Unspeakable ShaXXXspeares: Queer Theory and American Kiddie Culture* (1998) and *Licensed by Authority: Ben Jonson and the Discourses of Censorship* (1993). He is the editor of *The Administration of Aesthetics: Censorship, Political Criticism, and the Public Sphere* (1994), and co-editor of *Shakespeare, the Movie: Popularizing the Plays on Film, TV, and Video* (1997) and *Enclosure Acts: Property, Sexuality, and Culture in Early Modern England* (1994). Burt recently held a Fulbright scholarship in Berlin and is a member of the editorial board of *English Literary Renaissance*.

Janet Clare is a lecturer in English at University College, Dublin. She is the author of *Art Made Tongue Tied by Authority* (1990, 2nd edn 1999) and numerous articles on Renaissance literature in journals and collections of essays.

Richard Dutton is Professor of English at Lancaster University, where he has taught since 1974. He has published widely on early modern theatre and its reception, on ideas of authorship, and on censorship. His publications include *Mastering the Revels: the Regulation and Censorship of English Renaissance Drama* (1991), *Jacobean Civic Pageants* (ed.) (1995), *Ben Jonson: Authority: Criticism* (1996), *Women Beware Women and Other Plays by Thomas Middleton* (ed.) (1999) and *Buggerswords: Licensing and Authorship in Early Modern England* (2000).

Andrew Hadfield is a Professor of English at the University of Wales, Aberystwyth. He is the author of *Literature, Politics and National Identity: Reformation to Renaissance* (1994), *Spenser's Irish Experience: Wilde Fruit and Salvage Soyl* (1997), *Literature, Travel and Colonial Writing in the English Renaissance, 1545–1625* (1998) and *The Blackwell Guide to the English Renaissance, 1500–1620* (2000). He is the general editor (with Paul Hammond) of the Arden Critical Companions series and is currently working on a book on Shakespeare and political culture.

Arnold Hunt is a Research Fellow at the University of Nottingham. His book *The Art of Hearing: English Preachers and Their Audiences, 1590–1640* is forthcoming from Cambridge University Press.

David Loades is Professor of History Emeritus at the University of Wales, Bangor. He is the author of numerous works on early modern England, including *Politics and the Nation: Obedience, Resistance and Public Order* (1973), *The Reign of Mary Tudor* (2nd edn 1991) and *Power in Tudor England* (1997). He is currently editing John Foxe's *Actes and Monuments of the Christian Church*, a major project sponsored by the British Academy.

Stephen Longstaffe teaches English and drama at Saint Martin's College in Lancaster. He has written on Marlowe, Shakespeare's histories, and the history play genre.

Richard McCabe is a fellow of Merton College, Oxford, and university Reader in English. He is the author of numerous studies of early modern literature, including *Joseph Hall: a Study in Satire and Meditation* (1982), *The Pillars of Eternity: Time and Providence in The Faerie Queene* (1989), and *Incest, Drama and Nature's Law, 1550–1700* (1993). He has edited Edmund Spenser's *Shorter Poems* (1999).

Annabel Patterson is Professor of English at Yale University, having previously held a number of distinguished chairs in the United States. She is the author of many books, including *Censorship and Interpretation* (1984); *Fables of Power: Aesopian Writing and Political History* (1991) and *Reading Holinshed's Chronicles* (1994).

Alison Shell is a lecturer in the Department of English Studies, University of Durham. She is the author of *Catholicism, Controversy and the English Literary Imagination, 1558–1660* (1999) and numerous other articles and essays on early modern literature and religion. She is currently working on a study of early modern Catholicism and orality.

Preface

This collection of essays grew out of a colloquium, 'Literature and Censorship in Renaissance England', held at Gregynog Hall, Newtown, Wales, 18–19 July 1999. I organized the colloquium because I was keen to gather together a host of different perspectives on the question of censorship in the Renaissance and see whether any issues could be clarified or resolved. The results are largely enshrined in this book, and I will leave it up to readers to decide how far I have succeeded or failed in my aims.

I was delighted that so many of the principal participants in the debates were able to attend what proved to be an enjoyable event. My thanks to Richard Burt, Janet Clare, Cyndia Clegg, Arnold Hunt, David Loades, Stephen Longstaff and Alison Shell, for giving such stimulating and excellent papers. Richard Dutton, Barbara Freedman, Richard McCabe and Annabel Patterson were unable to attend the event but contributed essays later. My thanks also to the other participants, Tina Krontiris, Ceri Sullivan and Greg Walker, for contributing to the discussions, and those staff and students who made the journey from Aberystwyth and helped with the often tedious and thankless business of making the event run smoothly (and agreeing to repeat the mantras I taught them, 'It's not going as badly as you think it is'; 'They don't really hate you'; 'The train will be here soon'): Claire Jowitt, Rebecca Moss, David Shuttleton, Michael Smith and Teresa Walters. Joan Crawford and June Baxter, the English Department Secretaries at Aberystwyth, were a further help, as were the reprographic unit at the university and the staff at Gregynog Hall. A grant from the Learned Societies fund at Aberystwyth made the event possible.

List of Abbreviations

BIHR	*Bulletin of the Institute of Historical Research*
CSPD	*Calender of State Papers, Domestic Series*
EC	*Essays in Criticism*
EHR	*English Historical Review*
ELH	*English Literary History*
ELR	*English Literary Renaissance*
FQ	*The Faerie Queene*
HJ	*The Historical Journal*
HLQ	*The Huntington Library Quarterly*
IHS	*Irish Historical Studies*
IMC	Irish Manuscripts Commission
JBS	*Journal of British Studies*
JHI	*Journal of the History of Ideas*
MLR	*Modern Language Review*
MP	*Modern Philology*
MRTS	*Medieval and Renaissance Texts and Studies*
N&Q	*Notes and Queries*
P&P	*Past and Present*
PRO	Public Record Office
RD	*Renaissance Drama*
RES	*Review of English Studies*
R&R	*Renaissance and Reformation*
SEL	*Studies in English Literature, 1500–1900*
Sh.S.	*Shakespeare Survey*
SP	*Studies in Philology*
Sp.St.	*Spenser Studies*
SQ	*Shakespeare Quarterly*
STC	*A Short Title Catalogue of Books Printed in England, Scotland, and Ireland, and of English Books Printed Abroad, 1475–1640*, compiled by A. W. Pollard and G. R. Redgrave (1926).
TLS	*Times Literary Supplement*
UTSE	*University of Texas Studies in English*
Wing	*Short-title Catalogue of Books Printed in England, Scotland, Ireland, Wales, and British America, and of English Books Printed in Other Countries, 1641–1700*, compiled by Donald Wing, 2nd edn 1994.
YES	*The Yearbook of English Studies*

Chronology

1605–25	James burns various books at Paul's Cross.
1606	'Acte to restraine Abuses of Players'.
1610–22	Sir George Buc serves as Master of the Revels.
1614	Sir Walter Raleigh's *History of the World* called in by James.
1620–1	James issues proclamations warning his subjects not to write and talk about matters of state.
1622–3	Sir John Astley serves as Master of the Revels.
1623	James issues proclamation ordering his subjects to comply with decrees of Stationers' Company.
1623–73	Sir Henry Herbert serves as Master of the Revels.
1624	*A Game at Chess* suppressed.
1632	Printers required to include an imprimatur in published books; Archbishop Laud censors William Prynne's *Histriomastix*.
1637	Star Chamber decree to regulate printing.
1642	Theatres closed.
1643	Ordinance for the Regulating of Printing passed by parliament to control growth of printing presses.
1645–6	Licensing of newsbooks.
1647–8	Revival of drama suppressed.
1653	Act for the Regulation of Printing to control unlicensed press.
1660	Theatres reopen.

1
Introduction: the Politics of Early Modern Censorship

Andrew Hadfield

How and why were books censored in early modern England? Was it the case, as many have argued after F. S. Siebert, that a tyrannical state apparatus sought to silence the voices of potentially rebellious citizens?[1] Or, were the regimes of Elizabeth and James actually quite indifferent to what entered the medium of print unless a specific crisis loomed? Was there a game of cat and mouse played out between censor and writer, or is such a model rather too neat to approximate to the messy truth? The role of the censor has become a central concern of literary scholars, historians and other commentators on the English Renaissance. The answers given to the questions posed above go a long way to determining how we imagine and read the literature and culture of the sixteenth and seventeenth centuries.

It is clear that there is a lively and productive debate continuing among historians and scholars of censorship. Different readers configure the surviving evidence in divergent, sometimes mutually exclusive ways. All agree on the key cases and pieces of evidence: the calling in of John Stubbs' *The Discoverie of a Gaping Gulf* (1579); the censorship of key passages in Holinshed's *Chronicles* (1577, 1587); the Marprelate Crisis (1588–9); the 1599 Bishops' Ban of satire and epigrams (1599); the calling in of Dr John Hayward's *The First Part of the Life and Raigne of King Henrie the IIII* (1599); and the scandal over Thomas Middleton's *A Game at Chess* (1624). But how should each case be read and what – if any – connections are there between these examples and events?

Janet Clare, in an indispensable work on the subject, has made a strong case that the government authorities launched a coherent and systematic attack on the freedom of expression of the citizens it sought to rule and control, limited simply by the inefficiencies of the mechanisms they employed. Clare argues that 'the system of actual and discursive censorship which operated under Elizabeth I and James I was dynamic, unstable and unpredictable'. Individual works may have escaped from the eye of the censor but 'all the plays of our period were written in the shadow of the censor and ... no dramatist could unchain his thoughts from the agent of that most arbitrary and punitive instrument of state control.'[2] Clare argues that the Master of the Revels, the position held by the court official responsible for the relationship between the monarchy and professional playwrights and players, became 'the state's dramatic censor' after his role was expanded in 1581 and his office made 'a centralised agency of control'.[3] Clare points to a number of textual changes and omissions in plays and suggests that these were the result of the Master of the Revels insisting on cuts to prevent – usually political – offence. For example, Clare points out that in the folio text of Ben Jonson's play, *Cynthia's Revels* (first acted in 1600), a few lines appear which were absent from the earlier quarto text and which show a courtier trying to promote himself as the queen's favourite through his skill in dancing. Clare suggests that these lines were probably excluded because they probably referred to the rise of Sir Christopher Hatton, who was first noticed by Elizabeth when dancing and later became Lord Chancellor: 'The omission of these lines may well have been forced upon Jonson: precisely because of its strain of truth, the satire has a dangerous edge in making not only the favourite, but implicitly also the royal patron, its target.'[4]

A contrary case has recently been made by Cyndia Clegg. She argues that there was no grand plan of censorship, as many had previously assumed, but that censorship was an unplanned reaction to specific incidents that threatened to cause the government political problems or embarrassment: 'Press censorship was less a part of the routine machinery of an authoritarian state than an *ad hoc* response – albeit authoritarian – to *particular* texts that the state perceived to endanger the exercise of its legitimate and necessary authority [Clegg's emphasis].'[5] For Clegg, censorship was never part of a larger design: 'actual practices in government and the printing trade reveal multiple religious, political, economic, and social interests competing for expression and control.'[6] Clegg's analysis of the censorship of John Stubbs' *A Gaping Gulf* stands as a pointed contrast to Clare's approach to the question, and serves to illustrate how she reads the surviving evidence. Clegg argues that the book, which was an open appeal to the queen and her advisers not to marry François, Duke of Alençon, 'provoked suppression and the prosecution of its perpetrators because not to do so would have jeopardized Elizabeth's foreign policy.'[7] Stubbs, according to Clegg, pushed the queen into a position where, 'had she not proceeded by law against the libelers, she would have been perceived as ineffectual in domestic affairs.'[8] Stubbs, who had his right hand severed, as did the distributor of the book, William Page, was undoubtedly unfortunate that his book was as successful as it was, with a copy sent to the Pope and translations into French and Italian being produced. But his punishment did not prevent him from enjoying a long career in parliament afterwards, indicating that once the sentence had been passed and the consequences suffered, the incident was over. As Clegg points out, many similar criticisms of Elizabeth's plans were made elsewhere, including an open letter by Sir Philip Sidney. But these did not find their way into print and so risk widespread distribution in foreign, hostile states.[9]

Another perspective is provided by Richard Dutton, in his study of the office of the Master of the Revels. Dutton takes a different line to that of Janet Clare on dramatic censorship, one which might be read alongside the arguments of Cyndia Clegg. Dutton argues that the Master of the Revels was less a censor than an intermediary between the court and playwrights and performers. His role was to arbitrate between factions to ensure that a legitimate political process could take place, so that he was 'within the spectrum of court opinion, a consensus figure, there to filter out contentious material or over-personal comment but not to stifle all debate.'[10] Any problems and controversies that did occur, Dutton suggests, were not due to ideological conflict or repression, but 'occurred because the normal checks-and-balances had broken down, the conditions for reciprocity were temporarily missing.' Often patronage networks and other forms of allegiance failed to ensure straightforward and trouble-free relations between the theatre and the court.[11]

There is some corroborating evidence for Dutton's conclusions in other recent studies of the Jacobean court. Peter McCullough, in his study of Elizabethan and Jacobean sermons, has shown how often preachers were permitted not simply to advise but to criticize the incumbent monarch to the extent that Lent sermons at court 'dramatized the nation's religious divisions'.[12] A preacher so harangued the queen on the first Sunday of Lent in 1579, arguing that if she married the Duke of Alençon the country would go to rack and ruin, that she 'rose from her window seat, turned her back to the pulpit, and walked out'.[13] Significantly, she did not discipline him, in marked contrast to the fate of the unfortunate John Stubbs and William Page.

McCullough and Dutton argue that the court of James was even more liberal and tolerant. McCullough argues that directly contrary messages were received from the king's pulpit in 1614, 'one from the Calvinist Dean of the King's Chapel ... and another from the king's favourite Armenian preacher'. Such diversity shows that 'inside James's very household, we find further evidence of his masterly balancing of "inherently antipathetic religious tendencies" through delicate manipulation of patronage.'[14] Dutton argues that by the 1620s, 'freedom of speech [was] accorded to the king's advisers and ... by an unofficial extension (and suitably codified) to the drama of the day.' The Lord Chamberlain, Sir William Herbert, Earl of Pembroke, had 'a shrewd sense of the significance in the political dialogue of the day, both at court and in the public theatres,' and so made his relation, Sir Henry Herbert, Master of the Revels, a post he held from 1623 until the closing of the theatres in 1642.[15]

Herbert's long career can clearly be judged a success in most ways. He appears to have been keen to continue the lively, varied and politicized culture which existed at the Jacobean court and in the playhouses. Nigel Bawcutt has commented that this may not have been entirely due to political principle: '[I]t was in Herbert's interest to have the theatre in a vigorous and flourishing condition, and part of his activity as a censor was designed not to enfeeble the drama but to protect it and make it less vulnerable to Puritan objection.'[16] Herbert was, nevertheless, aware of his responsibilities and his brief to license plays. As he commented in 1633, plays needed to be scrutinized by him, 'since they may be full of offensive things against church and state; ye rather that in former times the poetts tooke greater liberty than is allowed them by mee.'[17] But if this makes Herbert sound like a keen censor we should bear in mind that he licensed Middleton's *A Game at Chess*, the most notorious case of non-censorship in Renaissance England (see Richard Dutton's chapter below, pp. 50–71).[18] We should also note that the remark was made just after a number of serious scandals involving plays which received licences, such as John Fletcher's *The Woman's Prize, or the Tamer Tamed* and William Prynne's *Histriomastix*, and that 'several major examples of dramatic censorship date from 1633 and 1634.'[19] Furthermore, Herbert, who was notorious for his objection to oaths, appears to have based his decisions more on plays' blasphemy and indecency rather than their political unsuitability.

Documents surviving from Herbert's period in office also provide evidence on other major questions of the role and practice of censorship. Having licensed John Shirley's play, *The Ball*, Herbert witnessed an early performance of it and was scandalized by what he saw:

> Ther was divers personated so naturally, both of lords and other of the court, that I took it ill, and would have forbidden the play, but that Biston [Christopher Beeston, an actor-manager] promiste many things which I founde faulte withall should be left out, and that he would not

suffer it to be done by the poet any more, who deserves to be punisht; and the first that offends in this kind, of poets or players, shall be sure of publique punishment.[20]

Several points arise from this entry. First, given that Herbert had licensed the play two days earlier, does this suggest that he did not read the works carefully, perhaps through pressure of time? Or, had the author smuggled through a work the satirical purpose of which only became apparent when it was acted, the script appearing innocuous enough?[21] Does the wounded tone of the note suggest that Herbert is attempting to compensate for his error, at least in word, and probably had no serious intention of carrying out his severe-sounding threats? Given that the theatres were closed in 1642, perhaps Herbert needed to cover himself against charges of weakness and complicity.[22] Indeed, although the note seems straightforward, it is a tantalizing piece of evidence that begs as many questions as it answers.

Herbert's papers illustrate another dilemma facing historians of early modern censorship. When marks survive in play texts, can we be confident that we know who made them? An interesting case is that of *The Honest Man's Fortune*, by John Fletcher, John Ford and Philip Massinger. The play was first licensed by Sir George Buc, Master of the Revels from 1610 until 1622, in 1613.[23] The original licence appears to have gone astray when attempts were made to revive the play in 1625, and Herbert granted a licence after scrutinizing the text. The manuscript contains a number of short passages 'so heavily deleted as to be almost illegible, and a larger number of passages have been marked for deletion by enclosure in lines or loops.'[24] The problem is, as Bawcutt points out, that 'none of these markings can be definitely attributed to Herbert ... and it is unlikely that he minutely scrutinized the play, since it contains numerous oaths that he would have deleted' (marks in Herbert's hand show that he was usually most concerned to prevent oaths and profane comments).[25] In 1623, Herbert had re-licensed *The Winter's Tale* on the word of John Hemmings (another actor-manager) that 'there was nothing profane added or reformed', suggesting that the same process could well have been applied to *The Honest Man's Fortune*.

If this is true, then it is most likely that 'the markings were made before the manuscript was sent to Herbert, and reflect the actors' understanding of what he would be likely to find offensive.'[26] Although some oaths remain, a number have been deleted, and a few topical satirical references have also been removed. However, other marks suggest revision and careful editing rather than fear of censorship, including the last 11 lines of the play (although 'stet' appears in the margin). As Richard Burt has concluded in his careful analysis of Thomas Middleton's *The Second Maiden's Tragedy*, 'Editing and censorship ... overlap ... the practice of using the same marks by the censor and by actors, authors, and bookkeepers in the playhouse suggests that censorship and theatrical revision were understood as parallel, complementary activities, not as opposed or different in kind.'[27] For Burt, there can be no original moment of the text as the author designed it which has been repressed or hidden, because all texts already exist as forms of negotiation between cultural and political authorities and are never pure: 'Any search for the origin of censorship will be frustrated by an infinite regression: court censorship (defined in its repressive and productive senses) generates self-censorship in the actors and the author that may be regarded with equal validity either as being an anticipation of court censorship or as following after the suggestions and demands of the censor.'[28]

Burt's comments serve to complicate the generally held liberal assumption that censorship is simply the repression of legitimate freedom. Deborah Shuger takes the argument a stage further – at least, in one direction – and makes a strong defence of the practice of censorship which she sees as essential for the establishment of civil society. Shuger argues that modern readers 'identify subversion with ideological critique' and political opposition, whereas the real purpose of censors was to prevent defamation and the spread of slander.[29] Shuger cites Edmund Spenser's famous image of the Blatant Beast, with its multiple tongues, firing out 'licentious words and hatefull things / Of good and bad alike, of low and hie', to illustrate what she sees as our misreading of the past:

> The Blatant Beast does not, of course, signify unlicensed printing but simply defamation, yet it was precisely the conviction that the latter profoundly threatened the foundations, both ethical and religious, of civil society that made it possible to perceive early modern censorship as a discipline of the Spenserian courtesy that 'spreds itselfe through all civilitie.'[30]

Shuger's point is well-taken and can be read alongside Clegg's analysis of Elizabeth's actions against dangerous books, although it is by no means so obvious that Spenser's other famous image of censorship, that of the poet, Mal(Bon)Font with his tongue nailed to a post at the court of Mercilla, can be read as a straightforward support of Elizabeth's struggle against defamation.[31] Lindsay Kaplan has also argued, although her point is rather different to that of Shuger, that we have tended to misrepresent the textual politics of the early modern period in concentrating on the question of the censorship of texts. Instead, she suggests, we should look at the laws governing censorship in terms of the wider question of slander and defamation, which would provide us with a much more productive and balanced understanding of power relations between state and individual:

> Slander can put you on the offensive; rather than defensively anticipating and perhaps incorporating your opponent's criticism into your thinking and writing, an accusation of slander enables you to delegitimate an opposing epistemological paradigm. You might not succeed in making your charge stick, but you nevertheless possess grounds to challenge your repressor. Slander offers a model of contestation, rather than repression and regulation, which demonstrates the material consequences linguistic instability has for the social order.[32]

Kaplan is responding to and attempting to revise the most influential model produced to describe the workings of censorship in the early modern period, that of Annabel Patterson. Patterson argued that both authors and censors played a 'game', the rules of which both understood. Censorship only took place – as was the case with John Stubbs' *Gaping Gulf* – when something went drastically wrong, usually with one of the sides overstepping the mark. For the most part, dangerous and subversive material could be made public, as long as it was not explicit. There existed a culture of '*functional* ambiguity, in which the indeterminacy inveterate to language was fully and knowingly exploited by authors and readers alike (and among those readers, of course, were those who were most interested in control)' [Patterson's emphasis]. As a consequence, 'authors who build ambiguity into their works have no control over what happens to them later.'[33] The reader has to base an interpretation of the text on the author's supposed intention, with the hope that the authorities cannot read the true meaning of the text, do not particularly care about the true meaning, feel that it has been sufficiently disguised to neutralize its subversive potential, or feel that the legal process would not be able to uphold their sense of the truth.[34]

A major impact of Patterson's model has been to move the question of censorship away from a straightforward analysis of what was actually censored and why, to the effects of an intellectual climate in which all writing was liable to be censored if it crossed certain boundaries. The fear of censorship may have had a far greater impact than the act of censorship itself, or, as Patterson puts it, 'The hermeneutics of censorship create their own paradoxes.'[35] Patterson suggests that such an approach can explain the changes Sir Philip Sidney made to the *Old Arcadia* when it was transformed into the *New Arcadia*. The *Old Arcadia* is a relatively straightforward work which 'offers to anyone who would listen carefully an analysis of Elizabethan culture, finding it wanting ... By working within the system, Sidney ... still maintained his commitment to a principle of moderate reformism.'[36] The *New Arcadia*, according to Patterson, shows how Sidney lost his faith that 'working within the system' could bring positive results:

> All of the other developments [apart from changes to the eclogues] – the generic shift from pastoral to chivalric romance, the massive expansion of the narrative to broaden the political perspective of the work and create the taxonomy of political theory and example ... – are consistent with a loss of confidence in indirect or covert discourse, or in messages accommodated to the forms of Elizabethan courtship.[37]

Janet Clare, while recognizing the beneficial impact of *Censorship and Interpretation*, has made an important objection to Patterson's analysis. Clare points out that Patterson has tended to assume that all literary genres and types of writing worked in the same way and were regarded as a seamless web by the authorities. But genre itself 'must to some extent determine modes of communication and evasion'. Some forms of writing clearly have to be more topical and risk drawing attention to themselves more than others:

> In the writing of romance, an author can employ allegory and fantasy to conceal actual intrigues and a network of relationships. The assumption of a cultural bargain struck between the professional playwright and those in power has to be revised in view of what we know about a body of drama which fell foul of censorship.[38]

For Clare, the rules were not so clearly on display or understood as Patterson maintains. Drama, the most dangerous and topical form of literary production, exposed the unstable and problematic nature of the alliance between rulers and writers and the central importance of censorship: 'no dramatist could unchain his thoughts from the agent of that most arbitrary and punitive instrument of control.'

The essays in this volume – many of them written by central figures in the debates outlined above – are all designed to illuminate our understanding of early modern censorship. Some adopt opposed perspectives and read the same evidence in differing ways. My hope is that by juxtaposing radically different ways of interpreting the evidence, readers will gain an insight into the problems and opportunities that surround the question of censorship, one of the most exciting and controversial subjects in literary history. I have also attempted to select a range of essays that will cover the main issues in early modern censorship from the late Elizabethan period to the Restoration. Of course, I could have extended or contracted the period covered, but, in line with my former aim, I wanted to gather together a series of arguments, and so I have let my contributors' interests help to determine the texts and issues contained in the volume. Many of the essays deal with literary texts, but I would be narrowing and distorting the history of censorship in the early modern period if I excluded histories, religious tracts and political works from the discussion. I hope the resulting compromises made satisfy most readers and stimulate those new to the subject to read more widely in the history and literature of censorship.

I have divided the book up into three sections for ease of reference and to collect debates together for readers, although no one section should be regarded as separated from any of the others. The first Part, 'Theatrical Censorship', as the title implies, contains essays dealing with the fraught relationship between drama and the authorities. Janet Clare, examining a series of plays including the *Isle of Gulls, Eastward Ho* and *Richard II*, demonstrates how censorship affected the working practice of the dramatist. Clare argues that, while there was a degree of agreed compromise and mutual understanding of what could and could not be said on the stage between theatre companies and the censor, boundaries were often crossed. According to Clare, 'textual negotiation must always have been incomplete and the interventions of the censor often unpredictable' (p. 29). The 'rules' were never as transparent as some theorists of censorship have suggested.

Stephen Longstaffe analyses the vexed and controversial question of the religious censorship of the theatre. Concentrating on the Oldcastle controversy and the play, *Sir Thomas More*, Longstaffe suggests that in the 1590s there was a concerted campaign to censor and so eliminate radical Protestant opposition to the ecclesiastical status quo, a campaign that went hand-in-hand with state-sponsored attempts to dismiss such opposition as the work of religious cranks ('puritans'). Subsequent scholarship has, more often than not, taken propaganda at face value, and so distorted not only our understanding of the content of the Elizabethan theatre, but also the relationship between the theatres in question, over-privileging the role of Shakespeare's Globe.

Richard Dutton's essay on Thomas Middleton's *A Game at Chess*, analyses one of the most frequently studied cases of censorship – or 'non-censorship', as the play was actually licensed and performed. Dutton makes the case that far from the censor – in this case, Sir Henry Herbert, Master of the Revels – failing to understand topical allusions smuggled past him by a cunning dramatist, he was all too aware of the political references in the play, but was happy to endorse them. In fact, the anti-Spanish line Middleton took was so widespread, that he did not need powerful court figures to sponsor him, as other critics have suggested must have been the case. Dutton argues that dramatists could, in fact, be extremely 'insolent' at the expense of the good and the great and would only be prevented from having their say if they went much too far.

Part II examines 'Religious Censorship'. Richard McCabe's essay scrutinizes the Bishops' Ban of 1599 when the Archbishop of Canterbury and the Bishop of London prohibited the publication of satires and epigrams, called in previously published works, and restricted the publication of histories and history plays. Most readings of this act have argued that the target was obscenity and indecency. McCabe makes a powerful case that this was simply a blind, and that the real purpose of the ban was to prohibit political discussion. What the authorities feared was the clandestine use of seemingly irrelevant or innocent subjects, often imitations of classical works, as a vehicle to smuggle in material hostile to the status quo. Alison Shell provides a subtle and historically informed reading of the fine distinctions between Protestant and Catholic poetry. Shell argues that Catholic writers often played a game of cat and mouse with the censor to disguise their work from hostile eyes, while enabling the faithful to read a true message to the faithful. However, it is hard to make a hard and fast distinction between Catholic and Protestant writing because Protestants, such as George Herbert, made use of Catholic imagery and ideas. Hence attempts to censor Catholic writing through 'the keyword-searches of a licenser' (p. 107), were always doomed to failure. David Loades provides an account of the publishing history of John Foxe's *Acts and Monuments of the Christian Church* (*Foxe's Book of Martyrs*). Foxe might not have had to face censorship himself but he defended its use as a means to 'protect the truth and suppress falsehood' (p. 124). Arnold Hunt suggests that the purpose of ecclesiastical licensing changed subtly but dramatically between 1580 and 1640, a process that can be understood only if we examine the mechanics of the licensing system as well as what has actually been censored. While late Elizabethan censors were keen not to intervene to alter an author's intention – unless it was deemed absolutely necessary – during the reign of Charles I,

Archbishop Laud tried to use his powers as chief licenser to police and control religious belief. There was no serious attempt to suppress anti-Catholic polemic *en masse*. However, criticisms of particular aspects of state religion were liable to be altered or removed.

The final Part in the book considers political censorship. I survey English writings on Ireland in the second half of Elizabeth's reign. I study the main texts in question – Spenser's *View*, Richard Beacon's *Solon his Follie*, William Herbert's *Croftus Sive De Hibernia Liber*, and Holinshed's *Chronicles* – and argue that once the Nine Years' War started in 1594, it became extremely difficult, for military as well as political reasons, to publish material on Ireland unless it was carefully disguised. Cyndia Clegg's ground-breaking survey of James I's attitude to censorship argues that James was less concerned with prohibiting his subjects from reading defamatory and subversive material than emphasizing his own importance as the monarch who was the central focus of the realm. When James publicly burned books it was 'an act of personal propaganda' (p. 183). One cannot analyse James's policy of censorship without reference to his political theories and beliefs. Annabel Patterson, following on from other essays in this collection such as those by Dutton and Shell, shows how censorship could be as productive as restrictive. Patterson suggests that Andrew Marvell was a poet and polemicist who worked especially well under a regime which placed limits to freedom of speech: 'Censorship was the kind of shade in which he peculiarly flourished' (p. 187). Patterson analyses Marvell's prose pamphlets and shows how time and again he outmanoeuvred his enemies, always writing works that were simply too enigmatic to be pinned down. Patterson also shows how it was often worse to be a censor than an author, as the political responsibilities and exposure to ridicule often made the position uncomfortable and sometimes untenable.

The collection concludes with Richard Burt's survey of images of Elizabeth from the late sixteenth century to the present, from Renaissance portraiture to television programmes. Burt provocatively suggests that we cannot properly analyse the 'censorship of Elizabeth's royal image ... without a consideration of her afterlives as a cultural icon' (p. 211). Burt points out that Elizabeth censored her own image so cannot be seen as purely the victim of censorship, which complicates our understanding of the process and practice of Renaissance censorship. Equally, Burt argues, our conception of Elizabeth and the Elizabethan age is heavily influenced by images and representations produced from the late sixteenth century onwards, and, therefore, these help to determine our conception of censorship. The afterlife inevitably becomes part of the event itself and cannot be removed as easily as we would like when we study the past.

Notes

1. F. S. Siebert, *Freedom of the Press in England, 1476–1776: the Rise and Decline of Government Censorship* (Urbana, Ill.: University of Illinois Press, 1952).
2. Janet Clare, *'Art Made Tongue-tied by Authority': Elizabethan and Jacobean Dramatic Censorship* (Manchester: Manchester University Press, 2nd edn, 1999), pp. ix, 236.
3. Ibid. p. 31.
4. Ibid. p. 105.
5. Cyndia Susan Clegg, *Press Censorship in Elizabethan England* (Cambridge: Cambridge University Press, 1997), p. 222.
6. Ibid. p. xii.
7. Ibid. p. 133.
8. Ibid. p. 134.
9. Ibid. p. 132.
10. Richard Dutton, *Mastering the Revels: the Regulation and Censorship of English Renaissance Drama* (Basingstoke: Macmillan, 1991), p. 47.
11. Ibid. pp. 46–7.
12. Peter E. McCullough, *Sermons at Court: Politics and Religion in Elizabethan and Jacobean Preaching* (Cambridge: Cambridge University Press, 1998), p. 55.
13. Ibid. p. 47.
14. Ibid. p. 114.
15. Dutton, *Mastering the Revels*, p. 231.
16. N. W. Bawcutt, ed., *The Control and Censorship of Caroline Drama: the Records of Sir Henry Herbert, Master of the Revels, 1623–73* (Oxford: Clarendon Press, 1996), p. 76.
17. Cited in ibid., p. 75.
18. Ibid. p. 65.
19. Ibid. p. 75.
20. Ibid. p. 177.
21. Ibid. p. 72.
22. See Martin Butler, *Theatre and Crisis, 1632–1642* (Cambridge: Cambridge University Press, 1984).
23. For different accounts of Buc's career, see Clare, *'Art Made Tongue-tied by Authority'*, passim; Dutton, *Mastering the Revels*, passim.
24. Bawcutt, ed., *Control and Censorship of Caroline Drama*, pp. 57–8.
25. Ibid. p. 58.
26. Ibid.
27. Richard Burt, '(Un)Censoring in Detail: the Fetish of Censorship in the Early Modern Past and the Postmodern Present', in Robert C. Post, ed., *Censorship and Silencing: Practices of Cultural Regulation* (Los Angeles: The Getty Research Institute, 1998), pp. 17–41, at p. 22. See also *Licensed by Authority: Ben Jonson and the Discourses of Censorship* (Ithaca: Cornell University Press, 1993).
28. Burt, '(Un)Censoring in Detail', p. 28.
29. Deborah Shuger, 'Civility and Censorship in Early Modern England', in Post, ed., *Censorship and Silencing*, pp. 89–110, at p. 95.
30. Ibid. p. 103.
31. See, for example, David Norbrook, *Poetry and Politics in the English Renaissance* (London: Routledge, 1984), p. 133.

32. M. Lindsay Kaplan, *The Culture of Slander in Early Modern England* (Cambridge: Cambridge University Press, 1997), p. 9.

33. Annabel Patterson, *Censorship and Interpretation: the Conditions of Writing and Reading in Early Modern England* (Madison: University of Wisconsin Press, 1984), p. 18.

34. See also John Barrell, *Imagining the King's Death: Figurative Treason, Fantasies of Regicide, 1793–1796* (Oxford: Oxford University Press, 2000).

35. Patterson, *Censorship and Interpretation*, p. 40.

36. Ibid. pp. 40–1.

37. Ibid. p. 41.

38. Clare, *'Art Made Tongue-tied by Authority'*, p. 16.

Part I
Theatrical Censorship

2
Censorship and Negotiation

Janet Clare

The Induction to John Day's *Isle of Gulls*, performed at the Blackfriars theatre by the Children of the Revels in 1606, provides some insight into the complex negotiations between playwright, players, audience and government which applied in the early modern period. Characteristic of the private theatre productions of Jonson and Marston, the play begins with on-stage auditors, here two gentlemen, questioning a player, as Prologue, about the nature of the drama. Exploiting the title's echo of the notorious and suppressed *Isle of Dogs*, of the previous decade, the first gentleman asks 'But why doth he call his play *The Ile of Gulls*, it begets much expectation.' The Prologue denies that the play contains any current political associations, maintaining that it does not 'figure anie certain state, or private government'. The first gentleman is unconvinced and persists in his suspicion of the playwright's intentions: 'Out a question, he hath promised thee some fee thou pleadest so hard for him.' Finally the prologue in mock exasperation confronts his interlocutors: 'Alas Gentleman, how ist possible to content you? you will have rayling, and invectives, which our Author neither dares nor affects . . . yet all these we must have, and all in one play, or tis already condemned to the hell of eternal disgrace.'[1] The words of the Prologue encapsulate one of the dilemmas of the early modern playwright. Audiences demanded plays which were referential and satirical in their dramatic intentions. This might betoken commercial success, but only at the attendant risk of the play's censorship or post-performance suppression.

The Induction to *The Isle of Gulls* serves as something more than merely a disingenuous expression of the Catch-22 situation of the Jacobean playwright. It also evokes certain current and related paradigms of early modern censorship which I want to explore in this paper. Negotiation, variously understood as aesthetic or pragmatic, would seem to inform current thinking on the operation of censorship. The first paradigm implies a textual act whereby a playwright might attempt to negotiate the boundaries of the permissible with both authority and his audience. The second suggests a relationship between patron and client or between the dramatist, theatrical personnel and theatrical licenser which might mitigate the operation and impact of censorship. In the case of *The Isle of Gulls*, on the premise that the author does not dare engage with contemporary satire, Day's Prologue denies that the play contains any critical or subversive material. If we take such a denial at face value, then we could say that the play is rendered innocuous by the very existence of a process of censorship. This view squares, to some extent, with Paul Yachnin's notion of the Renaissance theatre as rendered powerless through the twin pressures of censorship and commercialism.[2] Theatre must provide pleasure, Yachnin argues, and the commercial interests of the public theatres demanded that players please their audiences rather than follow what Yachnin sees as the factional preoccupations of the earlier drama. On the other hand, censorship produced indeterminacy of meaning. Thus Yachnin arrives at his idea of theatre as representing a profitable marginality. But the dialectic of the Induction to *The Isle of Gulls* and, moreover, the reaction to the play in performance suggest the very opposite. Audiences wanted – or, had come to expect by 1606 – political and satirical drama, to which demand the phenomenal success of Thomas Middleton's anti-Spanish *A Game at Chess* was later to attest.[3] As with similar paratextual denials of topical intentions in plays by Marston and Jonson, the Induction to *Isle of Gulls* cannot be read innocently. Instead of deflecting audience expectation of political resonance, the Induction serves to alert its members to the provocative and referential nature of the play. Far from employing indeterminacy, the play in performance was explicit in its satirical intentions. This much is clear from the post-production history of the play. In a letter to Thomas Edmondes, the French secretary, of 7 March 1606, Sir Edmund Hoby reported recent proceedings in the Commons: 'At this time was much speech of a play, where, in the Isle of Gulls from the highest to the lowest, all men's parts were acted of two divers nations. As I understand it sundry were committed to Bridewell.'[4] Hoby's brief reference to the enactment of all men's parts from two divers nations suggests that in performance the two dukedoms of Arcadia and Lacedemon were evocative of Scotland and England, unified by the unpopular Act of Union of 1606. At one point in the drama two Lacedemonians, Aminter and Julio – who are suitors to the daughters of Duke Basilius, a thinly veiled caricature of James I – list the oppressions and abuses suffered by their countrymen as the result of the duke's extended absence from his domain. Analogies are suggestive rather than exact and as such would not readily have been detected by a stage licenser, in this case Samuel Daniel, who had the special privilege of licensing plays for the Blackfriars company instead of the Master of the Revels.[5] If such critiques, latent in the text, were realized in performance, this would place the play in the context of anti-Jacobean plays such as *Eastward Ho*, *The Malcontent* and *The Fawn*, all of which suffered some kind of censorship or acquired a degree of notoriety soon after the accession of James I.[6] About nine months earlier Jonson and Chapman had been imprisoned for their contributions to *Eastward Ho*, in particular, a short diatribe against the Scots and a speech delivered in a mock Scottish accent presumably intended to evoke the king. Their collaborator Marston fled the city. What is clear is that in performance satirical meanings were far from indeterminate, and in the case of *The Isle of Gulls* several of the actors were imprisoned for their indiscretions in Bridewell, a short-stay prison where inmates were punished by flogging.

Yachnin's argument about plays performed in conditions of censorship producing an indeterminacy of meaning is clearly indebted to Annabel Patterson's classic thesis concerning the hermeneutics of censorship. In *Censorship and Interpretation* Professor Patterson has argued that writing assumes a multi-valency and functional ambiguity in response to the restrictions of a specific artistic milieu.[7] This is a cogent argument, satisfying the literary critic's desire to decode and deconstruct a text. Indeed, it is one with which Elizabethan writers, experienced in the use and interpretation of metaphor, allegory and parallelism, were familiar. The practice is alluded to in the anonymous play *Woodstock*, where the schoolmaster discloses that his verses on the government of Richard II may be considered libellous. But, he adds, he has safeguarded himself by adding lines, neutering the critique of the government by means of a refrain in praise of the Lord Chief Justice. Commenting on his strategy of camouflaging libel, he discloses 'The carriage of a thing is all ... I have covered them rarely.'[8]

The question is how generally applicable to drama, which operates under a different set of cultural practices and employs different rhetorical strategies, is the concept of functional ambiguity. Does the spectator interpret as the reader? What difference does the additional stimulus of performance make? And how might the theatrical licenser, who until 1606 was a different authority from the press licenser of plays, apply a different set of priorities from the latter? Responses to these questions are complicated by the concerns of genre. As in the case of dramatic satire and such plays as *Eastward Ho* and *A Game at Chess*, performance makes what is implicit explicit. John Marston, for example, was perfectly conscious of how the text could be transformed in performance, acknowledging in the address to the reader of *The Fawn* (1604) that the life of the play 'rests much in the actors' voice'.[9] The added dimension of performance allows the playwright to exploit different strategies – locution of speech, mimicry, parody and visual imagery – while allowing a certain immunity from any accusations of intentionality. Satire may have been countenanced by the censor, just as verse satire had apparently been allowed at first by press licensers prior to the Bishops' Ban of 1599 and before its full potential was released.[10] But, as the reactions to Jonson's *Poetaster*, *Eastward Ho*, *The Isle of Gulls* and *A Game at Chess* exemplify, satire appears as the genre most vulnerable to post-licensing intervention and censorship.

On the other hand, certain history plays can indeed be deconstructed to reveal multi-valency of meaning, which, in view of their subversive potential, could be regarded as a consequence of censorship. To demonstrate and yet, in the context of theatrical performance, to qualify Patterson's thesis, one has only to focus on Shakespeare's *Richard II*, a play which usefully serves as a case study of censorship. *Richard II* depicts resistance to tyranny, while articulating passive obedience, particularly in the words of John of Gaunt. In a scene not in the play's sources, Gaunt refuses to respond to the Duchess of York's plea to him to avenge the death of her husband, Thomas of Woodstock:

> GAUNT: God's is the quarrel, for God's substitute,
>   His deputy anointed in his sight,
>   Hath caused his death, the which if wrongfully,
>   Let heaven revenge, for I may never lift
>   An angry arm against his minister.

> (I.ii.37–41)

But, in view of the dramatic outcome, this fundamental expression of Tudor orthodoxy does not disclose the play's commitments. Instead, it could be said that the passage appears early in the play in order to allay the censor's suspicions that the drama might condone resistance. The same strategy of anticipating censorial objection may also dictate the Bishop of Carlisle's speech before Richard's deposition in which he expatiates at some length on the doctrine of non-resistance (IV.i.115–49). His prophecy that in consequence of Bolingbroke's act 'the blood of England shall manure the ground' – a by no means hyperbolic reference to the Wars of the Roses – has been interpreted, in conservative readings, as signifying Shakespeare's own antipathy to the idea of the king's subjects rising against him. But in the event, Bolingbroke's advance to power is achieved without impediment. To all intents and purposes, a just regime replaces an unjust one.

If, then, Gaunt's and Carlisle's words are not to be taken at face value, does the text endorse the obverse ideology of resistance to tyranny? There is no such explicit ideological expression. It is surely significant that the only illustration of popular resistance articulated in the play is circumspectly metaphorical. That takes the form of an exchange between the gardeners, which is overheard by the Queen, as they discuss the state of the kingdom in terms of a neglected and unkempt garden, accepting as inevitable the deposition of a king who has been so easily swayed by sycophants and time-servers (III.iv). But if the play offers no explicit justification of resistance countervailing its expressions of passive obedience, the action – on and off stage – undercuts the ideological position of Gaunt and Carlisle. Bolingbroke is welcomed enthusiastically by the populace. 'So many greedy looks of young and old/Through casements darted their desiring eyes/Upon his visage' (IV.ii.13–15) is York's report of his public reception. He shows politic judgement in pardoning York's son Aumerle, and in his clemency towards Carlisle. The rebellion plotted at Oxford is quashed. The murder of Richard takes place without any intimation that Carlisle's prophecies of doom may materialize. Bolingbroke assumes power, in the event, with remarkable ease. A play in performance, moreover, adds a further dimension of meaning which I think the hermeneutical theory of censorship tends to gloss over. In production, drama has the advantage of conveying meaning through spectacle and iconography. In the case of *Richard II*, the doctrine of passive obedience is subverted in Richard's actual surrender of the crown to Bolingbroke, in the image of the empty throne and in the sight of Richard being conveyed by his erstwhile subjects to the Tower. As is well known, the scene was omitted in all Elizabethan versions of the text, an omission which, I will argue later, was due to stage censorship: it seems evident that the Master of the Revels had located the play's most subversive moment.

The corollary to Professor Patterson's thesis is that there was an implicit social contract between authors and authorities which determined the text's functional ambiguity. Consequently, writers rarely overstepped boundaries. Again, in relation to theatrical censorship, I would wish to qualify this paradigm. Annabel Patterson, as a historicist critic, is keen to stress the importance of locating the text and its possible interpretation within a precise context. She is aware that texts become charged with new meanings if their political contexts are reconfigured. Interestingly, she reads *Richard II* not in the context of the mid-1590s when the text was composed and came before the stage licenser, but in that of the play's revival in 1601 on the eve of the rebellion of the Earl of Essex.[11] Once the historical contingencies of censorship are taken into consideration, it must be acknowledged that the conditions of the time were constantly shifting. But this seems to me to present problems with the idea of there being a tacit understanding between authors and authorities. Unstable political situations shape inconsistent censorship, as was the case in the late 1590s. Writers may not anticipate the changing preoccupations of censorship. In other words, if an implicit social contract existed between playwright and theatrical companies on one hand and the censoring authorities on the other, it must surely have been a provisional one. It is axiomatic that the concerns of censorship are not trans-historical and may change within a very short period. This point can be demonstrated by a consideration of the two texts of *2 Henry VI*.[12] The play was first published in 1594 as *The First Part of the Contention of the Two Famous Houses of York and Lancaster*. The provenance of this text appears to be theatrical, possibly representing a version of the play performed by Pembroke's Men which toured outside London 1592–3. The play was not published again until it appeared in the Folio of 1623. There are notable discrepancies between the two texts, but I want to focus on one area of difference, that of the reporting of the offstage Irish rebellion. In *The First Part of the Contention*, Act III, scene i, a messenger arrives imparting news to the Queen of the rebellion in Ireland:

> MESS.   Madame I bring you news from Ireland
> The wilde Onele my Lords is up in arms,
> With troops of Irish kerns that uncontrolled,
> Doth plant themselves within the English pale,
> and burnes and spoiles the country as they goe.

The development is indeed serious: the native Irish have made incursions into the Pale, the area round Dublin which was subject to English jurisdiction. At this news the Queen orders the Duke of York 'to cross the seas,/With troops of armed men to quell the pride/Of those ambitious Irish that rebel.' The dialogue continues with the Duke of Buckingham undertaking to levy an army which will 'overcome those Irish rebels'. Yet, the reference to the Irish in the Folio text becomes notably more cursory and the response to the rebellion more perfunctory. A Post simply announces: 'Great lords, from Ireland am I come amain/To signify that rebels there are up,/And put the Englishmen unto the sword.' However, York, from personal animus, though ahistorically, then suggests that Somerset be sent as regent and in the ensuing mutual recriminations there is a deflection from the Irish material. The fact that the allusion to the Irish opposition has become so unspecific in the Folio text can, I think, be attributed only to censorship. The quarto represents an early and – since it was provincial – possibly an unauthorized performance. But the wars in Ireland from the mid-1590s to the close of Elizabeth's reign came increasingly to dominate the political agenda. Hugh O'Neill, Earl of Tyrone and head of one of the great Irish clans, was engaged with Spanish support in mobilizing forces against the English with the ultimate aim of making Ulster an independent kingdom. In 1595, he assumed the title of 'the O'Neill' and in Ulster was accorded almost monarchical status. He was declared a traitor; fears intensified as successive attempts to subdue the rebels miscarried.[13] Thus, by July 1599 it was forbidden 'on pain of death, to write or speak of Irish affairs'.[14] Elizabethan policy in Ireland evidently had an impact on the drama and its censorship, but it would be inconceivable that there existed some kind of consensus with the Master of the Revels as to what could be admitted into the drama concerning Ireland. The early text of *2 Henry VI* suggests that when the play was composed, Shakespeare felt able to project a notable historical parallel. Subsequently, at some point in the play's early performance history the detail was regarded as provocative, possibly even of treasonable import, and muted by censorship. Something similar happens to the text of *Henry V*, where in the Folio the fifth chorus pays tribute to the King by offering the audience the analogous image of the Earl of Essex returning to London as 'a conquering caesar' with the Irish rebellion, which he had been sent to quell, 'broached on his sword'.[15] This, and the other speeches of the chorus, are omitted in the 1600 quarto text. In the hiatus between composition and performance, early optimism as to the success of Essex's campaign had been replaced by knowledge of its debacle as the Earl, acting independently of the Queen's orders, reached a truce with Hugh O'Neill. Self-evidently, the triumphal allusion to Essex in the final chorus must have been composed in or before 1600 and could not have been a later, anachronistic addition. Its omission from the 1600 text can be accredited either to direct censorial intervention or at the least self-censorship. What can be deduced from the instability of textual references to Ireland in these plays of the 1590s is how the vicissitudes of Elizabethan policy impinged on both representation and subsequent censorship. The very instability of the Irish situation meant that it would be difficult for playwrights to ascertain permissible boundaries in attempting to project a topicality in their material.

A model of censorship which is in some way contractual rather than oppositional tends to inform more revisionist approaches to the subject. Here patronage and its networks become an influential factor. Richard Dutton concludes his study of the Office of the Revels with the assertion that the Master was as much a friend of the actors as their overlord.[16] To some extent this represents an extension of Annabel Patterson's thesis that there was an implicit contract between authors and authorities. But whereas for Patterson negotiation is textual and aesthetic and a tacit agreement between writer and reader, Richard Dutton posits a pragmatic negotiation with the Master of the Revels as guardian of court privileges. Yet, from these different premises both scholars draw attention to instances of so-called 'non-censorship' as evidence of a system which cannot be seen in terms of opposition or oppression. Attention is drawn to the case of *Richard II* and, in particular, to the performance on the eve of the Essex rebellion. The incident is familiar and we need rehearse the details only briefly here. On 7 February 1601, the evening before the disgraced Essex and his supporters rode through the capital attempting to amass popular support, they crossed the river to the Globe theatre to see a command performance of a play about Richard II, almost certainly Shakespeare's *Richard II*, performed by the Lord Chamberlain's company. One of the actors, Augustine Phillips, was subsequently to claim at the trial of Essex that the company had initially been reluctant to perform the play since it was 'so old and so long out of use that they should have small company at it', but the offer of 40 shillings, 'more than their usual fee', prevailed.[17] Their performance was given to a group of discontented magnates who may have found encouragement for their cause in the spectacle of a successful uprising. The fact that the Lord Chamberlain's company suffered no reprisal for their command performance of *Richard II* has been cited by both Patterson and Dutton as a curious case of non-censorship demonstrating the comparative tolerance of institutional controls.[18] But in 1601 the play had already been censored so that its most provocative material, that of the deposition scene, had been removed. In focusing on the play's post-history, the bibliographical evidence of earlier censorship tends to be ignored.

There is no doubt that the censorship of the deposition scene was an act of theatrical censorship and that the Master of the Revels had reacted to this scene just as he had done to the scenes of riot in *Sir Thomas More*. Editors have been reluctant unequivocally to claim theatrical censorship here, suggesting that press censorship may be responsible instead. But the significant factor is that the play was entered in the Stationers' Register in August 1597 on the authority of a warden of the Stationers' company alone.[19] There is no mention in the register of any ecclesiastical licenser. The powers of the warden related to the establishment of copyright not censorship. It appears that *Richard II* was one of the few plays licensed for the press by the authority of the wardens and, thus, any censorship of the text which can be deduced must be traced to the theatrical censor, the Master of the Revels, Edmund Tilney.

The first three quartos of *Richard II*, as is well known, were all published without the deposition scene, which first appeared in print in the Jacobean edition of 1608. In minimizing the political significance of the scene's inclusion, it has been pointed out that only one in ten of the extant quartos advertises on the title page the additional material of the deposition 'as it was lately acted by the king's men'.[20] But might not the absence of the advertisement betray a certain apprehensiveness about the publication of previously prohibited material? In Elizabethan and Jacobean censorship there was no mechanism for the re-checking of the texts of theatrical revivals, a practice introduced by Henry Herbert as late as 1633.[21] We know from the considerable number of variant texts of the same works that when plays were revived, material which in all probability had been censored was reinstated for performance and/or print. Nevertheless, if the material was as contentious as the deposition scene, it may not have been considered wise specifically to advertise its recent inclusion in theatrical production.

The textual evidence for the censorship of *Richard II* would seem to be indisputable, independently of contextual and circumstantial detail. Such detail does, nevertheless, strengthen the case for the censor's intervention. A primary method of exposing what was deemed censorable at a particular time in the absence of a record book, is to consider a cluster of texts and examine any bibliographical anomalies. As we know, *Richard II* was produced at the height of the popularity of the Elizabethan history play. Its concerns with rebellion, resistance to the crown and passive obedience to monarchy, represented as divinely constituted, are issues which are replicated elsewhere in the canon. As Cyndia Clegg points out in her examination of Elizabethan press controls, in 1571, parliament extended the treason laws to cover any discussion of Elizabeth's succession.[22] An edginess about oblique allusions to dynastic succession is displayed in the omission of certain passages in the history plays. The copy text of the Folio *2 Henry VI*, for example, omits lines by the Earl of Warwick in which he exhorts the Duke of York to claim the crown with the assistance of the popular support which he – Warwick – will rouse (II.ii). Again, in the two texts of *3 Henry VI* there has evidently been some censorial intervention. The earlier version *The True Tragedy of Richard Duke of York*, has a much briefer version of the scene in which Henry surrenders power to Warwick and Clarence (IV.vi). In the version in the Folio, Warwick and Clarence discuss in detail the terms of the abdication and the succession. Such omissions from the earlier text suggest that in the political climate of the early 1590s the Master of the Revels disallowed full theatrical realization of a monarch surrendering power and admitting a new line of succession.

In understating the effects of censorship on the text of *Richard II* as well as the role of active censorship in general, Richard Dutton draws attention to Marlowe's *Edward II*, which is often compared to Shakespeare's play for the similarity of its theme, that of the deposition and murder of a legitimate, but weak, monarch. Suggesting that the abdication scene of *Richard II* may as likely be an addition as a censor's deletion, Dutton points out, 'Those who would argue that depicting the removal of the monarch from the throne in any circumstance was potentially subversive have to explain how the abdication scene in Marlowe's *Edward II* was allowed into print in both 1594 and 1598, with no apparent interference from any censor.'[23] But to consider *Edward II* and *Richard II* within the same compass reveals more striking dissimilarities in dramatic dynamics and ideology than parallels. Despite Marlowe's radical and shocking aesthetic of cruelty, the framework of his play is essentially orthodox. In enacting Edward's killing as an image of sodomy, Marlowe is more than simply rehearsing Holinshed. Indeed, he appears to be engaging in the emblematic method of admonitory drama, but to such devastating effect that the audience recoils from the sight in disgust. For his crime in mounting opposition to the King, Mortimer is arrested and beheaded by the King's rightful heir. The fates of the usurpers, Bolingbroke and Mortimer, could not be more strongly contrasted than in the final scenes of the two plays. In *Richard II* Bolingbroke, now crowned and acknowledged king, follows Richard's hearse, whereas in *Edward II*, Edward's son follows the hearse of his father, which supports the head of Mortimer. If the deposition and murder of a king caused the stage licenser any unease, it was countered by the reminder of the hideous fate of traitors.

A revisionist view of censorship has further emphasized the importance of patronage in securing the performance of a play or in protecting the interests of playwrights. There are undoubtedly instances where the intervention of a patron seems to have deflected criticism or reprisal, as in the case of Jonson's relationship to Esme Stuart, a Gentleman of the King's Bedchamber, following investigations into *Sejanus*.[24] But this kind of relationship was not necessarily the norm and certainly was not enjoyed by all dramatists. Here, John Marston presents an interesting case, as a dramatist whose career was shaped by the exigencies of censorship and whose plays insistently formulate a discourse on poetic liberty, censure and censorship. From his beginnings, in the non-dramatic satires, his works were not sanctioned by the authority of a patron. Marston, acutely conscious of his lack of a sponsor, is anxious to see such a role occupied instead by the judicious, well-informed reader or auditor. In *The Scourge of Villanie*, the author, 'W. Kinsayder', constructs the prefatory material around the familiar dialectic of the just, discerning reader/critic and the ignorant misjudging critic.[25] The reader is shamed into an alliance with the satirist. Yet, as is well known, verse satire was included in the Bishops' Ban on certain satirical works in 1599. The nervous tone of Marston's appeal appears to have been justified in the suppression and subsequent burning of his satires only months after their licensing and publication.

In *The Malcontent*, his first Jacobean play, Marston both recovers the objects of his non-dramatic satire and articulates strong defences of the satirist's art. The prefatory material, comprising the address to the reader and Induction, serves the same function as the preliminaries to the earlier satire, as Marston defends his intentions but implies that he cannot desist from satirical attack. The recovery of the snarling tone and style of the satires is evident in the language of Malevole, whose speech, says the usurper Duke Pietro, 'is halter-worthy at all hours' (I.ii.28). In the persona of Malevole, Marston affords the same liberty of expression to the satirist as was traditionally associated in the drama with the fool. Malevole rejoices in the fact that his disguise gives him 'that/Which kings do seldom hear or great men use-/Free speech' (I.iii.161–3). This emphasis on the imperative of free speech is, however, in marked contrast with the textual censorship of the play, specifically of lines spoken by Malevole. Three different quartos of the play were published in quick succession in 1604 and several textual excisions, reflecting irregular procedures of censorship, can be detected in one or more of the editions.[26]

Marston's lack of patronage placed him in a vulnerable position. This emerges from the reaction to *Eastward Ho*, which caused him to flee the city. His collaborators Jonson and Chapman were imprisoned, but were able to appeal to patrons who may have intervened on their behalf.[27] Marston's satiric exposure of the patron/client relationship in *The Fawn* would seem to reflect his own antipathy to seeking accommodation within the patronage network.[28] To compensate for the absence of a patron, Marston appeals boldly to the good judgement of his audience and to right-minded criticism, and he articulates concepts of freedom of speech. Yet there remains an awareness that its opposite, censure, will prevail. The ironic dedication to *Antonio and Mellida*, in which Marston appeals, as patron, to the person of 'Nobody' as 'Lord Protector of oppressed innocence', registers such uncertain, ambivalent feelings about dramatic reception. In commenting on Marston's application at the beginnings of *The Malcontent* and *The Fawn* of the Juvenalian motto *Vexet censura columbas* – the judgement goes against the doves – G. K. Hunter has made the point that it would be anachronistic to identify judgement, or *censura*, with censorship.[29] Marston, however, employs the concept of censure in the most inclusive way, incorporating both its sense of sagacious opinion and that of adverse criticism. For Marston, censure and censorship were akin. From the beginning of his career in *The Scourge of Villainie*, he projects his fear of the censuring, hostile critic who will misreport and claim to find libels in his satire. His experiences of the suppression of the satires, the textual interferences with *The Malcontent*, reactions to *The Fawn* contributing to the company's loss of royal patronage,[30] and finally the reception of *Eastward Ho*, all serve to indicate how censure could lead to censorship.

The hope of imposing some kind of self-regulatory norms on the text, expressed initially by Marston, approximates to one contemporary paradigm of early modern censorship. With the aim of moving the debate about censorship away from concepts of freedom and authority, Richard Burt, in his study of Ben Jonson, has sought to establish further definitions of censorship, in particular those of 'court' and 'market'.[31] Richard Burt focuses on critical self-consciousness, whereby a dramatist such as Jonson, by appealing to an idealized literary community, sought to regulate the circulation of his writing and to establish norms of good and bad criticism. In a sense Marston, in attacking and deriding his hostile, censuring critic, the antithesis of 'true judging eyes, quick sighted censurers', anticipated the Jonson of *Poetaster*. Burt is right to contend that more than one concept of censorship circulated in the early modern period. In theory, censorship could be as much a critical as a political or ideological act. The conclusions that I would draw from this state of affairs are, however, rather different. While Jonson – and, I would suggest, Marston – sought to legitimate such innovatory forms of censorship, they could not, as Burt implies, control the reception of their texts. State censorship proved to be more powerful than any self-regulatory literary practice which aspired to exclude it. Free speech and poetic liberty, which are often regarded as post-Enlightenment concepts, and as anachronistic in relation to the early modern period, are consistently advocated as ideals in Marston's dramatic and non-dramatic satire. Such arguments are harnessed by appealing to wise judgement and right censure, familiar from classical satire. As is apparent from the vicissitudes of his career,

Marston did not, however, succeed in countering the arbitrary hand of institutionalized censorship.

In this essay I have attempted, with reference to specific case studies, an overview of concepts of censorship from the perspective of negotiation. It is evident that the concerns of censorship could not have failed to interact with the creativity of practising dramatists and to have induced degrees of compromise, ambiguity and re-presentation of material. Yet since the parameters of the possible were continually shifting, textual negotiation must always have been incomplete and the interventions of the censor often unpredictable. It seems to me that we cannot confine the practice of censorship to any contractual arrangement or tacit understanding between writers and licensers, or between acting companies and censor. Such a paradigm does not allow for the individual responses of dramatists to the system within which they had to work or the political and ideological dynamics which underpinned early modern censorship.

Notes

1. *The Ile of Gulls*, with an Introduction by G. B. Harrison (London: The Shakespeare Association, 1936).
2. See Paul Yachnin, 'The Powerless Theater', *ELR* 21 (1991), 49–74.
3. See Janet Clare, *'Art Made Tongue-tied by Authority': Elizabethan and Jacobean Dramatic Censorship*, 2nd edn (Manchester: Manchester University Press, 1999), pp. 211–20 and Richard Dutton's Chapter 4 below.
4. In Thomas Birch, *The Court and Times of James the First*, 2 vols (London, 1848), vol. 1, pp. 60–1.
5. See Clare, *'Art Made Tongue-tied by Authority'*, p. 122.
6. See Janet Clare, 'Marston: Censure, Censorship and Free Speech', in T. F. Warton, ed., *John Marston* (Cambridge: Cambridge University Press, forthcoming).
7. Annabel Patterson, *Censorship and Interpretation: the Conditions of Writing and Reading in Early Modern England* (Madison: University of Wisconsin Press, 1984), pp. 18–23.
8. *Woodstock: A Moral History*, ed. A. P. Rossiter (London: Malone Society, 1946).
9. John Marston, *The Fawn*, ed. David A. Blostein (Manchester: Manchester University Press, 1978), p. 68.
10. See Richard A. McCabe, 'Elizabethan Satire and the Bishops' Ban of 1599', *YES* 11 (1981), 188–94; Lynda E. Boose, 'The 1599 Bishops' Ban, Elizabethan Pornography, and the Sexualization of the Jacobean Stage', in Richard Burt and John Michael Archer, eds, *Enclosure Acts: Sexuality, Property, and Culture in Early Modern England* (New York and London: Cornell University Press, 1994), pp. 185–200, and Clare, 'Marston: Censure, Censorship and Free Speech'.
11. Patterson, *Censorship and Interpretation*, p. 17.
12. For a fuller discussion of the probable censorship of these texts see Clare, *'Art Made Tongue-tied by Authority'*, pp. 60–4. Quotations are from *The First Part of the Contention, Malone Society Reprint* (Oxford, 1985) and *The True Tragedy* (in fact an octavo), Shakespeare Quarto Facsimile (Oxford, 1958).

13. See T. W. Moody, F. X. Martin and F. J. Byrne, eds, *A New History of Ireland*, vol. 3, *Early Modern Ireland* (Oxford: Clarendon Press, 1976), pp. 115–29.
14. *CSPD 1598–1601*, CCLXXI, p. 225.
15. For a full discussion of the Irish associations of *Henry V* see Stephen O'Neill, '"Irish Affairs": Representing Ireland in Sir John Oldcastle', *Proceedings of the Graduate Shakespeare Conference*, I, ed. Janet R. Costa (The Shakespeare Institute, University of Birmingham, 2000), pp. 236–45.
16. Richard Dutton, *Mastering the Revels: the Regulation and Censorship of English Renaissance Drama*, (Iowa: University of Iowa Press, 1991), p. 248.
17. *CSPD 1598–1601*, CCLXVIII, p. 578.
18. Patterson, *Censorship and Interpretation*, p. 17; Dutton, *Mastering the Revels*, pp. 100, 117, 124.
19. See Janet Clare, 'The Censorship of the Deposition Scene in *Richard II*', *RES* 41 (1990), 89–94.
20. Dutton, *Mastering the Revels*, p. 125.
21. See N. W. Bawcutt, *The Control and Censorship of Caroline Drama: the Records of Sir Henry Herbert, Master of the Revels* 1623–73 (Oxford: Clarendon Press, 1996), p. 177.
22. Cyndia Susan Clegg, *Press Censorship in Elizabethan England* (Cambridge: Cambridge University Press, 1997), pp. 32–3.
23. Dutton, *Mastering the Revels*, p. 125.
24. This is apparent from Jonson's dedication to Esme Stuart, Lord Aubigny, in the 1616 Folio text. See *Sejanus*, ed. Philip Ayres (Manchester: Manchester University Press, 1990), p. 49.
25. *The Scourge of Villanie* in *The Poems of John Marston*, ed. Arnold Davenport (Liverpool: Liverpool University Press, 1961).
26. See *The Malcontent*, ed. G. K. Hunter (Manchester: Manchester University Press, 1975), pp. xxiii–xxxi.
27. See *Eastward Ho*, ed. R. W. Van Fossen (Manchester: Manchester University Press, 1979), pp. 218–25.
28. See Clare, 'Marston: Censure, Censorship and Free Speech'.
29. Marston, *The Malcontent*, p. 20.
30. See Clare, '*Art Made Tongue-tied by Authority*', pp. 139–45.
31. Richard Burt, *Licensed by Authority: Ben Jonson and the Discourse of Censorship* (Ithaca and London: Cornell University Press, 1993).

3
Puritan Tribulation and the Protestant History Play

Stephen Longstaffe

There is a strong contemporary consensus that in early modern England there was not a widespread and intentionally repressive censorship or regulatory regime; rather, analysis of specific cases shows that interventions were often quite exceptional responses to particular crises. To use a military metaphor, this was 'smart' censorship, suppression precisely targeted in order to minimize collateral damage. One of the advantages of the 'suppression' model, Cyndia Clegg argues, is that it avoids the assumption that 'imaginative writer', 'Catholic apologist', and 'religious reformer' all wrote under the same constraints.[1] All the same, such a model is not always useful when the 'imaginative writer' does not steer clear of the material of the 'religious reformer'. The Protestant history play of the late Elizabethan and early Jacobean era is, I will argue, an example of 'smart' suppression of religious writings (and, indeed, the larger campaigns against non-conformists of which they were part) inflicting a largely underestimated amount of collateral damage upon the stage. In turn, I will argue that one particular late-Elizabethan satirical project – the stage representation of the puritan – was itself enabled by this collateral damage.

Critics tend to see the history of the early modern London theatre through Globe-tinted spectacles. I should, therefore, like to make clear that although the opening of this essay is concerned with Sir John Oldcastle, and what a mysterious change of name might tell us about the representation of the stage 'puritan' in the 1590s and beyond, it will only touch peripherally upon Shakespeare's plays. The name change is in *1 Sir John Oldcastle*, written for the Admiral's Men at the Rose by Munday, Drayton, Wilson and Hathaway, which announces itself as a reply to Shakespeare's Falstaff plays, claiming to present 'fair truth' in contrast to Shakespeare's 'forged invention'. *Oldcastle*, however, introduces one

significant 'invention' of its own to its 'fair truth'. Oldcastle's chief
persecutor was Thomas Arundel, Archbishop of Canterbury, aided by the
Bishop of London. The play substitutes the Bishop of Rochester for the
Archbishop, and omits London's Bishop entirely. This seemingly trivial
change was first pointed out by R. B. Sharpe, who concluded, reasonably
enough, that the writers did not want to upset either Whitgift, the present
Archbishop, or Bancroft, Bishop of London since 1597, possibly because of
Anthony Munday's work as a pursuivant.[2] What Sharpe did not make clear,
however, was that such an identification between past and present clerics
would have cast the play as a libellous contribution to a bloody, bitter and
one-sided struggle between the church authorities, including Whitgift and
Bancroft, and those desiring either further reformation of the church or
separation from it, a struggle which the underdogs insisted was a
persecution of the godly to parallel those of the pre-Reformation years.[3]

Whitgift became Archbishop in 1583 with a commitment to the
ecclesiastical status quo. In one of his early sermons, significantly on
Paul's letter to Titus ('Put them in remembrance, to be subject unto
principalities and powers, to obey magistrates ...'), he divided 'such as are
disobedient' into three 'sorts of persons': 'papists, anabaptists, and our
wayward and conceited persons'.[4] He quickly moved against the
'wayward and conceited' who 'will obey, but it is what they list, whom
they list, and wherein they list themselves', defining conformity in a set of
articles, and requiring the clergy, through the High Commission, to
comply with these.[5]

The methods of the Commission were controversial from the start, for it
was inquisitorial in structure, questioning only after the respondent had
sworn an *ex officio* oath that they would answer truthfully. Because it was
not a court of law, no charges need be made, witnesses produced, nor
counsel allowed. Sooner or later, the 'accused' would incriminate
themselves, and would have to abjure their 'errors'. Refusal to take the
oath was contempt, and punishable with imprisonment. Opposition was
vocal from the start. Burghley himself wrote to Whitgift in 1584 to protest
that 'I am now daily charged by councillors and public persons to neglect
my duty in not staying these your Grace's proceedings so vehement and
so general against ministers and preachers, as the Papists are thereby
generally encouraged, all ill-disposed subjects animated, and thereby the
Queen's Majesty's safety endangered.' The articles themselves were 'in a
Romish style ... so curiously penned, so full of branches and circumstances, as I think the inquisitors of Spain use not so many questions to
comprehend and to trap their preys'.[6] Whitgift slackened off, but soon,
assured of the Queen's support, continued where he had left off.

Following the Marprelate affair of the later 1580s, Whitgift uncovered evidence of organized networks of reformers, and used the High Commission and then the Star Chamber to pursue some of the leading lights in the movement. Nine prominent ministers were selected for exemplary punishment; all refused the oath and were imprisoned, though not always too onerously. Though none of them were actually formally punished, it was two and a half years before they were all released, 'worn down and all but defeated' in the words of Patrick Collinson.[7] Many other preachers were harassed by the ecclesiastical authorities, banned from preaching, ejected from universities, imprisoned and deprived of livings. John Udall, one of the most prolific and learned reformist pamphleteers, was arrested in 1590 for the felony of writing *The Demonstration of Discipline*. He was sentenced to death in 1591, and died a year later just after he had been pardoned, after spending a year and a half in prison.

The more radical separatists were more severely dealt with. Fifty-odd were arrested in the winter of 1589/90. The two separatist leaders, Barrow and Greenwood, both arrested in 1587, were eventually sentenced to death for their writings, and executed in spring 1593, after a grim cat-and-mouse procedure involving two last-minute pardons from the Queen, the second of which arrived as the two, with halters already round their necks, had nearly finished their last words.[8] Two others involved with the publishing of these tracts died in prison; a third was deported. John Penry, who had fled to Scotland after printing some of the Marprelate tracts, and converted to separatism in 1592, was arrested in London in March 1593, and executed in May.[9] In addition, some 25 separatist men and women died in London prisons between 1589 and 1596.[10] In comparison, for the *whole* of Elizabeth's reign, 63 lay-Catholics are recognized as martyrs; more to the point, despite the range of treason legislation employed against them, and the resources put into their pursuit and capture, only 133 missionary priests were executed.[11]

Whitgift's *coup de grâce* came in 1593, when an Act to 'Retain the Queen's Subjects in Obedience' was passed 'for the preventing and voiding of such great inconveniences and perils as might happen and grow by the wicked and dangerous practices of seditious sectaries and disloyal persons'.[12] Though the Act was modified in its passage through parliament, it remained a powerful anti-separatist (and, to a lesser extent, anti-reformist) weapon.[13] Amongst other things the Act made non-attendance at service, attendance at conventicles – puritan scripture meetings – and writing against 'her Majesty's power and authority in cases ecclesiastical united and annexed to the imperial crown of this realm' punishable with imprisonment until conformity (and imprisonment was no soft option, as the casualty figures above indicate), and deportation on a second offence.[14] In effect it treated non-conforming Protestants as severely as Catholics, and banned expression of Protestant dissent concerning the royal prerogative.

Whilst one strand of opposition to Whitgift's campaigns was focused in parliament, and challenged the legality of his proceedings, the reformers and separatists themselves responded by petitioning and publishing. This latter activity should not be understood solely as an attempt to influence public opinion – most separatist writings were printed abroad illegally, and were not generally available in the market-place. None the less, they did convert individuals. Francis Johnson was converted, ironically enough, through his activities as a confiscator and burner in the Netherlands of the entire first edition of *A Plain Refutation*, written by Barrow in prison and smuggled out. Johnson read one of the two remaining copies of the book, travelled to London to meet Barrow and Greenwood, and himself became a separatist.[15]

It is perhaps more productive to suppose that the persecuted considered publicising their tribulations to be an end in itself, rather than a means to halt persecution via mobilizing 'opinion'. The influence of Foxe here is paramount, as 'separatist leaders embraced the tradition of the suffering church popularized by Foxe, including themselves in the company of faithful witnesses extending back to Hus that he had celebrated'.[16] It was crucial to both separatists and reformers to interpret their own situation as analogous to that of the pre-Reformation church. John Field, a former assistant of Foxe, had compiled by the time of his death in 1589 a register of some 250 documents covering 'puritan' tribulations since 1565.[17] Accounts of persecution had the dual effect of showing the sufferings of the righteous and reproducing their arguments against their persecutors.[18]

Indeed, Foxe's work had such cultural capital, Damian Nussbaum has recently argued, that Timothy Bright's 1589 abridgement of the *Acts and Monuments* was sponsored by Whitgift himself, to promote a conformist line on episcopacy, the *ex officio* oath, and the use of vestments.[19] But even Bright's text, published in the middle of Marprelate, is not completely monological. The title page has two epigraphs – from Psalm 44, 'All day long are we counted as sheepe for the slaughter', and from Apocalypse 6:10, 'How long Lord, holy and true?'[20] Foxe's title page of 1583 has neither. Both of these quotations refer to persecution. The full quotation from the Psalm is 'Yea, for thy sake are we killed all the day long; we are counted as sheep for the slaughter. Awake, why sleepest thou, O Lord? arise, cast us not off for ever.' It is itself quoted in the context of persecution in Romans, 8:35–6: 'Who shall separate us from the love of

Christ? shall tribulation, or distress, or persecution, or famine, or nakedness, or peril, or sword? As it is written, For thy sake we are killed all the day long; we are accounted as sheep for the slaughter.'

The quotation from the Apocalypse, whose 'how long?' echoes many of the Psalms, directly refers to martyrdom: 'And when he had opened the fifth seal, I saw under the altar the souls of them that were slain for the word of God, and for the testimony which they held: And they cried with a loud voice, saying, How long, O Lord, holy and true, dost thou not judge and avenge our blood on them that dwell on the earth?'[21] At the very least, the referent of these two quotations does not have to be a wholly confident 'elect nation', and their presence on the title page goes some way towards confirming the importance of persecution to what might justly be considered an official production of the church of England.

One of the key precursors of the reformed church was, of course, Sir John Oldcastle, and both separatists and reformers explicitly compared themselves to him.[22] The leading reformer Thomas Cartwright, imprisoned by the High Commission in the Fleet for refusing the oath, wrote that even Oldcastle was not required to so swear.[23] Francis Johnson cited Oldcastle's opinions in support of his own, which were 'accounted Lollardye and heresye in the holy servants and martirs of Christ in former ages'.[24] In a letter to Cecil, Johnson states that his aims 'are that the false offices, callings, and works of the prelacy and other clergie of this land might be quite abolished owt of it, and their lordships and possessions, which ... were fittly of olde, by the Lord Cobham, that blessed martir, sayd to be the venime of Judas shed into the church, might also be converted to Her Majestie's civill uses.'[25] Foxe's 1583 *Acts* itself had pointed to Oldcastle's continuing relevance, Foxe commenting on the Archbishop's insistence on due course when examining Oldcastle that 'al this dissimulation was but to colour their mischiefes, before the ignoraunt multitude. Consider herein (gentle reader) what this wicked generation is and how far wide from the just fear of God for as they were then, so are they yet to this day.'[26]

Oldcastle's persecution as a proto-Protestant martyr was thus claimed by both separatists and reformers as a type of their own predicament. The procedure is reversed in *1 Sir John Oldcastle,* in which the historical figure appears as a late-Elizabethan 'puritan', in a late-Elizabethan setting. Some examples of this have been listed in Mary Grace Muse Adkins' article on the play: references to complaints about ceremony, Oldcastle's refusal to come to mass, the identification of those meeting in fields and solitary groves as 'Protestants', the Bishop's intent to examine Oldcastle 'of Articles', Oldcastle's insistence on the Bible as guiding his faith, and the finding of 'books in English' at his house (on which Adkins comments that they might well be from the library of a contemporary puritan).[27] Adkins' listing is not complete. There are also references to Protestants meeting in 'conventicles' (1:107)[28]; Rochester intends to summon Oldcastle 'unto the Arches' (the ecclesiastical court for the Canterbury province) (2:113); King Henry protests to Oldcastle that 'the bishops find themselves much injured' (6:3), and Rochester characterizes Oldcastle's servant Harpoole as a heretic 'in contempt of our church discipline' for his attacking a sumner (13:124). Harpoole protests he is 'neither heretic nor puritan, but of the old church' (13:129–30).[29] The stock comic device of disguising oneself in another's clothes to make an escape is given a 'puritan' twist, as the proto-Protestant Oldcastle escapes from the Tower dressed in the bishop's robes (scene 14).

Though Oldcastle is clearly the victim of a personal campaign by an 'envious priest', critics have commented very little on the resemblances between this campaign and Whitgift's methods. The examination 'of articles', for example, is identified by Adkins as referring to the 39 articles; a much more topical set of articles were the three articles Whitgift required the clergy to subscribe to from 1583–4 onwards.[30] The machinery of ecclesiastical justice is realized with some care. A sumner (an ecclesiastical court officer) visits Oldcastle's estate to serve a process on him, and is forced by Harpoole to literally eat his words. On Oldcastle's arrest by Rochester, the sumner searches his rooms for books, finding 'not a Latin book, no, not so much as Our Lady's Psalter. Here's the Bible, the Testament, the Psalms in metre, *The Sickman's Salve, The Treasure of Gladness*, and all in English, not so much but the almanac's English', to which Rochester replies, 'Away with them; to th' fire with them' (13:145–9).

Metrical psalms are, of course, vernacular translations from the Latin (hence, Protestant). The two 'heretical' books named both were very popular works, first published in the 1560s. *The Sick Man's Salve* was 'a treatise containing the nature, differences and kindes of death; as also the right maner of dying well'.[31] *The Treasure of Gladnesse*, more interestingly, was a purported proto-Protestant collection of prayers and paraphrases (the latter predominantly from the New Testament), as its title page stated:

This Booke is called the Treasure of Gladnesse, and seemeth by the Copie, being a very little Manuell, and written in Velam, to be made above. cc. yeares past at the leaste. whereby apeareth how God in olde time, and not of late only hath bene truely confessed and honored. The Copie hereof, is for the antiquitie of it, preserved and to be seene in the Printers Hall.[32]

One of Oldcastle's heretical books, though first published in the mid-sixteenth century, claimed on its title page to have existed in manuscript in Oldcastle's time. Sixteenth-century orthodoxy is presented as fifteenth-century 'heresy'. The relationship is, in fact, reversed in the case of one of the other books referred to, for when *Oldcastle* was written a new *Our Lady's Psalter*, written by Thomas Worthington, 'president of Douai College', and printed secretly in England, was circulating under a false Antwerp imprint.[33] The fifteenth-century orthodoxy the sumner seeks is here topical as sixteenth-century 'heresy'.

The search for heretical *books* is, of course, anachronistic; but it was a feature of Whitgift's campaigns. The presence of seditious books was the ostensible reason for the pursuivants' searches of separatist homes, as the supplication delivered to the Privy Council in February 1592/3 suggests:

> Their manner of pursuing and apprehending us is no lesse violence and outrage. Their pursevants with assistants break into our houses at all howers of the night (for such times to these exploits they for the most part chuse to hide their unchristian and cruel dealing with us from the world). There they breake up, ransake, rifle and make havock at their pleasures, under pretence of serching for seditious and unlawfull books.[34]

Nor is Rochester's book-burning out of character for Whitgift, for in the June of 1599 – a few months before *Oldcastle* was first performed – he (with Bancroft) ordered the public burning of satires. This was not an isolated instance: Whitgift ordered burnings of religious works on at least two other occasions, in 1587 and 1595.[35]

A few other references can be placed within the context of Whitgift's campaigns. 'Unlawful assemblies, conventicles or meetings under pretence of any exercise of religion', were forbidden under the 1593 Act. Oldcastle is persecuted for refusing to attend mass; non-attendance at divine service had similarly been named in the 1593 Act (and, of course, many of those the act was aimed at considered the unreformed service to be as good as a mass anyway). The court of the Arches still existed under Elizabeth, and in the 1580s and early 1590s its dean was Richard Cosin, an assiduous participant in Whitgift's campaigns, who went into print several times in the early 1590s to defend them.

What are we to make of the change of Oldcastle's persecutor from the Archbishop of Canterbury to the Bishop of Rochester in the light of these details?[36] All it tells us is that somebody involved in the production of the text – one or more of the writers, or of the actors, or the Master of the

Revels – thought that somebody watching the play might otherwise be able to identify the villainous prelate with the *current* Archbishop of Canterbury.[37] From this it is possible to say that if anybody had wished to use the theatre to directly link Whitgift's campaigns against reformist and separatist Protestants with Catholic persecutions of proto-Protestants, they could not have done so without risk, even six years after Whitgift had routed his opponents. One of the main rhetorical strategies employed by reformers and separatists themselves was thus unavailable to the stage.[38]

No such restrictions appear to apply to satirical representations of such Protestants. In fact, the person responsible for introducing the stock satirical 'puritan' to the London stage, 'already equipped with the elements of an essentially simple and stable repertory: outward piety (indicated by the white of an upturned eye), inner corruption, consisting of avarice, lust and sedition – in a word, hypocrisy incarnate', was quite possibly Richard Bancroft himself.[39] During the Martin Marprelate affair, Whitgift employed anti-Martinist writers to answer satire with satire, on Bancroft's advice.[40] These anti-Martinist writers may also have written for the stage.[41] But whether or not the response to Marprelate actually staged the satirical portrait of the 'puritan' it constructed, it undoubtedly circulated it more widely than it had been hitherto, and was important in producing the dramatic satire of 'puritans' which burgeoned post-Marprelate.[42]

In addition, Marprelate seems to have led to Whitgift asserting some control over the professional stage. In November 1589 the Privy Council seems to have set up a commission (comprising Edmund Tilney, the Master of the Revels, and a nominee each from Whitgift and the Bishop of London) to vet all professional playbooks 'that they may consider of the matters of their comedyes and tragedyes, and thereuppon to stryke out or reforme suche partes and matters as they shall fynde unfytt and undecent to be handled in playes, bothe for Divinitie and State'.[43] Though there is no evidence that the commission was anything other than a one-off purge, letters subsequently addressed to Whitgift by the Lord Mayor of London indicate that he was seen to maintain an interest in (at least) regulating the stage more tightly.

For a long time, the particularity of the stage's hostile construction of the 'puritan' was traced to 'the puritan attack on the stage' which preceded it, and which ultimately led to the closure of the London theatres in 1642. It would, however, be a mistake to see all anti-theatrical writing as texts in which the precisians rehearse the downsizing of the London theatre. The anti-theatrical writings preceding the theatre's satirical construction of the puritan can only be lumped together by a tremendous and warping critical effort. As Tracey Hill has recently shown, Rankins and Munday, two 'anti-theatrical playwrights', were paid to attack their own profession; Gosson, another playwright against the stage, opposed puritanism.[44] Some reformers were undoubtedly opposed to the stage, as can be seen by their polemical uses of the 'theatricality' of popish church services, but they had far more important things to concern themselves with than the way in which a small percentage of Londoners amused themselves. Given the energy, diligence and bravery with which reformers continued to take on the church hierarchy, if they had seriously worried about the stage we should certainly have heard.

The 'puritan attack on the stage' has, however, functioned effectively to mask the origins of the stage's antipathy towards puritans, which lie in the efforts of Bancroft, Whitgift and others to brand critics of the established church – many of whom they had imprisoned without trial, and some of whom they were soon to execute – as hypocrites and seditionaries. Censorship and satire are often seen as opposed. The satirical portrayal of historical or actual figures was, after all, one of the main causes of intervention into the affairs of the London theatre in the 1590s.[45] But here the satirists are engaged in the same project as the ecclesiastical censors. And the 1590s play most obviously replying to the satirized stage 'puritan' (both in the sense of the 'hypocrite' character and, more locally, Shakespeare's 'Oldcastle') was unable to show its 'historical' Oldcastle pursued, as the chronicles indicated, by the Archbishop of Canterbury, because this would have involved too strong a parallel between Arundel and Whitgift, a parallel insisted upon by some of Whitgift's victims.

Whether because of the above restriction or not, the play does not primarily seek to 'libel' Whitgift or other prominent Elizabethan church-men. Rather, its focus is on the similarities between Oldcastle and the separatists and reformers pursued by the church authorities. Most of the parallels noted above function to establish continuities between the two persecutions.[46] Oldcastle is condemned for his links with treasons he knows nothing about or actively opposes. He cannot control which disreputable elements will claim him as a friend, or what a malicious prelate will say to the monarch. The play shows just how persecutions of the godly, despite a righteous monarch, can succeed. It is in anatomizing of the dynamics of persecution that the play most strongly replies to Shakespeare's, and the Queen's Men's, 'Oldcastle': the primary fact about Oldcastle is that he 'died a martyr'. The play's avoidance of the *ad hominem* approach of Marprelate and the separatists, signified by its focus on the martyr rather than the persecutor, is clearly deliberate; it signifies the return of the discourse of reform to its pre-Marprelate boundaries.

What the name change has undoubtedly contributed towards, how-ever, is the effacement of the topicality of persecution from modern critical accounts of the play, for its omission allows critics to discuss *Oldcastle* as a play relatively disengaged from English Protestantism's recent internal struggles. The result is a topicality in which there is nothing outside texts, with Marprelate, Hooker, the publications of assorted separatists and bishops, and of course Shakespeare, marking the boundaries of discourse.[47] For example, David Bevington's discussion of the play places Oldcastle as 'yet another in the imposing list of victimized intermediaries [that is, characters in plays] urging a moderate and lawful course of popular reform'.[48] Bevington mentions Whitgift several times. The play's presentation of the monarch as the supreme authority in the land 'reflects the decline of the Puritan "classical" movement and the effectiveness of Whitgift's no-nonsense discipline'. This 'discipline' remains only in the margins of what might be called 'thin description'. For example, though Bevington points out that 'the Catholic menace' in the play is 'comparable also to that of Whitgift's conservative Anglicanism in the 1590s', this is through both 'repression of all moderate reform and individual conscience'.[49] Conservative Anglicanism here is a system of thought rather than a breaker of bodies.[50] Bevington does note the Archbishop's name change, but justifies it by asserting (without evidence) that the Bishop of Rochester was 'a familiar and hated name to Oldcastle's Puritan audience'.[51] Such an elision of the constraints upon the writers of *Oldcastle*, and of the topicality of 'no-nonsense discipline', allows the play to be configured as a work of generalized political philosophy, teaching that reformers 'must learn from their past ... that moderates can win a more lasting triumph for truth than those who flout their duty to the state'.[52] Oldcastle's persecution in Bevington's account, like the crucifix-ion, metonymically refers to a greater whole: salvation, or the triumph of the 'elect nation'. Indeed, an influential article on the English history play places *Oldcastle* amongst a number of 'elect nation plays' in which 'the good character or his cause triumphs, not a victim of fate but its instrument, in an action not tragic but tragicomic, as is the action of the Christian drama itself'.[53] However, Foxe himself, as has been noted, was less than sanguine that the cause had triumphed, and his doubts were often quoted by Whitgift's opponents.[54]

Reading the history play as focused on the reprobate and persecuting nation of the staged action, rather than the implied elect nation to come many years later, may, oddly enough, provide a new vantage point on one of the most worked-over examples of Elizabethan censorship, *Sir Thomas More*, the first version of which was probably, like *Oldcastle*, written for the

Rose. The recent 'public order' focus on Tilney's censorship of the early parts of the play is consonant with a theory of censorship which sees interventions as often quite exceptional responses to particular crises, rather than issuing from a widespread and intentionally repressive censorship or regulatory regime. This theory, however, does little to explain Tilney's crossing out a line which can have had no conceivable impact upon public order: More's Latin line 'Ubi turpis est medicina, sanari piget' (IV.ii.83). This line, which comes in the context of Roper asking More to be the King's 'patient' and submit, means 'when the medicine is disgusting one is loath to be healed'. It is a quotation from Seneca's *Oedipus*, and in context refers obliquely to Oedipus's own death (it is Creon's response to Oedipus asking him whose life must be sacrificed to appease the gods).

Just what the medicine is, and why More should loathe it, is made clear in the preceding scene, which also caused Tilney concern. Sir Thomas Palmer arrives at a meeting of the Privy Council with 'articles ... first to be viewed / And then to be subscribed to' (IV.i.70–1). More refuses to immediately subscribe: 'Subscribe these articles? Stay, let us pause: / Our conscience first shall parley with our laws' (ll. 73–4), and is joined, ironically enough in the light of his namesake in *Oldcastle*, by the Bishop of Rochester, John Fisher. Rochester is then accused of 'capital contempt'; More, who again asks for more time, is told not to leave his house in Chelsea and sets off for it; other lords instantly subscribe to the articles; and Rochester is escorted off by Palmer 'to answer this contempt'. Tilney marked the scene 'all altr' from the point where Rochester directly refuses to subscribe to his exit with Palmer. The Revels editors of the play comment that 'Tilney seems more disturbed by the sympathetic presentation of More's and Fisher's acceptance of Royal displeasure than by historical inaccuracy'.[55] William B. Long points out that this disturbance did not extend to a command to cut material, as Tilney 'neither cut nor altered More's refusal to sign which is crucial to the whole play'.[56] If the substance of the scene was acceptable, what in its details did Tilney find objectionable?

Given the consensus that Tilney's objections to the play's riot scenes can be topically located to 1593, it is worth thinking a little more about the topical inflections of the interventions noted above. As well as being a year of public order worries in London, 1593 saw Whitgift's decisive triumph over both reformers and separatists, in the executions of Barrow and Greenwood and the passing of the 1593 Act to Retain the Queen's Subjects in Obedience. Three key points relating to Tilney's markings discussed above can be placed in the context of Whitgift's campaigns: the words 'articles' and 'contempt', and the vehemence of More's Latin tag. One of Whitgift's key tactics was, of course, the use of 'articles', particularly against clerics, who could be deprived of their livings for refusal to subscribe. Refusal to take the *ex officio* oath was 'contempt'; it was for this contempt that non-conformists could be imprisoned. It is worth noting that Rochester's refusal to subscribe to articles is twice identified as 'contempt' in the passage Tilney marks for alteration. Assuming Tilney was led to intervene in IV.i by the topical conjunction of 'articles' and 'contempt' enables a similarly topical explanation of his objection to the vehemence of More's Latin tag, for the combination of 'disgust' and learning was a hallmark of Barrow's face-to-face dealings with Whitgift, whom he at one point identified with Antichrist.[57]

Assuming the play's 1593 topicality may also help to explain its inclusion of a story from Foxe concerning an encounter between Thomas Cromwell and a long-haired man. In Munday's original manuscript, More encounters the long-haired Falkner, who has gone three years without a haircut 'upon a vow'. More retorts that, though he will not ask him to break the vow, he will imprison him in Newgate 'except meantime your conscience give you leave / To dispense with the long vow that you have made'.[58] Falkner is dragged off, but returns soon afterwards, having cut his own hair. He also 'doth conform himself / To honest decency in his attire.' Falkner, all humility, re-enters and is discharged. There are several topical resonances in this scene, including the conscientious refusal to conform and the vow, but the most important visual point made is Falkner's demeanour after his haircut, for short hair was particularly associated with puritans (hence, later, 'roundheads'). Munday's original draft thus provides a stage image of a prison 'conversion', after which Falkner reforms his manners, and looks like a puritan.

However, in Dekker's revision of the scene, it is made plain that Falkner, far from reforming, resents having cut his hair precisely because it makes him resemble a godly separatist: ' 'S heart, if my hair stand not an-end when I look for my face in a glass, I am a polecat. Here's a lousy jest. But if I notch not that rogue Tom barber that makes me look thus like a Brownist, hang me. I'll be worst to the nittical knave than ten tooth drawings. Here's a head with a pox' (III.i.244–9). One of the effects of this alteration – perhaps even its point – clearly is to make it difficult to see Falkner as a type of reformed puritan, though its topicality then depends on arguments about the dating of the additions.[59]

William Long has speculated that the play was commissioned, '(or at least suggested or approved) by some government official(s)' in the light of 'steadily increasing anti-alien sentiment' so that players could 'demonstrate publicly the consequences of such socially disruptive actions'. Such a 'commission' is plausible for Long in the light of Anthony Munday's status as 'good and faithful servant' of the government, both as pursuivant and polemicist. Both the anti-alien action, and More's own refusal to subscribe, are simply examples of 'the unfortunate consequences of disobedience to the rule of the sovereign'.[60] In Long's account, the anti-alien point is the reason for the play's existence (he refers elsewhere to its 'pre-eminent topicality'); More's later downfall and death is simply a historically fortuitous repetition of the same basic 'lesson'. The play's orthodox didacticism, in turn, means that Tilney's interventions are an attempt to enable the production of the play, even though it had been overtaken by a drastic increase in anti-alien tensions.

Long's implication that the intention to write about Ill May Day entailed a full-length play centring on More is questionable. *Jack Straw*, a play dealing entirely with commons political action, and entered in the Stationers' Register in the year that *More* is assumed to have been written, is only slightly longer than the 'riot' scenes in *More*. It is also possible to argue with Long's sense that putting on a play would be one of the methods of choice to defuse anti-alien sentiment. Simpler methods of control were used. When the now-famous libel against strangers appeared in 1593, the authorities' response was immediate and forceful: the setting up of a 'strong watch', and a special commission authorized to enter any premises in search of the author, with the liberty to torture suspects (one of their victims, of course, being the writer Thomas Kyd).[61] Most importantly, however, Long's conflation of More's and the London crowd's 'disobedience' risks simplifying the issues involved (and doing so by adopting the same strategy as the church authorities). Whilst it was undoubtedly a common representational tactic to point to the bad ends of 'rebels' as indicating the illegitimacy of their cause, the same cannot be said of religious dissidents, such as More.[62] The Church of England itself was founded on religious dissidence and martyrdom. Martyrs do not 'fail' because they die; 'rebels' do. Long's point requires an audience ignorant of (or uninterested in) the specifically religious grounds of More's 'disobedience', and his status as martyr.

More's Revels editors do support Long to some extent, commenting that one of the play's main sources, the 1587 Holinshed's *Chronicles*, 'shows a remarkable change of attitude towards More', presenting him in a much more positive light than the first edition, partly by quoting the words of John Aylmer, Bishop of London when *More* was written.[63] That More's Catholicism (and persecution of proto-Protestants) was no longer the most important thing about him is also argued by Ernst Honigmann, who places the play with *Dr Faustus, Friar Bacon, John of Bordeaux* and *John A Kent* as a 'wise man play'. For Honigmann, More's death is not a martyrdom but a 'fall' which allows him to display his 'special gifts': 'his quiet dignity, his independence of mind, courage, wit, and his impressive classlessness, equally at ease with earls and artisans'.[64] Munday's involvement in the play, given his well-known antipathy to Catholicism and employment as a pursuivant, thus presents less of a puzzle, because More's Catholicism no longer disqualified him from sympathetic public portrayal, and indeed was not a necessary component of such a portrayal.

To 'de-Catholicize' More's concern with freedom of conscience is not necessarily to secularize him, however. In fact, the non-specificity of the 'articles' More refuses not only plays down the Catholic grounds of his disobedience to Henry VIII, but also enables an interpretation of his situation as paralleling that of those Protestants subject to Whitgift's much more topical 'articles'.[65] In other words, paradoxically, the play's refusal to explore the Catholic nature of More's conscientious disobedience, as well as enabling it to be read by modern critics as a proto-liberal exploration of the individual's general right to freedom of conscience, also makes a topical and specific interpretation more possible.

This interpretation might be approached as follows. The Act to Retain the Queen's Subjects in Obedience was passed in the spring of 1593, at the same time as anti-alien feeling was at its height. It bracketed non-conforming Protestants with Catholic recusants, and in doing so redefined political dissidence to include the private, conscientious inaction of the subject. This 'Catholicizing' of Protestant dissent was particularly ironic given that anti-Catholicism was a distinguishing feature of both reformers and separatists, whose objections to the established church were precisely to its unreformed papist elements. Records of the proceedings in parliament, and the books and petitions of reformers and separatists, remain, but though there is little evidence of how Whitgift's campaigns, culminating in the 1593 Act, impacted upon the nation at large, it is clear that it affected many more lives than anti-alien feeling in some parts of London. How might the stage have refracted such a vital issue?

Given Whitgift's hard-line approach to censorship, his recent interest in the theatres, and Munday's dependence upon him, producing, say, *Sir John Oldcastle* in this year would have been impossible. But if now more Protestants were effectively recusants, then the two categories themselves blurred. The anti-Catholic Munday produced a play focused on the prominent recusant Sir Thomas More, because after the 1593 Act his situation was analogous to that of those Protestant reformers who, though they insisted that church government was not a matter for royal prerogative, found themselves redefined as the enemy within. The play can be seen, in this context, to present the consequences for a man of high degree of the redefinition of the political to include the private conscience's dissent from 'articles'. The Ill May Day scenes, on this interpretation, not only refract the topicality of anti-alien murmurings, but present, at length, More's articulate and wise loyal governance. The play seeks to make an absolute separation of loyalty from conscience, public from private life. More is willing to retire from office, but not to abjure his principles. Tilney's interventions into the later as well as the earlier parts of the play can thus be traced to topical pressures, albeit differing ones, pressures which perhaps also help to explain the differences between the Falkner scenes.

My account of *More* has assumed a deliberate attempt to stage a religious persecution at a time when this was very topical. Though attributing intentional oppositional stances to writers risks revisiting some of the relatively unsophisticated historicist interpretations of the last century, it is worth noting that both these plays were written by syndicates containing a writer with radical Protestant associations (Dekker and Wilson). More to the point, Anthony Munday, the writer employed by Whitgift to hunt out Marprelate and papists, a man consequently familiar with the leading Protestants of his day, worked on both (and indeed, may have acquired one of the sources for *More* from the confiscated papers of a recusant).[66] Whatever his personal morality, Munday was extremely well placed to understand how far a play could go, though this in itself still begs questions. But even if it were possible to provide a definite origin for the two plays I have discussed, it would still be clear that writers and censors understood that there were contingent limitations to the staging of religious history. The influence of the observance, rather than the breach, of these limitations is often overlooked because the contingent is mistaken for the necessary. Polemical orthodoxy looks like common sense once the limits on heterodox expression are forgotten. Censorship, and the power behind it, removes the satire of puritans from its dialogue with Foxean counter-justification evidenced through persecution, and reversibly, deprives Foxean plays of their own polemical topicality. The result is an early modern theatre in which, if the great Globe itself should disappear, not a wrack would be left behind.

Notes

1. Cyndia Susan Clegg, *Press Censorship in Elizabethan England* (Cambridge: Cambridge University Press, 1997), pp. 222–3.

2. R. B. Sharpe, *The Real War of the Theaters* (Boston: D.C. Heath & Co, 1935), p. 145.
3. Annabel Patterson recognizes, but does not pursue, the point with her passing comment that 'the play's sympathies seem to be decisively against the ecclesiastical authorities, with the bishop of Rochester standing in all too easily for Whitgift'; in 'Sir John Oldcastle as a Symbol of Reformation Historiography', in Donna B. Hamilton and Richard Strier, eds, *Religion, Literature, and Politics in Post-Reformation England, 1540–1688* (Cambridge: Cambridge University Press, 1996), pp. 6–26, at p. 23.
4. *Works of John Whitgift*, vol. III, ed. Reverend John Ayre (Cambridge: Cambridge University Press, 1853), p. 591.
5. *Works of John Whitgift*, p. 593.
6. *Select Statutes and Other Constitutional Documents*, ed. G. W. Prothero (Cambridge: Cambridge University Press, 4th edn, 1913), p. 213.
7. Patrick Collinson, *The Elizabethan Puritan Movement* (London: Methuen, 1967), p. 431.
8. John Knott, *Discourses of Martyrdom in English Literature, 1563–1694* (Cambridge: Cambridge University Press, 1993), p. 132.
9. Michael Watts, *The Dissenters: From the Reformation to the French Revolution* (Oxford: Clarendon Press, 1978), p. 39.
10. *The Writings of John Greenwood and Henry Barrow 1591–1593*, ed. Leland Carlson (London: George Allen & Unwin, 1970), p. 410.
11. A. Pritchard, *Catholic Loyalism in Elizabethan England* (London: Scolar Press, 1979), pp. 7–8.
12. G. R. Elton, *The Tudor Constitution: Documents and Commentary* (Cambridge: Cambridge University Press, 2nd edn, 1978), p. 458.
13. T. E. Hartley, *Elizabeth's Parliaments: Queen, Lords and Commons 1559–1601* (Manchester: Manchester University Press, 1992), pp. 98–9.
14. Watts, *Dissenters*, p. 39.
15. *The Writings of Henry Barrow 1587–1590*, ed. Leland Carlson (London: George Allen & Unwin, 1962), p. 87.
16. Knott, *Discourses of Martyrdom*, p. 120.
17. Patrick Collinson, *Godly People: Essays in English Protestantism and Puritanism* (London: Hambledon Press, 1983), p. 354.
18. So a posthumous 1595 Continental publication of Barrow's first examination before the High Commission in the mid-1580s states, 'now al posterites shal see their practises; and though they have spilt the blood of those men, which vexed them so sore, yet can they not bereave the world of their testimonie, which by word and writing they have left behinde them' (*Writings of Henry Barrow*, p. 90).
19. 'Whitgift's "Book of Martyrs": Archbishop Whitgift, Timothy Bright and the Elizabethan Struggle over John Foxe's Legacy', in David Loades, ed., *John Foxe: an Historical Perspective* (Aldershot: Ashgate, 1999), pp. 135–53.
20. Coincidentally, in one of Greenwood's supplications to the high court of parliament, he uses the same verse: 'Well, heere our brethren lye (how long Lord, holy and true, thou knowest) in dungeons, in hunger, in cold, in nakednes and all outward distresse' (*The Writings of John Greenwood and Henry Barrow 1591–1593*, ed. Leland Carlson, London: George Allen & Unwin, 1970, p. 409).

21. These quotations are from the Authorized Version.
22. Patterson, 'Sir John Oldcastle as a Symbol of Reformation Historiography', p. 6.
23. *Cartwrightiana*, eds Albert Peel and Leland Carlson (London: George Allen & Unwin, 1951), p. 42.
24. *Writings of John Greenwood and Henry Barrow*, p. 463.
25. Ibid. p. 455.
26. John Foxe, *Acts and Monuments of the Christian Church* (1583), p. 561.
27. Mary Grace Muse Adkins, 'Sixteenth-century Religious and Political Implications in *Sir John Oldcastle*', *UTSE* 21 (1942), 97–9.
28. Quotations are from the edition of the play in *The Oldcastle Controversy*, eds Peter Corbin and Douglas Sedge (Manchester: Manchester University Press, 1991).
29. Harpoole's refusal of the name 'puritan' should be read in the light of its currency as an insult. According to Patrick Collinson, 'the character of a puritan, both in the literary-generic sense and more generally, originated as an attributed character, charged with intensely polemical resonances' ('Ecclesiastical Vitriol: Religious Satire in the 1590s and the Invention of Puritanism', in John Guy, ed., *The Reign of Elizabeth: Court and Culture in the Last Decade*, Cambridge: Cambridge University Press, 1995, pp. 150–70, at p. 155).
30. Other critics also miss the topical possibilities here. Judith Doolin Spikes presents the play as bringing to the 'early seventeenth-century stage the religious controversies of the 1560s, the issues and polemics of which had become once again alarmingly pertinent' (Judith Doolin Spikes, 'The Jacobean History Play and the Myth of the Elect Nation', *RD* 8 (1977), p. 125). Another example might be G. K. Hunter's comment that Rochester 'is a malignant heresy hunter in a mode we can recognize from later portrayals of the sixteenth-century bishops Bonner and Gardner, memorably presented in Foxe as scapegoats for the religious traumas of the mid-sixteenth century'. See G. K. Hunter, *English Drama 1586–1642: the Age of Shakespeare* (Oxford: Clarendon Press, 1997), pp. 243–4.
31. 1595 edition, title page.
32. *The Treasure of Gladnesse*, 1579 edition, title page.
33. The British Library Catalogue records editions dated 1598 and 1600, with the latter ascribed to Worthington.
34. *Writings of John Greenwood and Henry Barrow*, p. 400.
35. See Clegg, *Press Censorship*, p. 60.
36. There is the further complication that at 20:4 Rochester is referred to as 'envious Winchester'.
37. I am assuming that the Rochester was part of the play-as-performed rather than added to the play-as-printed, because Rochester is often referred to as 'bishop' in metrically regular lines.
38. Cyndia Clegg argues that 1599 was an atypical year for censorship, with Whitgift and Bancroft being unusually ready to censor non-religious texts in order to deflect criticism of the government during Essex's Irish campaigns (Clegg, *Press Censorship*, p. 202).
39. Patrick Collinson, 'The Theatre Constructs Puritanism', in David L. Smith, Richard Strier and David Bevington, eds, *The Theatrical City: Culture, Theatre and Politics in London, 1576–1649* (Cambridge: Cambridge University Press,

1995), p. 167. But the image of the puritan thus promoted was not Bancroft's invention. Whitgift, in his sermon at St Paul's on 17 November 1583, characterizes the hypocrisy and self-love of 'these wayward and conceited fellows' using, amongst other references, St Paul's second letter to Timothy and the book of Jude (*Works of John Whitgift*, vol. III, p. 593). Most of the characteristics of the satirized 'puritan' appear in St Paul's invectives.

40. Though Kristen Poole has convincingly argued that anti-Martinist writings made use of the Bakhtinian grotesque, her assertion that therefore 'stage puritans were widely expected to be comically grotesque figures', and indeed that this was a 'more pervasive' representation of the puritan than the austere hypocrite, is unsupported by reference to anything other than Marprelate ('Saints Alive! Falstaff, Martin Marprelate, and the Staging of Puritanism', *SQ* 46 (1995), pp. 63–4.

41. Collinson, 'Theatre Constructs Puritanism', follows C. J. Sissons in stating that 'the evidence is skimpy, but just sufficient'.

42. Collinson, 'Theatre Constructs Puritanism', p. 166. Theatrical gibes can be found soon after Marprelate. *A Knack to Know a Knave* (entered in the Stationers' Register on 7 Jan. 1593/4) contains the lines 'The next knave is a Priest, calde John the precise, / That with counterfeit holinesse blinds the peoples eyes, / This is one of them that wil say it is a shame, / For men to swear and blaspheme Gods holie name: / Yet if a make a good Sermon but once in a yeare, / A wil be fourtie tymes in a Taverne making good cheere, / Yet in the Church he will read with such sobrietie, / That you would thinke him verie precise, and of great honesty' (lines 1759–66).

43. Quoted in Richard Dutton, *Mastering the Revels: the Regulation and Censorship of English Renaissance Drama* (London: Macmillan, 1991), p. 77.

44. See Tracey Hill, ' "He Hath Changed his Coppy": Anti-Theatrical Writing and the Turncoat Player', *Critical Survey* 9 (1997), 59–77.

45. See Janet Clare, *'Art Made Tongue-tied by Authority': Elizabethan and Jacobean Dramatic Censorship* (Manchester: Manchester University Press, 1999), pp. 94–114.

46. G. K. Hunter notes that the play conveys 'the Establishment message that true Christian conscience is innocent of any political threat; but when the ecclesiastical arrangements are corrupt, even conscientious loyalty cannot guarantee to save the Christian's life, though it can preserve the soul'. However, he does not see any topical resonance in this point ('Religious Nationalism in Later History Plays', in Vincent Newey and Ann Thompson, eds, *Literature and Nationalism* (Liverpool: Liverpool University Press, 1991), pp. 88–97, at p. 93.

47. One recent example is Douglas Brooks' assertion that *Oldcastle* 'takes most of its cues not from an identification with a community, but from an individual playwright named Shakespeare' ('Sir John Oldcastle and the Construction of Shakespeare's Authorship', *SEL* 38 (1998), 347).

48. David Bevington, *Tudor Drama and Politics: a Critical Approach to Topical Meaning* (Cambridge, Mass.: Harvard University Press, 1968), p. 257.

49. Ibid. pp. 259, 257.

50. Similarly, there is no hint in David Scott Kastan's work on Oldcastle that what he calls 'Whitgift's vigorous promotion of uniformity', after which 'radical Protestantism ... was in retreat, at least as a political movement', had anything to do with imprisonment without trial or executions (David Scott Kastan, *Shakespeare after Theory*, London: Routledge, 1999, p. 101).

51. Though Bevington supports this statement only with a reference to Sharpe's *The Real War of the Theaters*, the latter makes no such claim.

52. Bevington, *Tudor Drama and Politics*, p. 259.

53. Judith Doolin Spikes, 'The Jacobean History Play and the Myth of the Elect Nation', *RD* 8 (1977), 119.

54. G. K. Hunter makes the point that 'Foxe's conception of England as an "elect nation" is thus by no means untroubled, and, in political terms, it is remarkably limited and circumspect'; see 'Religious Nationalism', p. 89.

55. Anthony Munday and others, *Sir Thomas More*, eds Vittorio Gabrieli and Giorgio Melchiori (Manchester: Manchester University Press, 1990), p. 166.

56. William B. Long, 'The Occasion of *The Book of Sir Thomas More*', in T. H. Howard-Hill, ed., *Shakespeare and Sir Thomas More: Essays on the Play and its Shakespearean Interest* (Cambridge: Cambridge University Press, 1989), pp. 45–56, at p. 46.

57. *Writings of Henry Barrow 1587–1590*, p. 188.

58. Munday and others, *Sir Thomas More*, p. 217.

59. The Revels editors place them around 1593, but Gary Taylor and Scott McMillin both favour a much later date (see their chapters in Howard-Hill, ed., *Shakespeare and Sir Thomas More*).

60. Long, 'The Occasion of *The Book of Sir Thomas More*', p. 50.

61. Giorgio Melchiori, 'The Master of the Revels and the Date of the Additions to *The Book of Sir Thomas More*', in Bernhard Fabian and Kurt Tetzeli von Rosador, eds, *Shakespeare: Text, Language, Criticism* (Olms-Weidmann: Hildesheim and New York, 1987), pp. 164–78, at p. 167.

62. Though Whitgift himself argued on 17 Nov. 1583, in one of his first major sermons as Archbishop, that 'Long life is a promise to obedience. Therefore short life [is the reward] to disobedience' (*Works of John Whitgift*, vol. III, p. 588).

63. Anthony Munday and others, *Sir Thomas More*, p. 7.

64. Ernst Honigmann, 'The Play of *Sir Thomas More* and Some Contemporary Events', *Sh.S.* 42 (1990), 78.

65. Though the Revels edition points out the potential appeal of the play to Protestants, it stops short of suggesting a directly topical resonance: 'Freedom of conscience was a question that interested the Puritan and non-conformist London middle class even more than the Roman Catholic dissidents. It is exactly this sort of audience – the puritanically inclined City middle class – that Munday seems to have had in mind in the later extant plays in which he had a hand ... [which] denounce the prevarications of Church and State against the rights of the individual' (Munday and others, *Sir Thomas More*, p. 16).

66. Ibid. p. 8.

4
Receiving Offence: *A Game at Chess* Again

Richard Dutton

Annabel Patterson dubbed *A Game at Chess* one of 'those famous puzzling incidents of *noncensorship*' in the early modern world.[1] She assumed it ventured on contentious issues and depicted notable individuals in ways not normally acceptable in Jacobean England: yet somehow it was performed. Albert Tricomi similarly assumes that the controversy which surrounded the play after its performance points to a work that was genuinely and distinctively subversive: 'Why did this play so threaten the Jacobean authorities?'[2] These comments encapsulate what remain perhaps the commonest views of the play and its censorship. But neither is beyond dispute, and critics as varied as Jerzy Limon, Trevor Howard-Hill and Thomas Cogswell have challenged them, as we shall see.

This is an oft-told tale, and I shall only recite it as far as I have to, in order to contextualize some new observations I shall develop. I particularly want to focus:

1) on the practice here of Sir Henry Herbert as Master of the Revels;
2) on the role of the Spanish Ambassador in protesting about the play;
3) on suggestions that the play might have been sponsored by someone in real authority – Prince Charles, the Duke of Buckingham, or the Earl of Pembroke – in such a way as to circumvent conventional censorship;
4) conversely, on suggestions that, within a general patriotic spirit, the play contrives to be critical of Charles and Buckingham, and perhaps even of the King himself.

I want to signal early that, if we are to make any real headway in these disputed waters, we need to be much clearer than commentators have commonly been in distinguishing between what a censor ought or ought not to have found objectionable in the script and what the investigation after the event actually found objectionable.

The role of the Master of the Revels

In assuming that *A Game at Chess* was unusually free-spoken (and so perhaps specially sponsored), modern critics often overlook the fact that Jacobean commentators on the play also felt it went beyond the bounds of what was acceptable and might well have been specially protected. If so, Sir Henry Herbert, Master of the Revels, would have to have been involved, since it was precisely his function to prevents scandals of the kind the play had become. John Holles, eye-witness to one of the unprecedented nine consecutive performances (interrupted only by a Sunday, when playing was forbidden), observed 'me thinks this is a hardy part, & b[o]eyond my understanding: & surely thes gamsters must have a good retrayt'. 'Hardy part', I think, means 'foolhardy affair' and he certainly believed that the actors needed protection, 'a good retrayt', if they were to avoid the consequences of their actions.[3] Another commentator, George Lowe, reported that 'it is thought that it will be called in and the parties punished', while at least two others recognized that the performances were anomalous and that it was only a matter of time before they were stopped. John Woolley observed that 'the Players looseth no tyme, nor forbeareth to make haye while the Sunne shyneth', while Sir Francis Nethersole noted that 'they play no thing els, knowing there time cannot be long'.[4]

Woolley later reported that 'Middleton the Poet' was likely to be imprisoned for writing the play 'if he doe not cleere him selfe by the Master of the Revells, who alowed of it; and it is thought not without leave, from the higher powers I meane the P. and D. if not from the K. for they were all loth to have it forbidden, and by report laught hartely at it'.[5] Woolley was on the fringes of the court and writing to the diplomat William Trumbull, then in Brussells, so his reports are not without interest. Unfortunately, there is no evidence that he had access to really privileged information, so that his suggestion that the Master of the Revels only licensed the play 'not without leave, from the higher powers' whom he coyly designates as the 'P'[rince], 'D'[uke of Buckingham] or 'K'[ing] really has no higher value than that of speculation or gossip. For what it is worth, however, he has difficulty believing that Herbert would have licensed it without specific authorization from the highest level.

When the play was actually performed at the Globe, the King and the court were on progress in the Midlands, two days' ride away – another circumstance which has fuelled conspiracy theories. Members of the Privy Council who were still in London, and asked to investigate the scandal, clearly also wondered what Herbert had been up to. They were themselves reprimanded in the first letter Secretary Conway wrote on the matter, voicing the King's complaint 'that the first notice thereof should bee brought to him, by a forrain Ambassador, while soe manie Ministers of his owne are thereaboutes and cannot but have heard of it'.[6] Their reply reads like an attempt to redirect the King's ire on Herbert: 'Wee have called before us some of the principall Actors, and demaunded of them by what lycence and authoritie they have presumed to act the same, in answer whereunto they produced a booke being an orriginall and perfect Coppie thereof (as they affirmed) seene and allowed by Sir Henry Herbert knight, Master of the Revells, under his owne hand, and subscribed in the last page of the said booke.' They returned this copy with their letter, suggesting that someone should 'call Sir Henry Herbert before you to know a reason of his lycenceing thereof, who (as we are given to understand) is now attending at Court'.[7]

We have separate confirmation that Herbert did license the play in the normal way, since Edmund Malone saw his office-book before it disappeared some time in the nineteenth century, and marked his Third Quarto copy of the play ' "A new play called *A Game of Chesse*, written by Middleton," was licensed by Sir Henry Herbert, June 12.1624. So his Office Book MS.'[8] But none of this tells us whether Herbert acted with or without special 'leave, from the higher powers'. If he was indeed examined, as the Privy Council suggested, no record remains of the outcome. Twentieth-century commentators, however, have not been deterred by the lack of evidence. Even at times in ignorance of the Jacobean opinion (the significance of the Holles letter, for example, has only been appreciated in the last decade), they have not been slow to suppose that 'higher powers' were involved in the staging of the play. Louis B. Wright argued in 1928 that 'the ruling favourite, Buckingham, and the Heir Apparent, Charles sponsored or, at least, actively approved' the play.[9] This conclusion was more recently endorsed by Jerzy Limon, who sees *A Game at Chess* as part of a 'consciously contrived campaign' to influence opinion about the conduct of English foreign policy: 'Because the play reveals striking congruity with the new ideology of "the war party" headed by the Duke of Buckingham and Prince Charles, it is therefore ... plausible that these two sponsored the production.'[10]

This argument ignores the doubts about the depiction of Buckingham and Charles within the play, which I shall discuss later. In her analysis of the play as 'oppositional drama', voicing a concerted, Puritan-centred opposition to the policies of the Stuart government (and so to Buckingham and Charles), Margot Heinemann suggested that William Herbert, the Earl of Pembroke, was a more likely sponsor: as Lord Chamberlain, Henry Herbert's immediate superior, indeed his kinsman and patron, Pembroke was better placed than anyone to support a play critical of the highest powers in the land.[11] He had been a long-standing opponent both of Buckingham's influence and of his (hitherto) pro-Spanish policies. But by the time of the play negotiations for a Spanish marriage for Charles had fallen through in a disastrous trip to Madrid undertaken by Charles and Buckingham (the subject of most of the final act of the play), Buckingham had openly declared in the House of Lords for war with Spain, and there had been a *rapprochement* between him and Pembroke.

T. H. Howard-Hill pointed out this, and much else besides, in a very sceptical review of all attempts to find evidence of 'higher powers' behind the play or indeed truly topical and contentious politics within it.[12] Elsewhere he suggests that the play as Middleton originally conceived it, reflected in the early-state Archdall-Folger manuscript, was 'predominantly moral', its tone 'prevalently satiric and ironic', its primary focus the attempted seduction of the White Queen's Pawn by two Black Pawns.[13] But this original conception was significantly altered by the addition of later material, notably the introduction of the Fat Bishop and the changed depiction of the White King's Pawn: 'The addition of the Black Knight's plot against the Fat Bishop – which had nothing to do with the politics of 1623–4 – dissipated the thrust of Middleton's moral design, and other revisions, notably the alterations to the White King's Pawn, emphasized the political dimensions of the play, so moving it further towards theatricality (in scenes V.i and iii), comedy and topicality. There is no reason to doubt that this significant wrenching of the play from the playwright's fundamental conception was inspired by the theatrical company after Middleton had shown them his early script' (p. 70). These moves towards 'theatricality . . . comedy and topicality' were reinforced by the 'extraordinary lengths' (p. 128) the King's Men went to in order to impersonate the former Spanish Ambassador, Gondomar, and (in the Fat Bishop) Archbishop De Dominis of Spalato, a Catholic prelate who had ostentatiously converted to Anglicanism, then equally ostentatiously returned to Rome. All of this is imagined as a dialogue of sorts between the author and the actors, without intervention from the censor or his superiors.

At the same time, while the revisions of the play may have moved it towards topicality of a kind, it was not *political* or contentious topicality:

'In the first place, *A Game* does not deal with any *current* political issue' (p. 105, my emphasis) – it may deal with the recent history of Anglo-Spanish relations, and of Jesuit activity in England, but none of this is contentious in a context where the King, his ministers and parliament were now at one in their opposition to Spain. 'Second, those White House characters that might be identified with English authorities are depicted with the utmost respect and, perhaps, a prudent brevity ... Third ... the villains represented men who had no popular constituency in England in 1624' (pp. 106–7). Rather, Middleton 'propagated attitudes to Spain fervently maintained by most politically aware Englishmen in the middle of 1624. The play cannot be considered to be propaganda because it did not seek to alter its audiences' attitudes to the matters of which it treated.' On the contrary, he celebrated what were essentially communal values *at the time*: 'This accounts for its popularity, its toleration by the authorities, and its initial approval by the censor. In short, the mystery of Herbert's licence is no mystery at all' (p. 108). Timing, in a sense, was all. As John Woolley commented in the earliest recorded response to the play's performance, 'had so much ben donne the last yeare, they had everyman ben hanged for it' (*Chess*, p. 193). While the King, Charles and Buckingham had remained in favour of the Spanish match, *A Game at Chess* was unthinkable. By mid-1624 there was no one with influence at Court who had cause to be offended by it.

So where for Limon the play is associated with the ascendancy of Charles and Buckingham, and for Heinemann it is ideologically consonant with the oppositional politics of Pembroke and his associates, for Howard-Hill it is (in factional terms) politically neutral, a celebration of the national mood. Although I have reservations about aspects of Howard-Hill's analysis (to which I shall return), his conclusions on its licensing substantiate my own earlier published view, in which I argued that 'While we cannot rule out a conspiracy behind *A Game at Chess*, there is no evidence for it, and it remains an unnecessary conjecture' – unnecessary in that, as a typical beneficiary of the patronage processes of the Jacobean court, the Master of the Revels was essentially a consensual figure. He tried to ensure that nothing was presented on stage which was provocatively offensive to persons of substance or to friendly foreign powers.[14] In the context Howard-Hill outlines there is no real reason to suppose that Herbert would have had any qualms about granting a licence to the play.

It may well be that the lengths to which the actors went to impersonate Gondomar – apparently acquiring his litter, chair of ease (with a hole cut in the seat, so that it would not aggravate his anal fistula) and a cast suit of clothes – breached normal levels of fictional veiling and so fuelled a level of popular success Herbert did not anticipate. In 1632 he was to insist that Queen Henrietta Maria's Men alter their production of Shirley's *The Ball*, which he had already licensed, because 'there were divers personated so naturally, both of lords and others of the court, that I took it ill' (Bawcutt, p. 177). Had Herbert recognized the implicit satire of those 'lords and others' in the play as he licensed it, but not thought it part of his function to remove it until it was made explicit by the 'personation'? In the case of Massinger's *Believe as You List* he clearly did recognize the target and refused a licence because it was not sufficiently disguised: 'I did refuse to allow of a play of Messinger's, because itt did contain dangerous matter, as the deposing of Sebastian king of Portugal by Philip the and ther being a peace sworen twixte the kings of England and Spayne' (Bawcutt, pp. 171–2). Nevertheless, when the play came back to him, transposed to classical antiquity but in other respects essentially the same, he granted it a licence.[15] That is, Herbert's practice seems to have been to sift out what was *provocatively* offensive to persons of influence, but not to attempt to police the intentions of dramatists and their players or to pry too closely into adequately coded and distanced works, whatever an audience might infer from them. To that extent Herbert's treatment of *A Game at Chess* is not, on the face of it, any different from his treatment of other plays.

The Spanish Ambassador's protest

In the case of *A Game at Chess* there was only one man in England likely to take violent exception to it – the man who did so, Don Carlos de Coloma, successor to Gondomar as resident Spanish Ambassador between April 1622 and September 1624. It might seem self-evident that a Spanish Ambassador would object to a play that was such an uninhibited attack on Spain, its king and his ministers. Foreign ambassadors regularly complained about such matters.[16] But – and I think this is a point no commentator has picked up – Coloma had very particular reasons for responding as he did. These may be inferred from the letter which he wrote about the play to the Conde-Duque Olivares, chief minister to Philip IV of Spain; it was written the day after he forwarded his protest about the play to King James.

The letter has been well known since E. M. Wilson and O. Turner first published an English translation in 1949, but mainly treated as the fullest account of the play in performance (until Holles's account became better known) and accorded virtual eye-witness status, though Coloma did not actually see it in person.[17] Yet most of it is less about the play than a justification of Coloma's own response to it, which has to be seen in the context of his situation in England at that moment: 'Had I followed the advice of the Marqués de la Hinjosa when he advised me to go away with him, such things would not have reached my ears, nor should I have seen the sacred name of my King outraged in so many ways by such low, vile people, nor his holy and glorious acts so unworthily interpreted; only this was lacking to let me describe my sufferings here as a true Hell. The greatest of these, materially, is to listen to the blasphemies uttered against God; I have been unable, too, to discover during the last two months whether I did right or wrong to stay on here; the question whether I served the King well or ill by so doing keeps me in that uneasiness that your Excellency will well understand in this true servant of his' (*Chess*, p. 195).

The Marqués de la Hinjosa had joined Coloma as ambassador extraordinary, after plans for Prince Charles to marry the Spanish Infanta all but collapsed, and the Prince and Buckingham had (with the reluctant acquiescence of the King) adopted an anti-Spanish stance. His brief was to work against this new direction in English foreign policy. In February 1624 the two of them had complained to James about a bill in parliament for the more effective repression of Catholic recusants; in April they conspired to discredit Buckingham, hoping to break his hold over the King and so reverse the anti-Spanish policy – James was sufficiently disturbed that he felt obliged to consult the Privy Council (3 May) on the truth of their charges. However, in June Philip IV formally broke off the marriage negotiations with James, all but ending the possibility of a *rapprochement* between the two countries. Shortly thereafter Hinjosa was obliged to leave England at short notice, ignominiously in a merchant ship and without taking formal leave of the King (26 June).[18] He advised Coloma to leave with him, but the latter remained in London for the next two months, totally isolated amid growing anti-Spanish feeling, and not even sure that he was doing what his masters in Madrid wanted him to do. Hence the tone of his letter, which at times is positively paranoid.

He had been appointed at a time when Anglo-Spanish relations were extremely cordial and seemed likely to be cemented by a royal marriage; two years later the situation had collapsed into a diplomatic nightmare. And just as Buckingham and his allies sought to scapegoat the British negotiators in Madrid (notably John Digby, Earl of Bristol) in the wake of the volte-face in Anglo-Spanish relations, Coloma could not be sure that people in Spain might not find if convenient to denounce his efforts in London. Coloma saw himself as a soldier rather than a diplomat: 'one who, from the time of his birth, took upon himself the obligations of a soldier, and . . . as I may be trusted in my quality as a soldier, I shall know how, with God's help, to make good those faults into which I have fallen as an ambassador' (*Chess*, p. 197). This is perhaps why Hinjosa was sent to reinforce his embassy and why the subtle friar known as Padre Maestro (Fray Diego de Lafuente) was dispatched from Madrid to conduct some private negotiations with James. Coloma had an exaggerated sense both of his duty to Philip IV and of his own honour: he quarrelled with Hinjosa, probably over a sensitivity about what the presence of the other man meant for his own exalted standing as the representative of the King of Spain ('his ambassador, who for that reason is owed so much outward respect and particular esteem': *Chess*, p. 197).[19]

Their joint attack on Buckingham had included the charge – sensational, though not entirely without foundation – that he had conspired to send James into forced retirement and replace him on the throne with Prince Charles. Faced with such accusations, Buckingham in turn 'commissioned Sir Robert Cotton to investigate precedents of proceedings against ambassadors, who had broken the rules of diplomatic protocol'.[20] Late in April 1624, Cotton circulated his 'Relation of the Proceedings against Ambassadors Who have Miscarried Themselves', which advised the Prince and the Duke to refer the matter to parliament, beginning a process which could lead to a declaration of war with Spain if the ambassadors were found guilty of undiplomatic activity and the King of Spain did not punish them and offer redress.[21] Cotton's recommendations were not actually followed, because James would not allow parliament to set the agenda of matters within the royal prerogative. But Buckingham did pursue a private vendetta against the Spanish ambassadors, which partly explains the ignominious treatment of Hinjosa.

And this did not end with Hinjosa's departure. From mid-July Sir Walter Aston, the British Ambassador in Madrid, informed Spanish ministers of the charges against Hinjosa and Coloma, and on 29 August presented a formal memorial of them to Philip IV himself. This made it plain that James did not blame Philip for the actions of his diplomats, but that he 'would and could by the Law of Nations, and the right of his own Royall Justice, proceed against them with such severity as their offence deserved ... but ... he would leave the reparation hereof to the justice of their King, of whom he would demand and require it.' In fact, nothing came of all this. Two months later (20 October) Aston reported to Buckingham: 'The Conde of Olivares with a strong and violent hand hath delivered the Marquis [i.e. Hinjosa] from an exemplary punishment which would certainly have been inflicted upon him had he been left unto the Council of State, and without care either of the King's master's honor or engagements has saved the Marquis and left the envy of it upon his Majesty if the King our master will so please to understand it.'[22] That is, Buckingham's Spanish counterpart had protected his diplomat from the supposed wrath of his royal master, in such a way that James might still (if he chose) regard the original offence as unpunished – though Philip IV could not himself be held responsible for any of this.

It is a typical early modern diplomatic square dance, which has interesting parallels with what happened in the wake of *A Game at Chess*. Among the rules of the dance it is important to remember that kings are never personally responsible for acts of discourtesy to their royal counterparts; that royal favourites may be held to blame but not normally to a pitch which calls into question their very status; that anyone else (including ambassadors) can be held personally responsible for anything, so that how they are treated by their masters becomes a public gauge of winning and losing, gaining and losing face, in a dispute; and that those who report these matters to their superiors always do so in such a way as to show their own part in the proceedings in the most favourable light.

All of this was in play when *A Game at Chess* became an issue.[23] Coloma knew that Buckingham was pushing for revenge, but could have no confidence that Olivares (or anyone else) would actually save him if diplomatic necessities required a scapegoat. Furthermore he could have had little confidence that Hinjosa, in Madrid, was not protecting himself by deflecting all the blame back on him (i.e. Coloma). All of which, I suggest, further explains the paranoid tones of his 10 August letter to Olivares. The play itself, and its popular reception, could only have underlined to Coloma just how vulnerable he then was in London. But at the same time it offered him an opportunity to strike back – to accuse James of unbecoming behaviour in allowing his players to stage this insult to His Most Catholic Majesty. This was hardly on a par with the ambassadors accusing Buckingham of plotting to overthrow James himself, but it was still a matter of public face and Coloma evidently determined to milk it for all it was worth, not least with a view to how it would look in Madrid. Naturally (under the rules of the square dance) he did not accuse James of personal responsibility, but these were his players, licensed under his authority, and Coloma demanded not only an end to public performance of the play but also that the authors and actors should 'be punished in a public and exemplary fashion' (just what James was demanding in respect of Hinjosa and Coloma himself). Tellingly, he prefaces the whole complaint with the information that he expects to be recalled home at any moment ('I expect at any moment the command of my master the King to go give his Majesty an account of my embassy'), yet offers James an alternative to punishing the players: 'or let Your Majesty order that I be given a ship to sail to Flanders with the appropriate safe passage which you give to the ambassadors of other Kings' – that is, to break off diplomatic relations, only one step short of declaring war. Coloma aimed to make the play the last straw in a seriously deteriorating situation, a twist on the situation which would allow him to withdraw with a shred of dignity. As he put it to Olivares: 'I have given the King of England this choice between punishing this roguery and sending me my papers, because every good reason and conjecture require that he should choose the first alternative, and it seemed to me that if he chose the second, he would find his actions condemned, not only by God, but also by the world' (*Chess*, pp. 196–7).

The whole affair might well have ended there if diplomatic relations had indeed been ruptured at that point, and Coloma had been either expelled or recalled. But James was not yet prepared for an open breach with Spain; so, as Robert Ruigh briefly observes, he was 'careful . . . to avoid offense' (p. 386). Nor apparently had Philip IV given up all hope of peace. And so the rules of the square dance continued to apply, and James's ministers (not unlike the Council of State in Madrid) went through the motions of looking for culprits – carefully assuring Coloma 'that justice will be done in this matter with proper publicity' and that 'complete satisfaction and content will be given in everything' (*Chess*, p. 201). Coloma equally carefully forwarded a translation of Secretary Conway's letter, shrewdly observing 'It remains to be seen whether the punishment that will be given to the actors and author of the play will prove that the [King's] indignation against them is genuine' (*Chess*, p. 202).

The question Coloma poses here is central to the wider debate about censorship. Was the well-documented Privy Council enquiry into the play's staging merely a diplomatic sham, or does it reveal genuine concerns about 'non-censorship' or about the play 'threaten[ing] the Jacobean authorities'? There are a number of reasons for supposing that James's own apparent annoyance with his players might be genuine. Although he had acceded to the new belligerently anti-Spanish policies of his son and favourite, he never did so with any enthusiasm. So he might well have been irritated that the play had placed him in a diplomatic embarrassment – at precisely the moment he was trying to take the high moral ground over Coloma and Philip IV. At a number of levels it would have brought home to the old man how much he was losing real control of his kingdom: he had seven months to live, and his bloated body could not walk unaided.

Most telling of all, his rebukes to the Privy Council for not dealing with the play sooner are prefaced by an unmistakably personal reminiscence:

'His Majestie remembers well there was a commaundment and restraint given against the representinge of anie moderne Christian kings in those Stage-playes' (*Chess*, p. 200). We do not know how James discovered that the actors 'take the boldnes, and presumption in a rude, and dishonorable fashion to represent on the Stage the persons of his Majestie, the Kinge of Spaine, the Conde de Gondomar, the Bishop of Spalato &c.' Coloma's complaint (unlike his dispatch to Olivares) gives no details of the play itself, beyond characterizing it as 'scandalous, impious, barbarous, and ... offensive to my royal master' (*Chess*, p. 193). We may suppose that the messenger who delivered the complaint (in fact, Coloma's English-language secretary) conveyed more verbally, but there is no way of knowing how accurate his information might have been.

James (like Elizabeth before him) was typical of his time in regarding an affront to a fellow monarch as an affront to himself: it was an issue which might well have moved him personally, especially if he believed (as the wording of the letter suggests) that both he and Philip had been 'personated' as disrespectfully as Gondomar and De Dominis. If that were so – whatever else the play contained – he had (through the insubordination of his actors) ceded face to Spain at precisely the moment that he was demanding redress for its ambassadors' undiplomatic behaviour. So, while the response to Coloma may well have been formulaic, it is not unreasonable to suppose that there was an element of genuine irritation in the King's rebuke to his Councillors and demand 'for the exemplarie, and severe punishment of the present offendors' (*Chess*, p. 200).

According to Howard-Hill, 'so far as can be determined at this distance of time, none of the other chessmen [i.e. other than Gondomar and De Dominis] was so strongly individualized', and he denies that the scandal of the play derived from any lifelike impersonation of King James, Prince Charles or Buckingham, however unmistakable their counterparts within the drama must have been.[24] This glosses over Coloma's clear contention to Olivares that 'the king of the blacks has easily been taken for our lord the King, because of his youth, dress, and other details' (*Chess*, p. 194). Moreover even the 'personation' of Gondomar, who had been the King of Spain's representative, and was still his minister, was a potentially serious issue – Coloma's assertion that a royal ambassador 'is owed so much outward respect and particular esteem' is not entirely self-aggrandizement. As we have seen, the Privy Council's response to Conway's letter (21 Aug. 1624) ignores this side of the issue altogether, just as it ignores the charge of dilatoriness levelled at themselves. They report their examination of the actors (Middleton had been expected but did not turn up), focusing almost entirely on questions of due process: had the play been properly licensed by the Master of the Revels? Had they changed or added anything since the licence? They do not mention 'personation': their apparent agenda was to redirect any blame onto the Master of the Revels. The actors were only punished by being prevented from performing and in having to put up a bond of £300 against any breach of this order.

Conway's prompt reply (27 Aug.) homed in on the Privy Council's omission, insisting that the King's 'pleasure is, that your LLordships examine by whose direction, and applicacion the personnatinge of Gondemar, and others was done. And that beinge found out, that partie, or parties to bee severely punished' (*Chess*, p. 206). Even the Earl of Pembroke's letter of the same day, which effectively signalled the last rites of the scandal in conveying the King's permission for his players to start performing again (though not *A Game at Chess*), pursues the same theme. He reminds the Council that the King had involved them in the enquiry into the play 'out of the tender regard hee has of that Kings honnour [i.e. Philip IV's], and those his Ministers who weare Conceived to bee wounded thereby,' and concludes his account of the King's terms under which the actors are to be allowed to perform again with the provision, 'Yet notwithstanding that my Llordships proceed in their disquisicion to fynd out the originall roote of this offence, whether it sprang from the Poet, Players, or both, and to Certefy his Majesty accordingly' (*Chess*, pp. 206–7). Pembroke is unobligingly vague about the nature of 'this offence', which is clearly more specific than the scandalous nature of the play as a whole. But taken in parallel with Conway's letter it is surely the issue of the impersonation, and specifically the impersonation of royalty and its representatives, which continued to rankle even as the general furore was dying down. The determination to apportion blame remains undiminished.[25]

At which point the official documentary record goes all but blank. John Woolley (28 Aug.) continues his gossip, but admits that he has no corroboration: 'Some say (how true it is I know not) that the Players are gone to the Courte to act the game at Chesse before the Kinge. which doth much truble the spanish Ambassador' (*Chess*, p. 207). One can imagine that it would indeed 'truble' Coloma, but it seems most unlikely – a kind of street fantasy of what might go on in royal palaces. And Coloma's paranoid vigil was almost over – his letter of recall to Madrid arrived a few days later, and he left the country in September. On 30 August Middleton's son, Edward, was required to appear before the Privy Council, and did so, but there is no record of what he said (*Chess*, pp. 207–8). That the enquiry into the play begins to dry up just when Coloma leaves might reinforce the suspicion that it was all for show, a matter of saving diplomatic face. Yet the questioning of Edward Middleton points to an ongoing investigation, which perhaps did result in the brief imprison-ment of his father, as the instigator of the impersonations.

The unspoken issue here may be the practice of some dramatists taking on the role of what in the modern theatre would be called the director – rehearsing the actors in how the text was to be played, including perhaps impersonations. We know that Jonson sometimes took this role. Did Middleton do it for *A Game at Chess*, or was it at least politic to channel the blame on to him and away from the company as a whole?[26] The various versions of verses said to have been addressed by Middleton to the King to effect his release may indeed testify to his having been imprisoned – whether as a convenient scapegoat or as the director (*Chess*, pp. 211–12). But in either case the root issue seems to have been that of the impersonation of royalty and its representatives, rather than the content of the play in general. Such impersonation was an affront in itself to royal dignity (*all* royal dignity) and also to the authority of the Master of the Revels, in betraying the trust which was implicit in the granting of the licence. So if Middleton was indeed imprisoned, it need not have been a complete sham for form's sake: someone, even King James himself, may have been determined that an example be made for such an affront.

The diplomatic context of *A Game at Chess* probably accounts for a number of the special features surrounding its scandal. The Master of the Revels was supposed to ensure that no offence was given in the public theatres to those – including friendly foreign ambassadors – with standing at court. When Philip Henslowe paid Chettle and Dekker to write *King Sebastian* in 1601, Edmond Tilney would have had no qualms in licensing a play on such a subject, given that England had virtually no diplomatic relations with Spain at the time. When Massinger tried to write on the same subject in 1631 Herbert stopped him, because diplomatic relations with Spain were good, and only allowed *Believe as You List* under a discreetly remote historical veil. *A Game at Chess* fell curiously between these two stools. Diplomatic relations with Spain were appalling, but not non-existent. So Herbert managed to allow something that actually caused offence, possibly miscalculating over whether Coloma would (given his circumstances) actually complain or whether, if he did, anyone would take it seriously. In the event, the King chose to take it sufficiently seriously that a formal process of enquiry was pursued, which may well have led to 'exemplary punishment'.

The evidence is not there to say that this did happen, but it would have been a perfectly logical consequence of Coloma's original protest and the terms in which it was couched. It would have been, in fact, what was *supposed* to happen if someone of sufficient standing chose to complain about a play – as, for example, Sir James Murray complained about *Eastward Ho!*[27] What made this different was that it required correspondence at Privy Council level and so left far more of a documentary record than is usually the case.

Buckingham and sponsorship

That documentary record thus relates exclusively to the offence to Spain, and specifically how that offence was exacerbated by onstage impersonation. Modern scholars, however, have not been slow to suppose that Middleton's targets in *A Game at Chess* did not only include Gondomar and the Jesuits, but implicitly those in authority in England who had allowed Spanish and Roman Catholic interests to flourish so strongly, prior to the reverses they had received in the year leading up to the play. When the Black Knight/Gondomar boasts of how he got a White House/ English fleet to deal with the Turkish pirates who threatened Spanish interests in the Mediterranean; or how he had made 'the jails fly open', in apparent reference to James's agreement to release 74 Catholic priests in 1618 (III.i.85–91), it is difficult to overlook the inference that James and his advisers had shown poor judgement in allowing him so much influence. In the former instance, since Buckingham as Lord Admiral was responsible for the 'gallant fleet', it is clear enough where implicit blame lay. When the Black Knight chortles how 'The court has held the city by the horns/Whilst I have milked her' (III.i.108–9) no individuals are implicated, yet there is no mistaking who is responsible.

By the same token, whoever is shadowed by the treacherous White King's Pawn (a matter I discuss below) it is difficult to avoid the reflection that a more vigilant master would have recognized the treachery sooner. There is some evidence that Middleton himself was conscious of this implication, and tried to answer it in having the White King say: 'And dost thou fall from the top-bough by the rottenness/Of thy alone corruption, like a fruit' (III.i.269–70). 'Thy alone corruption' could mean 'your unique corruption' (i.e. no one else was corrupt) or 'your corruption alone' (i.e. there were no other grounds for your fall); either construction amounts to an implied defence of both the court and the King – the Pawn is to be seen as a unique rotten apple in an otherwise blameless court. And it is earlier made clear that he had qualities which made it right for James to favour him, but that corruption was his undoing. In such ways Middleton defends James from a charge he never *quite* levels. The White King we actually see in the play is a model of rectitude and regal authority – but his improvidence (though never remarked upon) is actually responsible for the crisis in the play from which the nation needs to be saved.

The case of Buckingham (and, to a lesser extent, of Prince Charles) is more complicated. The play depicts their quixotic trip to Madrid – actually undertaken to pursue the deeply unpopular Spanish marriage negotiations – as a subterfuge to 'discover' Spanish double-dealing, and to this extent casts them in a heroic light. Here again, Middleton signals his own sensitivity to the issue by having the White Knight exhort his Duke: 'Let us prevent their rank insinuation/With truth of cause and courage' (IV.iv.2–3). That is, he resolves to anticipate and so thwart the foul rumours the Spanish themselves will spread about the marriage negotiations: which is entirely ironic, given that it was genuine English sentiment rather than Spanish 'insinuation' which made the Madrid trip so unpopular.

Furthermore, as Margot Heinemann points out, in the course of the trip they are obliged 'to feign a little' (IV.iv.17), and thus Middleton contrives to make the White Duke (Buckingham) 'accuse himself of faults well known to be his in reality – gluttony, fatness and lechery' (p. 164). She has in mind such passages as this: 'WHITE DUKE: Or I, beshrew my heart, for I fear fatness,/The fog of fatness, as I fear a dragon;/The comeliness I wish for, that's as glorious' (V.iii.58–60). As a young man Buckingham was notably tall, long-limbed and athletic, but he was fond of food and inclined to put on weight; he was, nevertheless, vain about his looks ('comeliness') and the need to make a splendid ('glorious') appearance. The banquets he served became legendary for their self-indulgence, another issue glanced at in the play, as the Black Knight castigates the 'White House gormandisers' (V.iii.49, and note). The ostensible joke of the scene is at the expense of the Spanish, whose hospitality for Charles's and Buckingham's entourage was reported to be meagre. But the more the Black King decries 'riot' and 'surfeit' (V.iii.2/3), and his Knight waxes poetic about epicurean practices which his House does *not* indulge in (while the virtuous White House does), the more apparent is the joke's double edge. In such ways, to pick up Heinemann's argument, the play may contrive to be 'oppositional' and to satirize Buckingham, even as it celebrates the anti-Spanish policies which he had latterly espoused.

Trevor Howard-Hill, however, refuses to accept that there is anything satirical here: the self-accusations are all a dissemblance undertaken by 'characters [who] have invited the highest respect heretofore'; he thinks it unlikely that 'the audience would be able to shift between a serious and a satirical understanding readily', and insists overall: 'None of the king, prince, duke, and archbishop could have read the play without gratification at the manner in which they were depicted. Certainly there is nothing offensive in their treatment in the play.'[28] But the issue is not so much the White Duke's 'treatment' in the play as the broader interpretive contexts within which his self-accusations are advanced – contexts about which, as I have shown, Middleton himself was clearly sensitive.

That sensitivity is further shown in the care with which he has built degrees of ambiguity into what may seem to be transparent identifications. At one level, for example, the White Queen has to 'be' Queen Anne, James's consort. Yet she died in 1618, and so had no literal place in the events of 1623 explicitly shadowed in the play. Nor would the lust which the youthful Black King declares for her (III.i.244) make any sense. Lust is the besetting vice of the Black House and is always at least partly a metaphor for their rapacious religious zeal. So the Black King's lust for the White Queen must relate to another entity, perhaps the Church of England (to which the White King could be said to be 'married'), a reading which chimes well with IV.iv, where the White Bishop saves the White Queen from the machinations of the Fat Bishop. At the same time, however, it was well known that Queen Anne had been a practising Roman Catholic, and in that context the desire of the Black House to 'take' the White Queen could make ready personal sense – if we do not hold the play to a consistent time-scale.

The ambiguities built into the 'identity' of the White King's Pawn can be traced more tangibly in the textual evidence. From the earliest conception of the play, as shown in the Archdall manuscript, the Pawn is characterized as a Roman Catholic convert, whose treachery looks for advancement in the Roman church. The Black Knight promises: 'There's an infallible staff and a red hat/Reserved for you' (II.ii.220–1) – the emblems of a cardinal. This would be appropriate for someone like Sir Tobie Matthew, who had advocated the restoration of the Catholic bishoprics in England and had furthered the marriage negotiations in Spain. On the other hand, on the Pawn's first appearance the Black Knight calls out '*Curanda pecunia*' (I.i.308) – 'Watch out for your money.' This scarcely seems relevant to Matthew, but might apply to Lionel Cranfield, Earl of Middlesex. As Lord Treasurer he had opposed war with Spain on grounds of cost, had incurred Buckingham's displeasure when the Duke's own policy changed in that direction, and paid the price, being convicted of corruption by parliament in May 1624. But Cranfield had no leanings towards Catholicism or the Jesuits. Yet later versions of the play point more strongly towards him:

WHITE KING: Has my goodness,
                      Clemency, love, and favour gracious raised thee
                      From a condition next to popular labour,
                      Took thee from all the dubitable hazards
                      Of fortune, her most unsecure adventures,
                      And grafted thee into a branch of honour

                      (III.i.263–8: italicized lines not in Archdall)

The inserted passage glances at his unique rise from city apprentice to rich merchant trader and speculator, to peer and Lord Treasurer. Other late insertions, such as his promise 'To cross ... with my counsel, purse and power' (I.i.319) anything unhelpful to the Black House, reflect on his opposition to war with Spain (construed as treachery) and the 'discovery' of the Pawn would thus equate to Cranfield's disgrace. But as Middleton developed the character he removed none of the earlier suggestions. The final White King's Pawn is thus an amalgam of treacheries rather than a specific individual – highly suggestive, yet irredeemably ambiguous in his suggestiveness. Strikingly, John Holles, the one man who actually saw the character onstage and committed his thoughts to paper, thought he represented neither Matthew nor Cranfield, but the Earl of Bristol, Buckingham's scapegoat for the failed Spanish marriage negotiations but neither a Catholic nor someone who had risen to the aristocracy from artisan labour (*Chess*, p. 199). Holles was a friend of Bristol's and so sensitive to the disgrace that hung over him. But that he could identify the White King's Pawn with him (though he clearly noted the reference to 'popular labour', quoting it virtually verbatim) suggests how indeterminate the play's allegory was, at least in some of its features.

It is this contextual ambiguity – this pointing in multiple directions simultaneously – which calls into question Howard-Hill's contention that it would be difficult for an audience 'to shift between a serious and a satirical understanding' of the White House characters. The more Middleton himself offers to preclude certain readings, the more it is apparent that they are actually available. This is especially true in respect of the White Duke's self-confessed lechery:

WHITE DUKE: Some that are pleased to make a wanton on't
                      Call it infirmity of blood, flesh-frailty,
                      But certain there's a worse name in your books for't.
BLACK KNIGHT: The trifle of all vices, the mere innocent,
                      The very novice of this house of clay: venery!

                      (V.iii.121–5)

Once he was securely in power, Buckingham became notorious for his (heterosexual) sexual appetite and quite indiscreet in his courtship; his advances to the wives of Spanish grandees in Madrid helped sour the marriage negotiations. Lust, as I observed, is the besetting vice of the Black House, a metaphor for their political and religious ambitions in pursuit of 'universal monarchy' (I.i.51), which is why the seduction of the White Queen's Pawn is so central to the plot. So it is all the more intriguing to find the White Duke identifying himself with this vice.

The intrigue deepens where these recurrent motifs of heterosexual lust are parallelled by one of sodomy. This is most apparent in III.ii, a clown scene. It takes its tone from the Black Jesting Pawn's fantasy of homoerotic sexual domination, in which whiteness equates with passivity; much of its 'business' involves three (male) Pawns contesting who can and will 'firk' the others; and it concludes: 'We draw together now for all the world/Like three flies with one straw through their buttocks' (III.ii.38–9). The Black Jesting Pawn is presumably the character identified by Holles as a Spanish eunuch (*Chess*, p. 199); if he was literally meant to be a eunuch, the joke about his sexual fantasies is that they are beyond his literal fulfilment. Perhaps, however, 'eunuch' is a euphemism for pathic or catamite which, whatever else, he certainly is. The focus is on homoerotic subordination as a metaphor for power relations. In the Counter-Reformation struggle between Catholic and Protestant, what is at stake is who 'firks' whom, a classic instance of political and sexual metaphors overlapping.

Middleton is more circumspect about associating the principal characters with homoerotic behaviour, but not entirely silent. Commentators have been rather coy about what follows the Black Knight's identification of the White Duke's 'venery': 'If I but hug thee hard I show the worst on't' (V.iii.127), which appears to mean 'If I embrace you closely I will show you the worst of [venery]': i.e. I will reveal my own sexual excitement. This may not be specifically homoerotic: it suggests a state of permanent sexual arousal, satyr-like, in tune with his utterly self-confident villainy. But again it is significant that it is the White Duke to whom he confides this. The whole theme treads dangerously on the nature of Buckingham's supposed relations with King James. Whether there was a physical relationship between them, contemporaries clearly thought there was, though naturally it could not be openly discussed.[29]

Perhaps the most remarkable evidence of the public perception of Buckingham's sexuality occurs in William Laud's diary for 3 July 1625, where (in Latin) he records: 'In my sleep it seemed to me that the Duke of Buckingham got into bed where he acted towards me most lovingly and it seemed to me that many people entered the room and saw it.'[30] Of course, this probably tells us a good deal about Laud's own sexuality and about the systemic conflation of political and sexual power relations in the early modern period. But I think it also gives us an unguarded glimpse into the public imagination of Buckingham.

In *A Game at Chess* by far the most pointed sodomitical reference occurs right at the end of the play, when the White Duke 'bags' his Black counterpart: 'WHITE DUKE: Room for a sun-burnt, tansy-faced beloved,/An olive-coloured Ganymede, and that's all/That's worth the bagging' (V.iii.211–13). 'An olive-coloured Ganymede' is a greenish catamite; 'olive-coloured' clearly identifies Olivares as the Black Duke. On the whole, the relationship between Philip IV – a young and new king – and his grand chamberlain would have meant very little to English audiences; besides, the Black Duke is a very minor character in the play, who never speaks more than two lines at a time, and only ever in support. It is therefore rather surprising that he is accorded the prominence of being the last character into the bag. Most striking of all, Olivares was significantly older than his king (37 in 1624 as against Philip's 19), so, whether or not there was anything sexual in their relationship, to dub *him* the 'Ganymede' is pointedly inappropriate. It is difficult not to conclude that English audiences were expected to 'apply' (laterally) the Jove/Ganymede relationship of the Spanish king and duke to the aging James and his own young duke/favourite.

In short, I think there are compelling reasons to suppose that Middleton was being satirical at the expense of the senior members of 'the White House', and especially of the White Duke, even as he celebrates their conversion to the anti-Spanish cause. For this reason I agree with Heinemann that Buckingham was an unlikely sponsor for the play, but I am still not persuaded that any other sponsor (such as Pembroke) was necessary. It seems to me likely, on the evidence of his acute reading of other texts, that Sir Henry Herbert recognized and understood some of the implications I have been outlining; but if so, they did not disturb him. This is less surprising than many would suppose, given the example of *Believe As You List*. Everything I have outlined here remains a matter of ambiguity, of implication, or of inference. On the surface, Howard-Hill is absolutely right: 'None of the king, prince, duke, and archbishop could have read the play without gratification at the manner in which they were depicted.' Which is precisely what it was Herbert's function to ensure. It was not part of his remit to police Middleton's private intentions or an audience's capacity to think laterally.

In one of the most striking passages in his office-book Herbert records Charles I's own response to Massinger's lost *The King and the Subject*, a play evidently more openly critical of Charles's personal rule than Middleton had ever been about 'the White House'. Yet the King, 'readinge over the play at Newmarket', merely marked that passage and said 'This is too insolent, and to bee changed' (Bawcutt, p. 204). Which suggests that he was quite used to (suitably veiled) insolence, and only drew the line at excessive provocation, at something being 'too insolent'. Herbert, I suggest, judged that the veiled and indirect satire of the White House in *A Game at Chess* fell short of that line, at least until 'personations' tipped the balance. If this 'reading' of the era's dramatic censorship does not square with common notions of Stuart absolutism, I suggest it is entirely consistent with a very patrician (some would say very English) response to a medium whose significance literary scholars are sometimes inclined to get out of proportion. In most circumstances aristocrats were secure enough in their status not to acknowledge veiled satire against themselves; they would not dignify it with their notice.[31] Ironically, of all people, Don Carlos Coloma best put this into words in his protest about the play: 'so offensive to my royal master (if, indeed, the grandeur and inestimable value of his royal person could receive any offense from anybody, and especially from men of such low condition as ordinarily are the authors and actors of such follies:)' (*Chess*, p. 193). For reasons we have observed, Don Carlos *chose*, on behalf of his royal master, to 'receive ... offense', thus precipitating the enquiry. None of the English deigned to be offended on their own behalf.

Notes

1. Annabel Patterson, *Censorship and Interpretation: the Conditions of Reading and Writing in Early Modern England* (Madison: University of Wisconsin Press, 1984), p. 17.
2. *Anticourt Drama in England, 1603–1642* (Charlottesville: University of Virginia Press, 1989), p. 144.
3. Letter of John Holles, Lord Haughton, to the Earl of Somerset, Wed. 11 Aug. 1624; quoted from T. H. Howard-Hill's Revels edition of *A Game at Chess* (Manchester: Manchester University Press, 1993), Appendix I, 'Documents Relating to *A Game at Chess*', p. 199. All references to the play will be to this edition, unless otherwise specified. All contemporary documents relating to the play will be cited from this edition, hereafter cited parenthetically as *Chess*. On Holles's letter, see T. H. Howard-Hill, 'The Unique Report of the Performance of Middleton's *A Game at Chess*', *RES* 42 (1991), 168–78; and A. R. Braunmuller, ' "To the Globe I Rowed": John Holles Sees *A Game at Chess*', *ELR* 20 (1990), 340–56. Holles is presumably thinking of the kind of 'retrayt' apparently accorded Chapman by the Duke of Lennox during the storm over his *Byron* plays; see John Margeson, ed., *George Chapman: the Conspiracy and Tragedy of Byron* (Manchester: Manchester University Press, 1988), p. 11.

4. George Lowe to Sir Arthur Ingram, 7 Aug. 1624; John Woolley to William Trumbull, 11 Aug. 1624; Sir Francis Nethersole to Sir Dudley Carleton, 14 Aug. 1624 (*Chess*, pp. 193, 198, 202 respectively).
5. John Woolley to William Trumbull, 20 Aug. 1624 (*Chess*, p. 203).
6. Sir Edward Conway to the Privy Council, 12 Aug. 1624 (*Chess*, p. 200).
7. Privy Council to Sir Edward Conway, 21 Aug. 1624 (*Chess*, pp. 204–5).
8. N. W. Bawcutt, *The Control and Censorship of Caroline Drama: the Records of Sir Henry Herbert, Master of the Revels 1623–73* (Oxford: Clarendon Press, 1996), p. 152. Hereafter cited parenthetically as 'Bawcutt'.
9. Louis B. Wright, 'A Game at Chess', *TLS* 16 Feb. 1928, p. 112; J. Dover Wilson also suggested Buckingham as a sponsor of the play in his review of R. C. Bald's edition, *The Library*, 4th ser., 11 (1930), 105–16.
10. Jerzy Limon, *Dangerous Matter: English Drama and Politics 1623/24* (Cambridge: Cambridge University Press, 1986), p. 98.
11. Margot Heinemann, *Puritanism and Theatre: Middleton and Opposition Drama under the Early Stuarts* (Cambridge: Past and Present, 1980), pp. 166–9.
12. T. H. Howard-Hill, 'Political Interpretations of Middleton's *A Game at Chess*', *YES* 21 (1991), 274–85.
13. T. H. Howard-Hill, *Middleton's 'Vulgar Pasquin': Essays on 'A Game at Chess'* (Newark: University of Delaware Press, 1995), pp. 8, 69.
14. Richard Dutton, *Mastering the Revels: the Regulation and Censorship of English Renaissance Drama* (Basingstoke: Macmillan Press, 1991), p. 245.
15. Ibid. pp. 97–8; on *The Ball*, see pp. 92–3.
16. Ibid. pp. 22–24; Margeson, ed., *George Chapman*, pp. 9–12.
17. E. M. Wilson and O. Turner, 'The Spanish Protest against *A Game at Chess*', *MLR* 44 (1949), 476–82; reprinted in *Chess*, pp. 194–7.
18. For a detailed account of the activities of the Spanish Ambassadors in the first half of 1624, see Robert E. Ruigh, *The Parliament of 1624: Politics and Foreign Policy* (Cambridge, Mass: Harvard University Press, 1971), pp. 257–302.
19. See Roger Lockyer, *Buckingham: the Life and Political Career of George Villiers, First Duke of Buckingham 1592–1628* (Cape: London, 1981), p. 172.
20. See G. P. V. Akrigg, *Jacobean Pageant* (Cambridge, Mass: Harvard University Press, 1963), p. 386; Ruigh, *The Parliament of 1624*, pp. 285, 289.
21. Cotton's paper was not published until after his death, when it was the first item in *Cottoni Posthuma* (London, 1651).
22. Ruigh, *The Parliament of 1624*, p. 302.
23. The text of Aston's 'memorial' is actually endorsed '5 August 1624', more than three weeks before he actually delivered it, and the day of the play's first performance.
24. Howard-Hill, *Middleton's 'Vulgar Pasquin'*, pp. 130, 113–14.
25. Howard-Hill's review of the same territory reaches a very different conclusion: 'I cannot detect in the official correspondence much enthusiasm to handle the matter' (*Middleton's 'Vulgar Pasquin'*, p. 104). But he overlooks James's initial criticism of the Privy Councillors in London, and that they (either deliberately or otherwise) did not do what he asked of them; he also ignores the fact that Pembroke's letter keeps the issue of 'the originall roote of this offence' alive.
26. Christopher Beeston, the manager of the Queen's Men, and Sir Henry Herbert seem to have reached a convenient understanding that Shirley was responsible for the impersonations in *The Ball* (Bawcutt, p. 177).

27. See Dutton, *Mastering the Revels*, p. 172.

28. Howard-Hill, *Middleton's 'Vulgar Pasquin'*, p. 107 and n. 46.

29. David Bergeron most fully argues the case for a physical relationship between James and Buckingham in *Royal Family, Royal Lovers* (Columbia: University of Missouri Press, 1991). Roger Lockyer cautiously agrees (*Buckingham*, p. 22; see also pp. 33, 233–4). Maurice Lee remains sceptical: *Great Britain's Solomon: James VI and I in His Three Kingdoms* (Champaign: University of Illinois Press, 1990), p. 248.

30. Quoted in W. Lamont and S. Oldfield, eds, *Politics, Religion and Literature in the Seventeenth Century* (London: Dent, 1975), pp. 44–5.

31. See Paul Yachnin, 'The Powerless Theater', *ELR* 21 (1991), 49–74.

Part II
Religious Censorship

5
'Right Puisante and Terrible Priests': the Role of the Anglican Church in Elizabethan State Censorship

Richard A. McCabe

Few documents in the history of Elizabethan censorship have occasioned such controversy as the extraordinary order issued to the Stationers' Company on Friday 1 June 1599 by the Archbishop of Canterbury, John Whitgift, and the Bishop of London, Richard Bancroft.[1] Its nature was both reactive and proscriptive: it prohibited the publication of satires and epigrams, tightened the procedures for licensing 'Englishe historyes' and plays, and commanded the confiscation of certain formerly printed works including the verse satires of Hall, Marston, Guilpin and Middleton.[2] On Monday 4 June all but two of the offending items were burned in Stationers' Hall. The 'ecclesiastical position' of the ban's 'authors' convinced John Peter that its principal target was obscenity, and Bruce R. Smith and Lynda Boose have recently employed it to illustrate the phenomenon of state intrusion into the realm of private sexual morality.[3] Yet while the regulation of the body private was certainly deemed essential to that of the body politic, there were many who regarded the Elizabethan government as culpably negligent in the business of moral censorship. Philip Stubbes complained that books 'full of all filthines, scurrilitie, baudry, dissoluteness, cosenage, conycatching and the lyke ... are either quickely licensed, or at least easily tollerate[d], without all denyall or contradiction whatsoever'.[4]

Bruce and Boose credit the bishops with an essentially 'pastoral' choice of texts, the chief criterion being the perceived indecency of the prohibited works. In order to support this notion, Boose advances the odd argument that my own account of the bishops' political motivations arose from the 'erroneous conclusion' that Nashe's *Choice of Valentines* had been printed prior to 1599 and would certainly have been banned had the object of the exercise been the defence of public morality.[5] But it is common knowledge that *The Choice of Valentines* circulated in manuscript, nor did I ever suggest otherwise. What was at issue was the identification, in Elizabethan terms, of the category of the 'wanton' or 'licentious'. Mindful of the salacious reputation of Nashe's poem, and of its likely influence upon other erotic works, I argued that 'had the bishops been attempting to suppress pornographic literature there were surely many works (of the *Choice of Valentines* variety, for example, or even some of the sonnet sequences) which would have taken precedence'.[6] My point was general not specific and did not depend on the availability in print of any particular title. Had the bishops been disturbed by perceived sexual 'deviance', for example, Barnfield's *The Affectionate Shepherd* (1594) or Marlowe's *Hero and Leander* (1598) might have served their purposes. The fundamental naivety of Boose's approach lies in her treatment of Whitgift and Bancroft as though they were Victorian churchmen, disturbed by 'masturbatory strategies of inhibited desire' (p. 192), and desperately attempting to stem the tide of 'pornography', a term invented in the nineteenth century in response to changing attitudes towards sexual mores. Boose works not from the original Stationers' Registers but from Edward Arber's Victorian transcript with its misleading annotations. She accepts without question Arber's insinuation that the printers specifically mentioned in the ban are unsavoury characters 'from whose presses any further publication of these banned works might be expected to come' (p. 186). If this were so, the omission of James Roberts would be quite remarkable, since he printed Marston's *Scourge of Villanie* which, according to Boose, was 'perhaps the most obscene piece of literature listed in the Bishops' Ban' (p. 193). But even Roberts was nothing like the dubious, backstreet character required by Boose's argument: he was a freeman of the Stationers' Company from 1564 and shared with Richard Watkins a lucrative patent for the exclusive privilege of printing almanacs and prognostications.[7] Far from being maverick printers who 'earned their living by printing under unauthorised conditions' as Boose alleges (p. 186), some of those specifically mentioned in the bishops' order were highly respected, liveried (i.e. senior) members of the Stationers' Company: John Windett, whose name heads the list, was not only liveried but was acting as the company's under-warden for 1599. Peter Short and Richard Braddock had also been admitted to the livery, and the former was one of the printers of Foxe's *Acts and Monuments*.[8] Boose has supported a misinterpretation of the text with a misrepresentation of the parties.

The presence upon the bishops' list of *Caltha Poetarum, Of Marriage and Wiving* and *The xv Joyes of Marriage* has lent credence to the notion that its target was obscenity. Yet the record of Whitgift and Bancroft's interventions in the affairs of the press indicates a very different agenda. Like the

'right puisante and terrible priests' to whom Martin Marprelate provocatively dedicated his first *Epistle*, they acted not primarily as ministers of
the Church but as ministers of the State.[9] Whitgift had been a member of
the Privy Council since 1586, and by 1599 both he and Bancroft were
senior members of the High Commission, the supreme high court of the
Anglican Church. Bancroft was largely responsible for the discovery and
destruction of the Marprelate press, and his service in that matter was
cited by Whitgift in support of his nomination to the see of London.[10] In
theory we might expect the High Commission to deal primarily with
heresy, the Privy Council or Star Chamber with treason, but in practice
the Acts of Supremacy and Uniformity (1559) made it difficult to
discriminate between them: it was treasonable, for example, to deny the
spiritual authority of the monarch even on purely 'religious' grounds, and
the insistence that no one in England was prosecuted solely for religious
reasons ironically clarified the state's priorities.[11]

The letters patent which established the High Commission in 1559
(addressed to Matthew Parker, Archbishop of Canterbury, Edmund
Grindal, Bishop of London, and 17 other nominees) made it clear from
the outset that its principal purpose was the enforcement of the Acts of
Uniformity and Supremacy: 'such persons as shall hereafter offend in
anything contrary to the tenor and effect of the said several statutes to be
condignly punished'. It was designed as an instrument of state and its
activities were directed against 'divers seditious and slanderous persons'
who 'have set forth divers seditious books within this our realm of
England, meaning thereby to move and procure strife, division and
dissension amongst our loving and obedient subjects, much to the
disquieting of us and our people.' The Commissioners were therefore
required to enquire into 'all and singular heretical opinions, seditious
books, contempts, conspiracies, false rumours, tales, seditions, misbeha-
viours, slanderous words or showings, published, invented or set forth'.[12]
The rhetoric is pervasively 'moral' but the concern is the political stability
of the state – characteristically represented as a 'moral' cause in itself. So
far as censorship is concerned, the danger is not obscenity but sedition.
The subsequent 'Injunctions' issued to the High Commission on 19 July
1559 required the licensing by the stipulated public authorities of all
'pamphelettes, playes and balettes ... wherein regard wold be had that
nothing therin should be either heretical, sedicious, or unsemely for
Christyan eares' (item 51), but despite the pious overtones of the final
clause the High Commissioners concerned themselves almost exclusively
with suspected cases of subversion not indecency.[13] Nothing was deemed
more 'unsemely for Christyan eares' than treasonable utterance.

In 1566 a set of ordinances for 'reformation of divers disorders in pryntyng and utteryng of Bookes' was issued by the Privy Council through the Star Chamber at the request of the High Commission. The first ordinance stipulated that,

> no person shall prynt, or cause to be imprynted, nor shall bryng, or cause, or procure to be brought into this Realme imprynted, any Booke or copye agaynst the fourme and meanyng of any ordinaunce, prohibition, or commaundement, conteyned, or to be conteyned in any the statutes or lawes of this Realme, or in any Iniunctions, Letters patentes, or ordinaunces, passed or set forth, or to be passed or set forth, by the Queenes most excellent Maiesties graunt, commission, or aucthoritie.[14]

It was also decreed that 'whosoever shall offende agaynst the sayde ordinaunce shall ... forfayte all suche bookes and copies' and that 'all bookes to be so forfayted shalbe brought into Stationers hall' to be 'destroyed or made waste paper'.[15] This is precisely what happened on 4 June 1599, and the fifth ordinance supplies a good idea of the activities over the preceding weekend since it empowers the officers of the Stationers' Company to 'make searche' for prohibited items 'in all workehouses, shoppes, warehouses, and other places, of Prynters, Booksellers, or such as bryng bookes into this Realme to be solde, or where they shall have reasonable cause of suspition'.[16] Cyndia Clegg has recently argued that the searches immediately resulting from the ordinances of 1566 demonstrate 'that protecting privilege was as important to the Stationers' Company as confiscating Catholic imprints'.[17] This may well be the case but it does not follow, as Clegg seems to imply, that the High Commission's intentions in initiating such searches were any less draconian than has traditionally been imagined. However imperfectly policed, the ordinances established both the authority and the mechanism for censorship as and when required. The government shrewdly relied upon the worldly motivation of commercial self-interest to effect its own peculiar aims.

In 1586 the Star Chamber issued a set of 'newe Decrees ... for Orders in Printing' reaffirming the ordinances of 1566 and stipulating that no 'book, woork, coppye, matter, or any other thinge' be printed without being 'first seen and perused by the Archbishop of CANTERBURY and Bishop of LONDON'.[18] It was in this capacity that Whitgift and Bancroft issued their order to the Stationers on 1 June 1599. They were acting, that is to say, under the special powers delegated to them by the Privy Council through the court of Star Chamber. Clegg has argued, however, that viewed from the perspective of 'trade interests' the Star Chamber Decrees of 1586 should properly be seen as 'a genuine triumph for the Stationers' Company and the privileged printers' and therefore 'requires considerable revision of pervasive views that through the Decrees Elizabeth imposed press control to censor religious dissent and political opposition'.[19] But while Clegg is certainly correct in asserting that the Star Chamber was responding to pressure from the privileged printers, it does not follow that the promotion of 'trade interests' was its exclusive concern. Nor does it follow that the protection of 'trade interests' was necessarily inimical to the business of censorship. A well-regulated press, dependent upon the Star Chamber for its financial security, was likely to be more amenable to government control than a disorganized commercial free-for-all. The preamble to the Decrees asserts that disorderly printing has occasioned 'intollerable offences and troubles and disturbances ... aswell in the Churche, as in the Civill governement of the state and common wealthe of this Realme'.[20] In this respect the political and social anxieties occasioned by the Elizabethan press were not dissimilar to those currently occasioned by the Internet. The Elizabethan government was well aware that the press was, by nature, a potentially anarchic medium. By protecting the vested interests of privileged printers, and increasing the self-regulatory powers of the Stationers' Company, the Star Chamber hoped to regulate the message by securing the medium. The confiscation of Robert Waldegrave's press in 1588 by the Stationers' Court 'according to the late decrees of ye Starre chamber' for publishing John Udall's *Diotrephes* is a case in point.[21] Yet no sooner had Waldegrave's press been confiscated than he involved himself in the surreptitious production of the Marprelate pamphlets. The Star Chamber Decrees had confined the business of printing to three locations, London, Oxford and Cambridge, but the Marprelate press was both illicit and mobile and therefore anathema to the government. Since it had put itself beyond the intervention of the Stationers' Company, it took the combined efforts of the High Commission and the Privy Council to track it down. Although neither could be proved to be the author of the Marprelate pamphlets, John Udall was subsequently sentenced to death, and John Penry was executed, not for heresy but for treason. As one might expect, the Marprelate pamphleteers represent the High Commission as little better than an English version of the continental Inquisition, but Clegg argues that 'what looks like hegemony in conception, in practice emerges riddled with contradictions shaped by competing interests'. In support of this view she points to 'the far greater liberty (within limits) for radical reform ideas within the printing establishment and the Church than earlier studies of print culture have allowed'.[22] The crucial phrase in this formulation, however, is the parenthetical 'within limits'. What Clegg represents as tolerance was actually indifference. The Thirty-nine Articles are deliberately ambiguous on certain key issues of doctrine, and the authorities were largely unconcerned by heterodox opinions which did not tend to undermine the Acts of Supremacy or Uniformity and thereby pose a threat to the government of the realm.

The surviving correspondence of Whitgift and Bancroft amply illustrates the range and nature of their concerns in the matter of press censorship. Writing to Robert Cecil on 29 September 1597, for example, Bancroft enclosed 'an history in latine very lately come over'.[23] The author, he asserts, 'is one, who favours the gospel, and is out of question no papist' and who writes 'more honourably . . . of her Majesty and of her actions then any stranger hitherto hath done.' Yet while there is much that is 'commendable' in the work, it also contains material that 'might . . . have been better omitted' and which may possibly constitute an 'impediment' to its publication. Cecil's attention is directed to p. 473 where the author supplies the contents of Sextus V's bull of 1588 against Elizabeth. Although he has been careful to delete 'all the popes raylinge, and slanderous imputations to her Majesty's person' he has included Cardinal Allen's 'malitious calumniations' against her government. The work may therefore prove harmful to those 'who are allredy popishly addicted'. It also treats of such dangerous matters as the queen's excommunication (p. 83), of her policy in refusing to appoint an heir apparent (p. 424), and of her relationship with the Duc d'Alençon (p. 322). The latter was particularly sensitive and had occasioned one of the most notorious acts of censorship in living memory. In 1579, following the publication of the anti-Alençon tract *The Discoverie of a Gaping Gulf Whereinto England is like to be Swallowed*, the author John Stubbs, and the publisher William Page, 'had their Right hands cut off with a Cleaver, driven through the Wrist by the force of a Mallet, upon a Scaffold in the Marketplace at Westminster'.[24] They had been convicted of seditious libel. Although the matter is 20 years in the past, the issue is still taboo because the author alleges the existence of a formal betrothal between the queen and 'Monsieur'. Bancroft has no option, therefore, but to prohibit the sale of the work until he has learned Cecil's 'pleasure' in the matter.

A letter from Whitgift to Robert Cecil on 10 May 1600 relating to the *Apology against those which falsely taxe him*, attributed by its printers to the Earl of Essex, indicates the exhaustive measures that were taken in order to secure prohibited matter when the political stakes were high:

Yesterday in the afternoon, Mr. Cuffe, the Earl of Essex his man, came from his Lord unto me to signify that he had understanding of the printing of this book which I send unto you herewith. Whereupon I presently sent to the Master and Wardens of the Stationers to make enquiry for the same, which they did accordingly, and found out both the press and the printers; the press in one Dawson's house, the printers two of Dawson's servants, whom I sent for yesternight, and examined so far forth as the time then served, and committed them to close custody in several prisons ... They confess that they have printed 292 copies, whereof I have gotten into my hands 210 or thereabouts, and am in good hope to recover most of the rest some time this day. Their examinations I purpose to bring with me tomorrow to the Court, because they are not yet finished.[25]

Notable here is the determination to secure exact information about the whereabouts of the press, the identity of the printers, and above all the size of the print-run. As Essex, who denied all involvement in the publication, was currently awaiting trial on a number of serious charges relating to his activities in Ireland, the 80 or so copies unaccounted for represented a considerable danger to public order. On 27 February 1601, just two days after Essex's execution, Bancroft advised Cecil that,

Since I came home from the Court, I am informed that a fellow goeth about the street, selling the ballads whereof here is a copy enclosed. He giveth it out that the Countess of Essex hath made it, which procureth many to buy it. I have sent divers up and down the city to see if they can meet with him. I am told that the ballad was made half a year since upon some other occasion, and that the knave, to make his gain, doth affirm as is before mentioned. I have sent for the Warden of the Stationers and will take as quick a course as I can. These villainous printers do trouble me more than I will write of.[26]

The concluding sentiment aptly expresses the frustrations of a lifetime. As the enterprising ballad seller realized, there was nothing so commercially viable as topicality – or at least the perception of topicality. The same realization, rather than any concern with sexual mores, motivated Whitgift and Bancroft's concern with satires, epigrams, histories and plays in 1599.

Elizabethan formal verse satire was the product of a turbulent decade. Social and economic unrest combined with political uncertainty to create a climate of complaint which the satirists expertly exploited, and fostered, using the pretence of classical imitation as a cloak for topical comment. Marston disingenuously explained that it was the purpose of satire 'under fained private names, to note generall vices' and that only ignorant or malicious readers would 'wrest each fayned name unto a private unfained person'.[27] It now seems clear, however, that the primary effect of such disclaimers of slanderous intent was the promotion of a slanderous hermeneutic. It was a device borrowed from Juvenal, who undertook in his first satire to speak ill only of the dead owing to the political danger of the times: 'experiar quid concedatur in illos,/quorum Flaminia tegitur cinis atque Latina' ('I will see what may be said of those whose ashes lie under the Flaminian and Latin roads', ll. 170–1).

Contemporary habits of marginal annotation show how avidly particular identifications were made by Elizabethan readers. *The Faerie Queene* was a case in point, and the calling in of *Mother Hubberds Tale* in 1591 for scandalous aspersions upon Lord Burghley and his children can only have intensified the search for similar instances throughout the Spenserian canon.[28] In his prefatory remarks to *Volpone* Ben Jonson complained that the practice of 'application' was so widespread that even genuinely non-specific texts were construed as topically relevant.[29] Yet, as manuscript evidence suggests, few satiric texts were genuinely non-specific. In the earliest manuscript of Donne's fourth satire, for example, the lines 'A / Pursevant would have ravish'd him away / For saying of our Ladies psalter' (ll. 215–17) read 'Topcliffe' for 'pursevant', alluding to the licensed informer and torturer dreaded by the Recusant community into which Donne was born.[30] Had the satire been published, 'pursevant' would certainly have been used, but the substitution indicates the ease with which generalized statements might encode particular allusions. As Spenser's 'Letter to Raleigh' makes clear, political allegory relies upon such strategies, for 'in that Faery Queene I meane glory in my generall intention, but in my particular I conceive the most excellent and glorious person of our soueraine the Queene'.[31] The satirists negotiated a similar correlation between 'particular' and 'general' intentions and their public responded accordingly: Donne's vague reference to 'two reverend men / Of our two Academies' is glossed by one reader as John Reynolds and Lancelot Andrewes.[32]

Within the fourth satire Donne is careful to attribute the worst accusations against prominent persons not to the first-person narrator, but to an unidentified scandal-monger who acts 'like a privilegd'd spie / Whom nothing can discredit' and freely 'libells now 'gainst each great man' (ll. 119–20). Although the general situation is borrowed from Horace (I.9), the acute sense of danger is original to Donne. Horace's interlocutor is simply a bore; Donne's may actually be 'a privilegd'd spie', attempting to lure his victim into self-incrimination. There were draconian laws against seditious rumour and as the tirade continues the fear becomes palpable:

> Who wastes in meat, in clothes, in horse, he notes;
> Who loves whores, who boyes, and who goats.
> I more amas'd than Circes prisoners, when
> They felt themselves turne beasts, felt myselfe then
> Becomming Traytor ... (ll. 127–31)[33]

Annabel Patterson aptly refers to the speaker's 'deeply divided and half-felonious self', but the passage is also designed to mirror the reader's self-consciousness.[34] What Donne represents himself as feeling is precisely what anyone who came into possession of a covertly circulated manuscript of Satire IV might feel. This is dangerous matter not because it involves obscenity *per se* – 'Who loves whores, who boyes, and who goats' – but because it uses obscenity as a satiric device. The distinction between the issues arising from eroticism and satire is clearly marked by Donne in a letter of 1600 in which he refers to his 'satyrs' as works to which 'belongs some feare', while to his elegies belongs only 'shame'.[35] The central theme of Satire IV is satire itself, and as such it constitutes perhaps the best contemporary commentary upon the atmosphere of suspicion and apprehension in which the genre developed. The relationship between Elizabethan satire and Elizabethan censorship is disturbingly symbiotic.

The publication of formal verse satire on the Latin model began in 1595 with Thomas Lodge's *A Fig for Momus* but came properly into vogue two years later with the appearance of Joseph Hall's *Virgidemiarum*. Hall's *Tooth-lesse Satyrs* of 1597 were quickly followed by the more acerbic *Byting Satyrs* which closely engaged with the social problems occasioned by enclosure, dispossession, inflation and unemployment.[36] Coming so soon after the Oxfordshire riots of December 1596 when armed gangs attempted to pull down the 'hedges' enclosing common land, Hall's evident sympathy for the protesters was little short of inflammatory: in a desolate landscape of deserted villages and 'starved Tenements' the 'thriftie Yeoman' is warned to 'hedge in nought, but what's thine owne', and scorn is cast upon the local aristocracy who have abandoned traditional habits of 'good hospitalitie'.[37] The pattern was set, and the publication of formal verse satire accelerated apace. Sir John Davies's *Epigrammes* appeared in 1597 and in May 1598 William Rankin's *Seven Satyres* and John Marston's *The Metamorphosis of Pigmalions Image and*

Certaine Satyres were entered in the Stationers' Register. Marston's *The Scourge of Villanie* was published in September of the same year as was Everard Guilpin's *Skialetheia: or, a Shadowe of Truth in certaine Epigrams and Satyres*. 1599 saw two further editions of *The Scourge of Villanie* augmented by the 'Satira Nova', an attack on Hall whose *Byting Satyres* were also reissued. John Weever's *Epigrammes in the Oldest Cut, and Newst Fashion* appeared the same year as did Thomas Bastard's *Chrestoleros, Seven Bookes of Epigrames* and Middleton's *Micro-cynicon: Sixe Snarling Satyres*. As all of these works employed the same techniques of cryptic allusion, the range of potential 'application' was expanding exponentially. The pamphlets of the Harvey–Nashe controversy – also banned on 1 June 1599 – had established a lucrative market for personal slander which the satirists exploited with alacrity. References to topical events, popular 'ordinaries' and new-fangled fashions (such as the Cadiz beard) seemed to offer the reader hints and to invite the very speculation that Marston and his fellow satirists pretended to deplore. Readers were manipulated into making identifications by direct appeals to their own experience, to what, according to Guilpin, they can 'observe' in the aisles of St Paul's.[38] Thus Middleton can ask 'Who knows not Zodon?' with the same confidence with which Spenser can ask – in a poem that invites personal identifications throughout – 'who knowes not *Colin Clout?'*.[39] Readers were repeatedly brought to the verge of a dangerous political revelation, reminded of the problem of the succession, and then left to their own devices:

> O is not this a curteous minded man?
> *No foole, no, a damned Machevelian.*
> Holds candle to the devill for a while,
> That he the better may the world beguile
> That's fed with shows. He hopes though some repine,
> When sunne is set the lesser starres will shine ...
> But bold-fac'd Satyre, straine not over hie,
> But laugh and chuck at meaner gullery.[40]

Then there was Guilpin's 'great Foelix', alias 'Signior Machiavell', who attempted, like Shakespeare's Bolingbroke, 'with curtesie',

> T'entrench himselfe in popularitie,
> And for a writhen face, and bodies move,
> Be Barricadode in the peoples love.[41]

Both Bolingbroke and Foelix have traditionally been associated with the Earl of Essex and the issuing of the Bishops' order coincided with the suppression of John Hayward's *Life and Raigne of King Henrie IIII*, a work controversially dedicated to the earl.[42] The association has led Cyndia Clegg to argue that the ban's principal purpose was the suppression of material hostile to Essex. Whitgift, she claims, 'seems to have extended his own authority according to the bonds of friendship'.[43] There is no documentary evidence to support this, however, and such partisan behaviour would surely have proved unacceptable to Whitgift's fellow Privy Councillors. As Clegg herself points out, the Privy Council closely 'monitored' the activities of the High Commission and occasionally rebuked it for overstepping its authority.[44] The order of 1 June 1599 must therefore be seen as an act of state rather than an act of personal patronage. In view of this I would reiterate my earlier view that it was to the general climate of social unrest and political danger that Whitgift and Bancroft reacted, intervening on behalf of the Privy Council and the High Commission. Essex was very much the product of his times, a symptom rather than a cause of the general malaise, and the ultimate object of satire was the crown, as the repeated attempts to suppress seditious rumours and libels demonstrate.[45] Hence the deep suspicion of 'anti-feminist' works.

Together with the satires of Hall, Marston, Guilpin and Middleton the following works were banned outright:

Caltha Poetarum
Davyes Epigrams, with marlowes Elegyes;
The booke against woemen, viz'; of marriage and wyvinge
The xv ioyes of marriage

It was further stipulated,

That noe Satyres or Epigramms be printed hereafter
That noe Englishe historyes bee printed excepte they bee allowed by somme of her maiesties privie Counsell
That noe playes bee printed excepte they bee allowed by suche as have aucthorytie[46]

As the clause concerning histories indicates, matters of state rather than sexual ethics are involved. There is no mention whatsoever of indecency or obscenity. Rather, the juxtaposing of satires, histories and plays speaks to the major concerns of the Privy Council in the matter of censorship over the years 1597–9. The recent affair of *The Isle of Dogs* had served to remind Elizabeth's ministers of the potentially seditious nature of public theatre. Having effectively ignored the moral complaints of the city fathers for over a decade, the Privy Council suddenly ordered the theatres to be demolished and banned all professional acting within London and its environs.[47] The fact that the theatres were not demolished and that performances resumed within a few months is, I think, less surprising than is often imagined. The point had been made. The players, playwrights and impresarios had received a clear shot across the bows: the vulnerability of their position had been demonstrated as had the severe financial repercussions of contumacy.

The clause regarding 'Englishe historyes' was probably occasioned by the furore surrounding John Hayward's *The First Part of the Life and Raigne of King Henrie IIII*. Whitgift had ordered the suppression of its second edition on 28 May, just a few days prior to issuing his 'ban' to the Stationers' Company.[48] He had earlier ordered the suppression of the dedicatory epistle to the first edition even though the text had been licensed by Bancroft's chaplain, Samuel Harsnett. Writing of Hayward's work to his friend Dudley Carleton, John Chamberlain explained that,

> here hath ben much descanting about yt, why such a storie shold come out at this time, and many exceptions taken, especially to the epistle which was a short thinge in Latin dedicated to the erle of Essex ... for my part I can finde no such buggeswords, but that every thinge is as yt is taken.[49]

As the phrase 'why such a storie shold come out at this time' suggests, the affair says as much about the state of mind of the censors, and the reading public, as of the author. The concern was not merely with what had been said, but what might be thought to have been said. Hayward became one of the first English writers to be accused of what might be termed 'seditious anachronism' – of having adopted Juvenal's strategy of writing about the living under the pretence of writing about the dead and leaving the business of 'application' to the reader.

Whatever the truth in Hayward's case, the satirists were certainly perceived to be playing a similar game under the guise of classical imitation. This is demonstrated by the nature of the works proscribed along with theirs. The prohibition of Marlowe's elegies was necessitated by their publication with Davies' epigrams as *Epigrammes and Elegies by J. D and C. M* (ca. 1575), and it is therefore notable that the list of books burned in Stationers' Hall on 4 June omits all mention of Marlowe and gives the title simply as 'Davies Epigrams'. *Caltha Poetarum: Or the Bumble*

Bee (1599), a satire masquerading as an erotic epyllion, is a more interesting case. The title page attributes the work to 'Thomas Cutwode', but Leslie Hotson has convincingly demonstrated that this is merely a pseudonym for Tailboys Dymock, the brother of Sir Edward Dymock, the Queen's champion.[50] Throughout his life he conducted a bitter feud with his uncle the Earl of Lincoln and was called before the Court of Star Chamber in 1590 on a charge of producing a malicious libel 'published in most foul, slanderous and riming and railing sort, as it were by way of poetry'. A similar accusation was levelled against him in 1601.[51] *Caltha Poetarum* is advertised to the reader as an allegorical work touching the author's contemporaries but 'without offence or fault': 'by Flower, Plant, or Tree, / Persons of good worth are ment, conceale thus doth hee'.[52] It seems clear, however, that Dymock took yet another opportunity to satirize the Earl of Lincoln while also considerably expanding his range of scurrilous reference. As Hannah Betts has argued, the poem constitutes 'the most fantastically erotic vision of Elizabethan court politics to survive from the period'.[53] Spenser's Belphoebe – said in the 'Letter to Raleigh' to represent the private person of Elizabeth Tudor – seems to be parodied in the figure of 'La sancta Caltha', and the bee's devotion to her beauty reads suspiciously like a sly comment on the 'cult' of the Virgin Queen with all of its Marian associations:

> With Virgin wax he makes a hony alter,
>   And on it stands, the torches and the tapers,
> Where he must sing his Rosarye and Psalter,
>   And pray devoutly to his holy papers,
> With book, with candlelight, with bels and clappers.[54]

The royal image was peculiarly vulnerable to iconoclasts when seen as the mere displacement of a discredited theology. In the event, however, *Caltha Poetarum* was not burned on 4 June. Together with Hall's *Virgidemiarum* it was merely 'staid', or confiscated, presumably pending further investigation. At the same time, *Willobie His Advisa. or The True Picture of a Modest Maid, and of a Chast and Constant Wife* (1594), a work not originally on the bishops' list, was ordered 'to bee Called in'. This is highly suggestive in view of the likelihood that it deals allegorically, and critically, with the complex relationship between the Queen's private life and public policy.[55] As *Caltha Poetarum* is the most overtly salacious work on the list, its 'staying' clarifies the nature of the bishops' priorities. It would indeed be ironic if the work were spared primarily on the grounds that it was judged to be merely obscene rather than libellous or seditious.

Neither *The xv Ioyes of Marriage* nor *Of Marriage and Wiving* were so fortunate. Both were committed to the flames.[56] Neither could reasonably be termed obscene but both mine a rich vein of misogyny and reflect very severely, albeit obliquely, on the subject of 'the monstrous regiment of women'. 'What new spouse is she', asks Ercole Tasso in *Of Marriage and Wiving* 'that scarce hath bin two daies in her husbands house, but will straight (as if she were a Princesse) make newe laws and orders?'[57] The parenthesis suggests a highly dangerous dimension of political 'application' even though, or possibly because, the translator pointedly makes an exception of the Queen. By describing *Of Marriage and Wyvinge* as 'the booke againste woemen' the bishops would appear to have identified its satiric anti-feminism as its offending aspect. It fact it is comprised of two orations, one extremely hostile to women the other highly favourable – but even the latter implies that the proper status for women is that of wife and mother. A few sentences prior to its praise of the 'famous English Queen' it declares marriage to be essential for 'the preservation of Realmes, [and] the glorie of Princes'.[58] This was not a message that the ageing virgin queen liked to hear, particularly when coupled with the assertion that female nature was inherently 'vile ... perverse and Diabolicall'.[59] In a state ruled by a female sovereign the ultimate political referent of anti-feminism was the monarch herself. The authorities were facing a rising tide of discontent expressed in seditious rumour, slander and libel. Hayward was accused of portraying Richard II in such a way as to suggest an 'application' to Elizabeth, an application she acknowledged when she told William Lambarde 'I am Richard II know ye not that?'[60] She was apparently referring not to Hayward's history but to the play (probably Shakespeare's) performed before the conspirators on the eve of the Essex rebellion. The association seems to have gained wide currency. It was all the more alarming, therefore, that Guilpin had sought to 'keepe *Decorum* on a comick stage' by 'bringing a foule-mouth Iester who might sing, / To rogues, the story of the lousie King'.[61] In February 1601 a lawyer's clerk was hanged in Smithfield for seditious libel and in April a royal proclamation offered an hundred pounds reward for information concerning the dissemination of 'libels ... tending to the slander of our royal person and state'.[62] Taking their cue from the bishops' prohibition of satire, contemporary commentators were quick to associate its authors with such political malcontents. John Weever, for example, asked in 1601: 'Was not one hang'd of late for libelling? / Yes questionlesse. And you deserve the same.'[63] Weever's change of heart was highly self-serving, but the point has a certain validity. Since his own epigrams were not specifically mentioned in the order of 1599 he takes the opportunity to distance himself from the wider political and social implications of engaging in topical satire:

> Well looke the rowles, no office overskippe,
> And see if you can finde the Satyrshippe.
> If not, dare you usurpe an office then
> Without the licence of her Maiestie,
> To punish all her Subjects with the pen,
> Against the Law of all Civilitie?
> I have him up, t'is petty treason all,
> And therefore fears to breake his necke and fall.[64]

In writing a satire against satires, however, it is questionable whether Weever is himself in breach of the bishops' order.

In the immediate aftermath of 4 June 1599 a close watch was kept on the press. Although Breton's anaemic 'Pasquil' poems were entered in the Stationers' Register and apparently printed without objection in 1600, other works fared less well. Samuel Rowlands' *The Letting of Humours Blood in the Head-Vein* was entered in the Stationers' Register on 16 October of the same year, perhaps because of its somewhat misleading title. The Hayward affair had revealed a less than conscientious attitude on the part of the official licensers to whom Whitgift and Bancroft habitually delegated their powers: Harsnett claimed to have read no more than a page of the offending work – although it was admittedly in his immediate interest to make such a statement.[65] Just 13 days after its entry, Rowlands' work was called in and burnt. Some attempt would appear to have been made to circumvent this action, for on 4 March 1601 a number of persons were fined 'for their disorders in buyinge of the bookes of humours lettinge blood in the vayne beinge newe printed after yt was first forbydden and burnt'.[66] Inevitably, as time passed, the order was enforced less rigorously: Rowlands' work was reissued in 1603, 1607 (under a new title), 1611 and 1613. During the period from 1600 to 1608 many works of a satiric nature were printed quite openly, but the authorities were not disposed to ignore anything that seemed to overstep the mark and the nature of their concerns remained quite consistent: the Privy Council ordered action to be taken against the players at the Curtain theatre in 1601 on the grounds that scandalous personal allusions were being made 'under obscure manner, but yet in such sorte as all the hearers may take notice both of the matter and the persons that are meant thereby'.[67] George Wither found himself incarcerated in 1613 following the publication of *Abuses Stript and Whipt*.

Satirists have traditionally claimed not merely a talent but a privilege to abuse. On 1 June 1599 that privilege was officially revoked, and the purpose of the action, as I see it, was to indicate that such revocation lay within the government's power. The 'all licensed fool' might lose his licence at any moment. Opposing Annabel Patterson and earlier commentators, Cyndia Clegg has argued that such instances of press censorship were 'less a part of the routine machinery of an authoritarian state than an *ad hoc* response – albeit authoritarian – to particular texts that the state perceived to endanger the exercise of its legitimate and necessary authority'. Once again the parenthesis considerably qualifies the main statement. 'The imaginative writer,' Clegg concludes, 'must have enjoyed considerably more freedom than has heretofore been allowed.'[68] But this is to configure the 'imaginative' and the 'political' as mutually exclusive categories whereas all of the major literary genres – such as epic, pastoral and romance – are notable for their fusion. To say that the 'imaginative' writer enjoyed the 'freedom' to deal with non-political issues is to say that he was not 'free' in either the political or the imaginative sense. There comes a point at which a pattern of '*ad hoc*' prohibitions constitutes a form of 'repression' in itself. As Patterson has valuably pointed out, Ben Jonson was imprisoned for *The Isle of Dogs* and again for *Eastward Ho*, was summoned before the Lord Chief Justice for *Poetaster*, before the Privy Council for *Sejanus*, and before the High Commission for *The Magnetic Lady*.[69] In the Elizabethan state there were few faculties so politically potent as the imagination, and satire, the genre most likely to foster an aggressively uncompromising stance, was correctly perceived to be particularly dangerous. The difficulty was that satire is more properly a mode than a 'genre': it may inform epics, eclogues, plays and even panegyrics, since one may be damned as effectively by over-praise as by faint praise. It is not surprising that the bishops' action was doomed to 'fail' in the long term, but this does not argue their intentions, nor those of their political masters, to be any the less 'authoritarian'. As King Lear points out, 'the great image of Authority' may itself be satirically configured as no more than a dog in office (IV.vi.160–1).

Notes

1. For the background see Richard A. McCabe, 'Elizabethan Censorship and the Bishops' Ban of 1599', *YES* 11 (1981), 188–93. The present essay is intended to update and complement this article in the light of subsequent comment and scholarship. I am grateful for advise on various points to Dr Ian Gadd and Dr Peter Blayney.

2. *The Stationers' Register, Register C*, fols. 316a, 316b. The text is printed in *A Transcript of the Registers of the Company of Stationers of London: 1554–1640*, ed. Edward Arber, 5 vols (London, 1875–94), III (1876), 677–78. Hereafter Arber. The transcript should be used with caution. As Peter Blayney has recently demonstrated, the 'licensing' or authorizing of material for publication by the appropriate public authorities was distinct from the granting of a 'licence' to print by the officers of the Stationers' Company. The former was a matter of public censorship, the latter of commercial interest – although the Stationers' Company might refuse a 'licence' to print on the grounds that a work had not received proper authorization. The entry of a work in the Stationers' Register was not mandatory but was seen as advantageous in securing the publisher's rights in his copy. Blayney concludes that 'authority [i.e. authorization by the public censors] was officially compulsory, but in practice the company officers could decide when it was or was not required. License was mandatory, and the company punished evasion whenever it was detected. But entrance was voluntary, and its absence is *never* sufficient reason for suspecting anything furtive, dishonest or illegal'. 'The Publication of Playbooks', in John D. Cox and David Scott Kastan, eds, *A New History of Early English Drama* (New York: Columbia University Press, 1997), pp. 396–405, at p. 404.
3. John Peter, *Satire and Complaint in Early English Literature* (Oxford: Clarendon Press, 1956), pp. 149–50; Bruce R. Smith, *Homosexual Desire in Shakespeare's England: a Cultural Poetics* (Chicago: University of Chicago Press, 1991), p. 164; Lynda Boose, 'The 1599 Bishops' Ban, Elizabethan Pornography and the Sexualization of the Jacobean State', in Richard Burt and John Michael Archer, eds, *Enclosure Acts: Sexuality, Property and Culture in Early Modern England* (Ithaca: Cornell University Press, 1994), pp. 185–200.
4. *Philip Stubbes's Anatomy of the Abuses in England in Shakespeare's Youth*, ed. F. J. Furnivall, *New Shakespeare Society*, 6th series, no. 4 (1877), p. 69 of the introduction. A bill specifically directed against obscenity was dropped after its first reading in the Commons in 1580 and never became government policy. See Arber II, 751–3.
5. Boose, 'The 1599 Bishops' Ban', pp. 187, 190. Further references are supplied parenthetically in the text.
6. McCabe, 'Elizabethan Censorship and the Bishops' Ban of 1599', p. 190.
7. Roberts also printed Guilpin's banned *Skialetheia*. See R. B. McKerrow, *A Dictionary of Printers and Booksellers in England, Scotland and Ireland, and of Foreign Printers of English Books 1557–1640* (London: The Bibliographical Society, 1910), p. 229.
8. Ibid. pp. 46–7, 244–5, 294–5. Twelve of the 14 printers mentioned in the Bishops' order are elsewhere said to have been 'present' at its issuing. See *Records of the Court of the Stationers' Company 1576–1602*, eds W. W. Greg and E. Boswell (London: The Bibliographical Society, 1930), p. 72.
9. *Oh read over D. John Bridges for it is a worthy worke: Or an epitome of the fyrste Booke of that right worshipfull volume written against the Puritanes* (1588), p. 1.
10. See Leland H. Carlson, *Martin Marprelate, Gentlemen: Master Job Throckmorton Laid open in his Colours* (San Marino: Huntington Library, 1981), p. 53.
11. For the history of the High Commission see Roland G. Usher, *The Rise and Fall of the High Commission*, introduced by Philip Tyler (Oxford: Clarendon Press, 1968).

12. See G. R. Elton, ed., *The Tudor Constitution: Documents and Commentary*, 2nd edn (Cambridge: Cambridge University Press, 1982), pp. 226–7.

13. *Injunctions geven by the quene's majestie* (1559), sig. D1r.

14. I quote from the text reproduced in Cyprian Blagden, 'Book Trade Control in 1566', *The Library*, 5th series, 13 (1958), 287–92 (plate XII). For variant readings see Arber, I, 322 and John Strype, *The Life and Acts of Matthew Parker*, 3 vols (Oxford: Clarendon Press, 1821), I, p. 442.

15. Blagden, 'Book Trade Control in 1566', plate XII, items 2, 4.

16. Clegg, *Press Censorship*, pp. 58, 59.

17 Cyndia Susan Clegg, *Press Censorship in Elizabethan England* (Cambridge: Cambridge University Press, 1997), p. 46.

18. See Arber, II, pp. 807–12 (p. 810).

19. Clegg, *Press Censorship*, pp. 58, 59.

20. Arber, II, p. 807. See Janet Clare, *'Art Made Tongue-tied by Authority': Elizabethan and Jacobean Dramatic Censorship* (Manchester: Manchester University Press, 1999), p. 17.

21. *Records of the Court of the Stationers' Company*, eds Greg and Boswell, pp. 27–8.

22. Clegg, *Press Censorship*, pp. 51, 54.

23. Hatfield MSS, 55.83. For an accurate synopsis see *Calendar of the Manuscripts of the Most Honourable the Marquis of Salisbury K.G. preserved at Hatfield House, Hertfordshire*, 24 vols (1883–1973), VII (1899), p. 406. Hereafter *Calendar of Hatfield MSS*. Spelling and punctuation are modernized in the *Calendar*.

24. See H. J. Byrom, 'Edmund Spenser's First Printer, Hugh Singleton', *The Library*, 4th series, 14 (1933), pp. 121–56; Richard A. McCabe, '"Little Booke: Thy Selfe Present": the Politics of Presentation in *The Shepheardes Calender*', in Howard Erskine-Hill and Richard A. McCabe, eds, *Presenting Poetry: Composition, Publication, Reception* (Cambridge: Cambridge University Press, 1995), pp. 15–40, at p. 19.

25. *Hatfield MSS*, 79.40; *Calendar of Hatfield MSS*, X (1904), pp. 142–3.

26. *Hatfield MSS*, 77.1; *Calendar of Hatfield MSS*, XI (1906), pp. 88–9.

27. *The Poems of John Marston*, ed. Arnold Davenport (Liverpool: Liverpool University Press, 1961), p. 176.

28. See John Dixon, *The First Commentary on 'The Faerie Queene'*, ed. Graham Hough (privately printed, 1964); Richard S. Peterson, 'Laurel Crown and Ape's Tail: New Light on Spenser's Career from Sir Thomas Tresham', *Spenser Studies* XII (1991 – but pub. 1998), 1–35.

29. See *Works*, eds C. H. Herford, P. Simpson and E. Simpson, 11 vols (Oxford: Clarendon Press, 1925–52), V (1937), pp. 18–19.

30. John Donne, *The Satires, Epigrams and Verse Letters*, ed. W. Milgate (Oxford: Clarendon Press, 1967), p. 162.

31. *The Faerie Queene*, ed. Thomas P. Roche, Jr. (Harmondsworth: Penguin Books, 1978), p. 16.

32. *Satires, Epigrams and Verse Letters*, p. 153, ll. 56–7.

33. For seditious rumour see *Tudor Royal Proclamations*, eds Paul L. Hughes and James F. Larkin, 3 vols (New Haven: Yale University Press, 1964–9), II (1969), pp. 534–5.

34. Annabel Patterson, *Censorship and Interpretation: the Conditions of Writing and Reading in Early Modern England* (Madison: University of Wisconsin Press, 1984), p. 93.

35. See Evelyn M. Simpson, *A Study of the Prose Works of John Donne* (Oxford: Clarendon Press, 1924), p. 298.
36. See Richard A. McCabe, *Joseph Hall: a Study in Satire and Meditation* (Oxford: Clarendon Press, 1982), pp. 53–72.
37. *The Poems of Joseph Hall*, ed. Arnold Davenport (Liverpool: Liverpool University Press, 1969), pp. 77, 78, 81, 85.
38. *Skialetheia or A Shadowe of Truth, in Certaine Epigrams and Satyres*, ed. D. Allen Caroll (Chapel Hill: University of North Carolina Press, 1974), p. 84.
39. *The Works of Thomas Middleton*, ed. A. H. Bullen, 8 vols (London: J. C. Nimmo, 1885–6), VIII (1886), p. 120; *The Faerie Queene*, 6.10.16.
40. *The Poems of John Marston*, p. 75.
41. *Skialetheia*, p. 65.
42. See *King Richard II*, ed. Peter Ure (London: Methuen, 1966 – first pub. 1956), pp. lvii–lxii. For a recent discussion see Howard Erskine-Hill, *Poetry and the Realm of Politics: Shakespeare to Dryden* (Oxford: Clarendon Press, 1996), pp. 40–3.
43. Clegg, *Press Censorship*, p. 208.
44. Ibid. pp. 42–3.
45. Clare, '*Art Made Tongue-tied by Authority*', pp. 26, 61.
46. The full text is given in McCabe, 'Elizabethan Censorship and the Bishops' Ban of 1599', p. 188.
47. See Richard Dutton, *Mastering the Revels: the Regulation and Censorship of English Renaissance Drama* (London: Macmillan, 1991), pp. 107–9.
48. See Clegg, *Press Censorship*, pp. 202–4.
49. *The Letters of John Chamberlain*, ed. N. E. McClure, 2 vols (Philadelphia: The American Philosophical Society, 1939), I, p. 70.
50. Leslie Hotson, 'Marigold of the Poets', in *Essays by Divers Hands: Transactions of the Royal Society of Literature of the United Kingdom*, new series, 17 (1938), pp. 47–68.
51. Ibid., pp. 51, 53.
52. *Caltha Poetarum*, sig. A8r.
53. ' "The Image of this Queene so Quaynt": the Pornographic Blazon 1588–1603', in Julia M. Walker, ed., *Dissing Elizabeth: Negative Representations of Gloriana* (Durham, NC: Duke University Press, 1998), pp. 153–84, at p. 173.
54. Ibid., pp. 173–4; *Caltha Poetarum*, sig. C4v.
55. For a political reading of this work see B. N. De Luna, *The Queen Declined: an Interpretation of Willobie His Avisa with the text of the Original Edition* (Oxford: Clarendon Press, 1970).
56. A work entitled *The xv Ioyes of Marriage*, a translation of *Le Quinze Joies de Mariage*, was printed around 1509 by Wynkyn de Worde and the banned book may possibly be a later edition of this. However, a new translation (probably by Thomas Dekker and Robert Tofte) appeared in 1603 under the title *The Batchelars Banquet* and it is more likely that it was an earlier version of this work to which the bishops took exception. See *The Batchelars Banquet*, ed. F. P. Wilson (Oxford: Clarendon Press, 1929), pp. xvi–xvii; *The Batchelor's Banquet*, ed. Faith Gildenhuys, Medieval and Renaissance Texts and Studies, 109 (Binghampton, NY: Dovehouse Editions, 1993), p. 23. *Of Marriage and Wiving* (1599) is a translation by R.T. (possibly Robert Tofte) of a dialogue between Ercole and Torquato Tasso originally published in 1595.

57. *Of Marriage and Wiving*, sig. D3v.
58. Ibid., sig. L2r.
59. Ibid., sig. D4v.
60. See *King Richard II*, p. lix.
61. *Skialetheia*, p. 58.
62. *Tudor Royal Proclamations*, III (1969), pp. 233–4.
63. *The Whipper Pamphlets*, ed. Arnold Davenport (Liverpool: Liverpool University Press, 1951), p. 22.
64. Ibid., p. 33.
65. See W. W. Greg, 'Samuel Harsnett and Hayward's *Henry IV*', *The Library*, 5th series, 11 (1956), pp. 1–10, at p. 6.
66. *Records of the Court of the Stationers' Company 1576–1602*, p. 79.
67. Dutton, *Mastering the Revels*, p. 114.
68. Clegg, *Press Censorship*, pp. 222, 223.
69. Patterson, *Censorship and Interpretation*, p. 49.

6
What is a Catholic Poem?: Explicitness and Censorship in Tudor and Stuart Religious Verse

Alison Shell

What *is* a Catholic poem?[1] This is a question crucial to a proper appreciation of post-Reformation religious verse, but surprisingly hard to answer. Louise Imogen Guiney, the first and only anthologist of recusant verse, made her choice from among poems written by Catholics, often regardless of subject; but most critics would be less catholic than she, limiting the designation to verse demonstrating devotional or religio-political sentiments. Any religious poem written by a Catholic is, in one sense, a Catholic poem; yet the distinctiveness of Catholic poetry rests in those elements which a Protestant could not have imagined or condoned. To make things more awkward still, identifying such elements is very problematic. In the past, the label of Catholic, or of Catholic-influenced, has seemed appropriate for the kind of poem containing elements traditionally attributed to Catholic sources – but in full recognition of the fact that these poems might or might not actually be *written* by Catholics. This is particularly true of poems which in some way show the influence of Ignatian meditational discipline, many of which were written by converts from Catholicism, like Donne, or lifelong conformists like Herbert.[2] Is a Catholic poem one that was read only by Catholics, or could it reach Protestants as well? Was it copied only by Catholics? – and if one finds what one thinks of as a Catholic poem in a manuscript miscellany, can one automatically assume that the compiler was Catholic? Or ought one to be suspicious of all binary oppositions, not only between Catholic and Protestant poems, but between Catholic and Protestant writers and readers? This is not, in short, an area in which there has been much taxonomical rigour. This essay, based around a limited number of case-studies, makes a preliminary attempt to answer the question, arguing in particular that a satisfactory response needs to address the circumstances of early modern censorship, both of an external and an internal kind.

Hard cases, though, are not the whole story. Some kinds of Catholic poem are very easy to define as such, and four provisional categories – to be taken as overlapping rather than discrete – can be identified straight away. First, early modern Catholic writers produced many uncompromising, usually polemical poems, unmistakably setting Catholics up in opposition to Protestants: Catholic martyr-ballads are obvious examples, such as the anonymous 'Why do I use my paper, ink and pen?', written on the death of Edmund Campion. Secondly, some non-religious poems deserve the definition because they are known to be written by a Catholic, and have traditionally been read in relation to their religious context: these can be political, or linked to a biographical event. One example is Chideock Tichborne's exercise in *contemptus mundi*, 'My prime of youth is but a frost of cares', composed the night before Tichborne's execution for his part in the Babington Conspiracy. Thirdly, it seems reasonable to count as Catholic any religious poems which do not touch on areas of Catholic/Protestant difference, but are always or usually found in the company of more obviously Catholic poems, in the context of a manuscript miscellany or printed anthology. Lastly, non-polemical religious poems of Catholic origin, most usually devotional, could be transferred into the Protestant mainstream, perhaps with relatively minor rewritings. Robert Southwell's *St Peter's Complaint*, a best-selling item in the publishing mainstream after Southwell's execution in 1595 and for many years thereafter, is a well-known example of this phenomenon.[3]

With the fourth of these categories, we come on to censorship. Not all poems of Southwell's enjoyed mainstream popularity – as is well known, certain poems of his were circulated in the sixteenth and seventeenth centuries, yet not printed until the nineteenth because of their content – and even poetry printed in the mainstream could be edited to remove Catholic matter.[4] This illustrates a larger point: every poem, or sequence of poems, which survives both in a Catholic version and in a version doctored for Protestant tastes provides a checklist of what a censor or censors, at one particular point in time, thought too objectionable to leave in.[5] A consciousness of censorship tells us that we ought to supplement the question 'what is a Catholic poem?', with a further one: 'which *elements* of a poem, or a poet's work, were thought too Catholic by Protestant contemporaries?'. But this entails, in the first instance, admitting that common ground among Tudor and Stuart religious poets is vastly more important than difference. Much writing on the topic is marred both by insufficiently rigorous definitions of the Catholic, or the Protestant, or the puritan aesthetic, and, conversely, an unwillingness to admit areas of overlap. Though differing theological emphases certainly have differing imaginative knock-on effects, criticism is often unwilling to search for counter-examples when identifying the Protestant, or Catholic, elements of a text. One is, perhaps, least likely to get it wrong if one takes one's bearings from contemporary controversial theology: going, unashamedly, for the obvious first.

An awareness of censorship is valuable here, because censors at this date – or at any other – have a pronounced tendency towards literalmindedness. Censors have no interest in, for instance, the precise nature of imaging undertaken by a poet; they go straight for the polemical flashpoints, looking for the transubstantiationist statement[6] in eucharistic verse, or the implications of mentioning the Virgin Mary, the saints or purgatory. Yet, if those expecting subtlety in a censor are likely to be disappointed, even consistency can sometimes be elusive. A black-letter, much-adapted broadside version of the Catholic sacred ballad 'Jerusalem, my happy home', printed in the mainstream and recorded in the 1624 list of ballads in the Stationers' Register, omits one verse which does survive in manuscript versions, 'Our Ladie singes *magnificat,*/with tune surpassinge sweete,/And all the virginns beare their partes,/sitinge [about] her feete' – but it leaves in other saints, Augustine, Ambrose and Mary Magdalen.[7]

Even with sole-authored ballad texts, verses have a pronounced tendency to float and evolve during the process of transmission.[8] Nevertheless, one is probably entitled to assume an official or unofficial censorship here, since the verse appears in another mainstream – if shadily mainstream – printed version of this poem, discussed below. If one places these two texts side by side, the intervention of a censor would suggest Catholic matter; but even if no manuscript evidence survived, the tolerant mention of saints might lead us to suspect, at least, a Catholic author for this particular poem. And this, in turn, points towards two conclusions: the limits of censorship as evidence; and a reminder that a Protestant audience could be surprisingly broad-minded – if more so as readers than as writers.

One cannot invariably assume, across the entire Elizabethan and Stuart period, that lines, or poems, about a topic challenged by the reformers bespeak a Catholic author. But trying to date a poem, then placing it in the context of conformity at the time it was written, can be a valuable way of alerting oneself to something unusual. To revisit an example cited above – the suppression in the mid-1590s of some of Southwell's poems – I know of no late Elizabethan Protestant verse on the Virgin Mary's death and assumption.[9] Yet during the 1630s and the ascendancy of Archbishop

Laud, a considerable degree of Marian veneration was practised by at least some members of the Church of England.[10] Crashaw's poem on the Assumption, for instance, was probably written during the 1630s in the high-church, highly-charged atmosphere of Peterhouse, and was published in the first edition of *Steps to the Temple* in 1646. Crashaw had long converted to Catholicism by this stage, though *Steps to the Temple* discreetly avoids mentioning this. But the poem on the Assumption was probably not left in on the grounds that Crashaw was probably, technically, a Protestant when he wrote it – censorship in the 1640s was, after all, a very hit-and-miss affair.

Looking at Crashaw's career more generally, one sees a widespread difficulty of defining the Catholic poem. How is one to define religious verse, dealing with Catholic matter, written by a Catholic convert before he converted? It would be possible to call Crashaw's religious poems Catholic by retrospection, since so many of them seem to be experimenting with Catholicism: yet how would we think of them if his Catholicism had remained at the experimental level, and he had stayed a member of the Church of England?[11] The fact of imaginative experimentation in religious verse reminds one of how important it is to give full weight to internal censorship, as well as external, and invites another question still: what, after all, did one do, when one wrote a religious poem in Tudor or Stuart England? To write any piece of Christian poetry – or, for that matter, any poetry addressing the tenets of an established religion – is an act of monitoring, testing a particular assortment of religious tropes against internalized standards of orthodoxy: one's own, and often other people's as well. This is not to deny that a writer of religious verse can be heretical or irreligious at times, either accidentally or – as so frequently with Donne – calculatedly, since the same standards define both conformity and deviation.

One can assume that there were several kinds of implied reader, differently foregrounded in different cases, for all religious verse at this date. God is the ideal, all-knowing reader. Then there is the orthodox reader, who agrees with the poet, without being able to see into his or her mind. To such readers, poets are generally anxious to demonstrate an orthodox position, which frequently entails defining their difference from other implied readers with who they are in theological disagreement: papists, puritans, Arminians, or the more exotically heterodox. This is where an internalized censorship could come into play, because of the necessity of not being misinterpreted – poets were constantly justifying themselves to an implied interlocutor who had, at least, the power of censure. I would argue that this was much more of an imaginative restriction to Protestants than to Catholics – yet all the same, Catholics were sometimes impelled to engage in explicit poetic *justification* of Catholic devotional practice, as if to a non-Catholic audience.

These could prove acceptable to a mainstream audience – here as elsewhere, one has to think beyond the old category of recusant writing. One such example can be found in the title-poem of a poetic miscellany which was issued by a mainstream publisher, William Ferbrand, in 1601, and registered at Stationers' Hall: *The song of Mary the mother of Christ: containing the story of his life and passion. The teares of Christ in the garden: with the description of heavenly Jerusalem.*[12] Despite the fact that the Bible would have validated Mary's song of praise, and the fact of her meditating on the life of Christ, Mary tends to define English Protestant poetics by her polemically-induced absence. The idea of writing a poem called 'The song of Mary' might just have been possible to a Protestant, although the pre-Laudian date would be very surprising.[13] Still, one begins reading the title-poem with a strong presumption of Catholic origin, which is borne out in the poetic preamble: a conventional declaration of authorial incapacity, unconventionally adapted to justify invoking saints. The poet begins 'Faine would I write, my minde ashamed is, / My verse doth feare to do the matter wrong ...' (f.A2a), and is reassured by God: 'To publish it unworthy art thou found, / Yet I accept the proffer of thy will ...' (p. 2). The poet then asks the saints, 'Lend me your notes, if now you sing no more'; but the saints reply 'No, thinke not so, our song for ever is ...' (p. 2) and invite him to join with them in praising the name of Jesus.

As the poet reports, collective humility makes them reluctant to begin: 'For none did thinke him worthy to be one, / And every one to other there gaue place:/But bowing knees to Iesus euery one, / They him besought for to decide the case. / Who said to me, most fit for this appeares / My mothers plaint, and sacred Virgins teares' (p. 4). The Virgin modestly agrees, and begins her narrative with a long hymn of obeisant praise to Jehovah. This stress on the Virgin's humility, on the saints' answerability to God and, most of all, Christ's legitimization of the Virgin's song is far from accidental; it pre-empts and counteracts any sense that the Virgin – as so often in late medieval piety – is acting in a semi-autonomous manner. This is not just a Christianized version of invoking the muses, but a poetic fictionalization of traditional Catholic doctrine, written explicitly to counter the assumptions and criticisms of an implied Protestant reader.[14] The poem would hardly have pleased all Protestants, but for many, the fictionality of a poem might have been acceptable where a tract justifying the invocation of saints would have been felt dangerous.

Later in the poem, the narrative of the Last Supper is doing something very similar:

> He caused them, the table for to lay,
> And eate the Lambe as vse was euery where,
> A figure of more sweet and heauenly cheere.
> Which he him selfe did institute and giue,
> Whereby his Church should euer eate and liue.
>
> There was that table furnished that night,
> With heauenly *Manna*, holy Angels foode:
> The Paschall Lambe, the honny, giuing light,
> The Testament, the holy sprinckled bloud,
> The tree of life, which midst the garden stood.
> The meale and oyle, which eaten lasteth still,
> *Elias* loafe, to walke from crib to hill.

(pp. 14–15)

This description imagines the Gospel scene in a manner which some non-Catholic *readers* would find acceptable, but with imaginative details to which a Catholic *writer* would have had easier access than a Protestant. This needs to be recognized with an eye to counter-examples. It would, for instance, be easy to point to the cornucopian abundance of eucharistic imagery in this passage, clearly owing something to late-medieval Corpus Christi devotions, and conclude simply from this that the last stanza reveals a Catholic author; but though there is certainly a high quantity and concentration of eucharistic language, reformers were far from uniform in holding a low doctrine of the Sacrament.[15] Most of the language is typological – the bread and wine is compared to the Israelites' manna, the sacrificial lamb of Passover, then seen as the redemptive antithesis of the apple in Genesis – and so would have been acceptable within the English reformed tradition. Yet the employment of typological instances is very much a matter for individual authorial imaginations: and in this passage, the last instance – the cake fed to Elijah in I Kings 19, giving him enough strength to walk for 40 days and 40 nights – is unmistakably described in terms of the physical body of Christ, seeming to invite literal identification between Elijah's loaf, Christ's crucified body and the bread and wine of the Eucharist. 'Elias's loaf' is literally, physically, imagined as walking from the crib to hill. While this is not spelling out transubstantiationist ideas, a transubstantiation takes place in the language: it is perhaps no coincidence that this comes last in the catalogue of sacred epithets.

The presumption of Catholic matter is borne out by the other poems in *The song of Mary*, mostly but not wholly mentioned on the title page: 'The teares of our Sauiour in the Garden'; 'A heauenly Prayer in contempt of the world, and the vanities thereof'; 'The description of heauenly Ierusalem' beginning 'Ierusalem thy ioyes divine ...'; 'Another on the same subiect,' beginning 'Jerusalem, my happy home ...'; and 'A sinners supplication, or the soules meditation.' Some of the titles and first lines are enough, on their own, to alert one to a possible Catholic compilation: for instance, the two hymns on Jerusalem are of frequent occurrence in the manuscript poetic collections of Catholics. This may have been a privately kept miscellany that fell into the hands of the printer or publisher – many anthologies came to be printed by just that route – or a compilation pieced together by them.[16] In either case, the book's bibliographical arrangement is far from innocent. As already argued, the title-poem is a very placatory piece of writing in the way it justifies itself to an imagined Protestant interlocutor; whether it was written for mainstream print publication or not, it is, at least, reasonably suitable for it. But some copies of the book included more inflammatory material. Most surviving copies are without the last four leaves, Signature F.[17] But surviving, more complete ones reveal that this portion of the book contains the unexpurgated version of 'Jerusalem, my happy home', the Catholic ballad discussed above, and another, fiercely polemical Catholic poem, 'O blessed God, O Saviour sweet'. One verse of the latter refers specifically to the rack, the torture strongly associated in mid-Elizabethan England with the methods of the priest-catcher Richard Topcliffe: 'Then would I boldly dare to say, / that neyther racke nor corde; / Nor all the torments in the world, / should make me loose my Lord' (f.F4a).[18]

One needs, perhaps, to remind oneself that the book *was* entered at Stationers' Hall.[19] But the printer of this text, Edward Allde, had a history of printing dubious matter, Catholic and other: he had his press seized in 1597 for printing a popish confession, and two years later is mentioned in an order of the Master and Wardens for printing certain satires which had been ordered to be burnt.[20] This is a collection similarly operating on the limits of legality, probably not sold to all and sundry, even if technically on the open market; many Protestants would have tolerated the content of – at least – the main book, but most would have found it antipathetic to some degree. As with censorable literature throughout the ages, there would have been *ad hoc*, irrecoverable ways for the right sort of customer to make their preferences known. But even if one assumes an under-the-counter element to the production and distribution of this book in general, one is still left with the fact that only some copies were upgraded with the supplement.[21] Here, then, there survives evidence of something which is normally very hard to gauge: an idea of what the *publisher* thought was the most potentially dangerous material in the book. For these semi-legal operators, it seems, the full catalogue of saints in 'Jerusalem, my happy home', and the exhortation towards martyrdom in 'O cruel death, o wounds most deep' *are* Catholic matter, but carefully negotiated invocations of saints, and transubstantiationist passages, are seen as all right in the mainstream – literal-mindedness, indeed.

A poem similar to 'The song of Mary' was issued 21 years later in 1622, John Bullokar's *A true description of the passion of our Saviour Jesus Christ*.[22] Bullokar is very easily identifiable as Catholic from his biography, but the print version of his poem was published in the mainstream.[23] The history of its circulation in manuscript, too, proves its suitability for a Protestant audience – perhaps fortuitously, perhaps because the author had a Protestant interlocutor in mind.[24] Again, the description of the Last Supper – quoted below – is the place most symptomatic of the writer's allegiance.

> O happy Feast held by a heavenly King,
> Where bread of Life with bounty was bestowd:
> No more a Type, but now a figured thing,
> True Rocke, whence pure sin-cleansing waters flowd:
> Sweet antidote, whose vertue sets man free,
> From deadly surfet of forbidden tree.
>
> When thou wert made, each ceremonious Rite,
> That had prefigur'd better things to come,
> By Gods appointment was abolisht quite;
> New Sacraments succeeding in their roome:
> Whose worth in Christ who worthily embrace,
> Adopted are new heires of heavenly grace.
>
> Cleare light was then in place of shadowes brought:
> Figures for better Truth exchang'd away: . . .
>
> But this is not yet all that then was done:
> For the new-spoused Church redeemed so deere,
> The precious Body of Gods only Sonne,
> Was instituted to be eaten heere:
> That blessed Body borne for sinners good,
> True Manna, farre exceeding Angels food.

Such wisedome did th' Almighty workman show,
In altering shadowes into substance true:
Such humble seruice did a God bestow,
Pure humbled thoughts in proud man to renue ...

(A7b–8b)

This description is strewn with translated quotations from Thomas
Aquinas, and allusions to him. 'O happy Feast held by a heavenly King'
gestures towards his *O sacrum convivium*;[25] the passage beginning 'When
thou wert made, each ceremonious Rite ...', and the exquisitely non-
committal 'No more a Type, but now a figured thing', each differently
render lines from *'Pange, lingua': et antiquum documentum / novo cedat
ritui*.[26] There is even a rapturous contradiction, or outdoing, of Aquinas's
Ecce panis angelorum: 'True Manna, farre exceeding Angels food.'[27]

Catholics, it should be said, were not necessarily the only people to use
Thomist reference at this date.[28] Aquinas was one of the few scholastic
writers who generally found favour with Protestants, and would have
been encountered by all those who underwent theological training at the
universities. But one can get further by looking at the suppressions of the
passage. While picking its way amid one of the most notorious minefields
of the Reformation, the passage says nothing that a Catholic might not
have found orthodox, but circumnavigates obvious confessional give-
aways. The line 'In altering shadowes into substance true' is primarily an
unexceptionable comment on how the New Testament has fulfilled the
typology of the Old. Only secondarily might it be interpreted as implying
transubstantiation; and, even then, the potential for disavowal is greater
than the suggestion. Aquinas's conception of the bread and wine of the
Eucharist as *figurae* was a congenial one to Protestants: so much so, that
Catholics themselves began to move away from Thomistic vocabulary for
fear of being misinterpreted. After the Council of Trent, it was unusual for
a Catholic theologian, writing in Latin, to use the term *figurae* in talking
about the sacraments.[29]

So why, then, do I see this passage as being typical of a Catholic writer?
First, there is a difference between knowing a text, and endorsing it by
allusion. If there was no reason in theory why Aquinas should not have
been drawn upon by poets within the Church of England, I have not so far
found this level of allusion to him among those whose conformist
allegiances were fixed: which emphasizes – were added emphasis
necessary – the considerable difference between the referential fields of
poetry and theology. Secondly, a narrative poem of this nature

commanded an audience beyond the theological specialist, and this would have increased a writer's need to be prescriptive. Among Protestants, as argued below, this would have tended to mean an explicit distancing of one's text from popery. But among Catholics, prescriptiveness might have taken the form of gently introducing material Catholic in origin, in a form to which a Protestant could have assented. Bullokar can, perhaps, be classified as a Catholic writer writing for an audience that included Protestants, and acceptable to them.

But reading is different from writing. No one would argue that readerly engagement with religious verse at this period was other than intense and discriminating; but readers of a poem are not answerable for it in the same way that authors are, and do not face internal interlocutors to the same degree. Much recent work has been done on the amount of Protestant devotional literature which, around this time, borrowed from Catholic sources with only minor alterations: an exchange facilitated both by the broad areas of similarity between the two traditions, and by the fact that devotional differences between Protestant and Catholic are less often simple opposites than matters of degree, level and addition. It would have been perfectly possible for Protestant devotional fervour, on topics like the Eucharist, to slip into language which could sound Catholic; and sometimes it does. But Protestants tend to reveal themselves as Protestants, because they were unwilling to be taken for Catholics.

George Herbert's poem 'The H. Communion' stirs up the speaker's devotion precisely through the *denial* of transubstantiation.

> ffirst I am sure, whether bread stay
> Or whether Bread doe fly away,
> Concerneth bread, not mee.
> But that both thou and all thy traine
> Bee there, to thy truth, & my gaine,
> Concerneth mee & Thee...
>
> Then of this also I am sure
> That thou didst all those pains endure
> To' abolish Sinn, not Wheat.
> Creatures are good, & have their place;
> Sinn onely, which did all deface,
> Thou drivest from his seat.[30]

Similarly, another of Herbert's poems, 'To all angels and saints', turns on the paradox of him addressing the Virgin Mary, only to explain why he cannot pray to her.

> I would addresse
> My vows to thee most gladly, Blessed Maid,
> And Mother of my God, in my distresse...
> But now, alas, I dare not; for our King,
> Whom we do all joyntly adore and praise,
> Bids no such thing...[31]

Because Protestantism forbids anything that is not explicitly bidden in the Bible, Herbert is 'now' unable to pray to the Virgin, whatever he might have been glad to do in former times. Though these poems address topics of hot debate, they do so in a faultlessly conformist manner; these are Protestant poems precisely because of Herbert's careful – though not unfriendly – distinction of his speaker's opinions from those held by Catholics. If the question 'What is a Catholic poem?' begs the counter-question 'How far can a Protestant poem go?', Herbert provides us with at least one answer: when approaching an area scattered with popish mines, Protestants made a poetic point of watching their step.

Sometimes their poems, like Herbert's, positively derive inspiration from this. This is also true of a vastly less self-aware writer: a late seventeenth-century poet, whose work survives in a manuscript in the Bodleian Library in Oxford. This contains a series of poems in which he argues that, even though he has a cross in his study, he is not an idolater or a papist. In the poem 'None But Christ', he tells us that he merely regards the cross as an emblem.

> If placeing of Some Emblems heere
> To anie Gives offence
> hee that shall Take offenc heereat
> Ile say has Little sence /
> If that an emblem for to make
> It cann bee proovd a sinne
> Its then Ile owne and not till then
> Ive in An error beene /...
> When I my Cross look on I think
> I nothing do amiss
> because when I look on my Own
> It mindeth me of His[.][32]

This personally defensive note reminds us again how religious verse, at this date, is most characteristically used to affirm the orthodoxy of its author. But, as we see here, the *need* for such affirmation can arise out of an initial doubt, formally postulated at the beginning of the poem, and resolved – or not – as the poem unwinds its argument. This forces the reader to try and locate the implied interlocutor. In the poems quoted above, Herbert is distinguishing his own position from the Catholic one with extreme care: less, perhaps, because he feels vulnerable from Catholics, than to pre-empt adverse judgements from members of his own church less sympathetic to ceremony than he is. One could see these poems, like 'None But Christ', as written *against* the imagined condemnations of an internalized censor, anti-Laudian or low-church. 'None But Christ' is thoroughly different, though, in its defensive tone; less poised by far than Herbert, and seemingly not written for any kind of circulation, it illustrates – more nakedly than Herbert ever could – the necessity of defining one's ecclesiological position against the importunate internal voice of dissent. Just as much as any anti-papal ballad does, these poems define themselves against Catholicism; the difference is that they rely less on abuse, more on an intimately, scrupulously negotiated dialectic with Catholic doctrine and practice. In these poems, Protestant sympathy becomes most pronounced and most necessary where the boundaries are thinnest; precisely because similarities are so easy to detect, differentiations have to be highlighted with especial care.

This may be because the onus was on the Protestant not to sound Catholic, not the other way round. Whereas certain topics – for instance, the uncertainty of being saved – would preoccupy a Protestant, especially a Puritan, writer but not a Catholic one, it is considerably more difficult to identify devotional areas forbidden to the Catholic but allowable to the Protestant. Just a Catholic poets could draw on a wider range of devotional reference than Protestant ones, they had – in theory at least – more room for imaginative manoeuvre than their religious opponents. They may not always have taken up opportunities as fully as a poet from the reformed tradition would have done – Barbara Lewalski may be correct in asserting the especial potency of the Bible as an inspiration to Protestant poetics – but the Bible was not forbidden to Catholic writers in the same way that, for instance, Marian devotion was frowned upon among pre-Laudian English Protestants.[33] Looked at another way, Herbert's moderation, so much praised by the back-daters of Anglicanism, can be characterized as one of alert and pious restraint from Catholic hyperbole. A typical Catholic religious poet would certainly have been obliged to be orthodox, but would not have had such a pronounced fear of recklessness in devotional poetry. He might, for any number of reasons, not have gone out of his way to parade his faith; as argued above, he might have derived poetic inspiration from Protestant-stimulated attempts to justify his doctrine; but both in his subject-matter and in his attitude towards it, he would not have minded being *taken* for a Catholic.

We think of internal censorship as repressive. Herbert gives conflicting testimony here: his poem to the Virgin sounds regretful, his poem on Holy Communion content. The latter is perhaps more typical; clearly, the vast majority of Protestant religious poets felt little sense of constriction at being restricted to the devotional language approved by the reformers. Such language must often, indeed, have been experienced as positively empowering; and puritans developed hyperboles of their own. A vocal minority of poet-converts to Catholicism, though – most coming, significantly, from a conformist background – found Protestant limitations indicative of hardness of heart. Some, like William Alabaster, write of a sense of release on their conversion which is as much linguistic as anything: his manuscript autobiography, preserved at the English College in Rome, tells us that an early sign of his change of heart was an exhortation upon the Passion, delivered with 'much more fervour and feeling of Devotion, and with a greater tendernes of harte towards Christes Crosse and Passion, than it seemed to the hearers that the protestantes were wont to feele or utter; or ther spirit abyde'. The holy sonnets written after his conversion were specifically designed to stir himself up to greater and yet greater heights of devotion, using language he suddenly felt himself able to employ. 'And I did sett some tymes a certayne strife and wager between my present affections and future, my present persuadinge to devise sonnets now and so full of fyerie love and flaminge ardour towards Christ, ... but on the contrarie parte my future devotions made offer so to maintaine <and> increase the heate and vigour of love and affection in me, that when I should come afterwardes to reed over my former sonnets I might wonder rather at the coaldnes of them then gather heate by them...'[34]

Can one see this release as the final murdering of an internal monitor, one who before had been constantly truncating, toning down and reforming the livelier excrescences of Alabaster's religious imagination? If so, one has to admit that there is more to a Catholic poem than the keyword-searches of a licenser, more even than the opposition proposed above between Protestant devotional limitation and Catholic devotional justification – a sense of freedom from censure, of stepping into the spaciousness of a wider orthodoxy. If Catholic poetry was pruned by external constraints and the necessity to justify, Protestant poetry had some of its buds pinched out in the mind.

Notes

1. I am grateful, for help of various kinds, to Victoria Burke, Elizabeth Clarke, Ian Doyle, P. J. FitzPatrick, Seán Hughes, Arnold Hunt, Steven May, Michael Questier, Ceri Sullivan, and all those who participated in the University of Wales conference at Gregynog, in July 1999, where this paper was first delivered.

2. This was a definition which informed Louis Martz's landmark study *The Poetry of Meditation* (New Haven: Yale University Press, 1954), and was challenged by Barbara Lewalski in *Protestant Poetics and the Seventeenth-century Religious Lyric* (Princeton: Princeton University Press, 1970). See my discussion of the Martz/ Lewalski debate in *Catholicism, Controversy and the English Literary Imagination* (Cambridge: Cambridge University Press, 1999), ch. 2.

3. Southwell's publication history has often been discussed: see James H. Macdonald, SJ, and Nancy Pollard Brown, eds, *The Poems of Robert Southwell, S.J.* (Oxford: Clarendon Press, 1967); James H. Macdonald, SJ, *The Poems and Prose Writings of Robert Southwell, SJ: a Bibliographical Study* (Oxford: Roxburghe Club, 1937); Nancy Pollard Brown, 'Robert Southwell: the Mission of the Written Word', in Thomas M. McCoog, SJ, ed., *The Reckoned Expense: Edmund Campion and the Early English Jesuits* (Woodbridge: Boydell, 1996), pp. 193– 213; Arthur Marotti, 'Southwell's Remains: Catholicism and Anti-Catholicism in Early Modern England', in Cedric C. Brown and Arthur Marotti, eds, *Texts and Cultural Change in Early Modern England* (Basingstoke: Macmillan, 1997), pp. 37–65; Shell, *Catholicism, Controversy*, ch. 2.

4. Southwell's translation of Aquinas's *Lauda Sion Salvatorem* was rewritten to remove references to transubstantiation, in the 1620 edition of his poetry and onwards (Macdonald and Pollard Brown, eds, *Poems of Robert Southwell*, p. 130). Compare the discussion of eucharistic verse below.

5. For instance, the poems on Mary's death and assumption which belong in Southwell's poetic sequence on Christ's life were not printed in contemporary mainstream editions. Sir John Beaumont's poetic output provides a case-study from the early seventeenth century, regarding both what could incur censorship at press stage, and what was perceived as too Catholic to print at all: Beaumont's poem about the 'Fatal Vesper' (an accident at Blackfriars in 1623, in which a number of Catholics lost their lives while attending a sermon) was cancelled from the first edition of his poetry (1629), while his poem on the Assumption was not printed till the nineteenth century. See *The Shorter Poems of Sir John Beaumont*, ed. Roger D. Sell, Acta Academiae Aboensis, Ser. A Humaniora, vol. 49 (Abo: Abo Akademi, 1974), pp. 46–7, 158–9, 177–8, 317, 329–30.

6. Though, as will be argued below, transubstantiationist *assumptions* could affect the nature of a Catholic poet's language and imagery.

7. It could have been the popish address 'Our Ladie' that was objected to, more than the actual presence of Mary. The ballad in its printed broadside version concludes with loyal addresses to the monarch: described in Tessa Watt, *Cheap Print and Popular Piety* (Cambridge: Cambridge University Press, 1991), appendix A, no. 22. Hyder Rollins, *Old English Ballads* (Cambridge: Cambridge University Press, first edn 1920), no. 24, takes the version from British Library Add. MS 15,225, attributed to 'F.B.P.', as the most authoritative. For the most exhaustive discussion to date of the borrowings and adaptations, see John

Julian, *A Dictionary of Hymnology* (London: John Murray, rev. edn, 1908), pp. 580–3.

8. The version of 'Jerusalem, my happy home' printed in *The song of Mary the mother of Christ*, discussed below, is differently ordered in some respects from that in Add. MS. 15,225. This, however, needs to be assessed in the terms of a literary culture where, as Arthur Marotti argues in *Manuscript, Print and the English Renaissance Lyric* (Ithaca: Cornell University Press, 1995), creative textual instability was not uncommon in the short poem.

9. A check of the most thorough reference tool to date, Roman R. Dubinski, *English Religious Poetry Printed 1477–1640: a Chronological Bibliography* (Ontario: North Waterloo Academic Press, 1996), subject index under Marian headings, suggests that there may have been a strong association between poetry about the Assumption and rosary-centred worship.

10. See Erica Veevers, *Images of Love and Religion* (Cambridge: Cambridge University Press, 1989), ch. 3.

11. I discuss this point more fully in *Catholicism, Controversy*, ch. 2. As has often been observed, there is a very high level of similarity between the contents of Crashaw's two major poetic collections, Steps to the Temple (first edn, 1646), and *Carmen Deo Nostro* (1652), the latter of which was published after Crashaw's departure to the continent. See *The Poems, English, Latin and Greek, of Richard Crashaw*, ed. L. C. Martin (Oxford: Clarendon Press, 1972).

12. Printed by Edward Allde (*STC* 17547) and entered for William Ferbrand at Stationers' Hall on 23 July 1601: see Edward Arber, *A Transcript of the Registers of the Company of Stationers of London, 1554–1640 A.D.*, 5 vols (London: privately printed, 1875–1894), III, f.72b.

13. Though occasional counter-examples can be found: e.g. John Weever, *An Agnus Dei* (1601), which mentions the birth of the Virgin.

14. Cf. the comment in Victoria James, 'English Catholic writing in the reign of Charles I (1625–1649)' (D.Phil., University of Oxford, 1999), p. 68, discussing Marian texts of the 1630s: 'while [they] certainly partake of polemic ... they seem curiously non-committal about pushing their engagement to its usual conclusion ... Instead we find Catholic authors modifying their own overstatement, emending the grammar of the church's canonical scripture, taking scrupulous pains to justify their language.'

15. See Arnold Hunt, 'The Lord's Supper in Early Modern England', *P&P* 161 (1998), 39–83, esp. the Introduction.

16. See Marotti, *Manuscript, Print*, esp. the Introduction.

17. *STC* lists Signature F as occurring only in the British Library and New York Public Library copies. Andrew Maunsell's *Catalogue of English Printed Bookes* (1595) has, analogously, a manuscript addendum listing prohibited books: see Shell, 'Catholic Texts', pp. 48–9.

18. For 'O blessed God, O Saviour sweet' see Rollins, *Old English Ballads*, no. 16.

19. Arber, iii, 677–8. Entered 23 July 1601 (Arber, iii, 188).

20. For Allde, see R. B. McKerrow, *A Dictionary of Printers and Booksellers in England, Scotland and Ireland, 1557–1640* (London: Bibliographical Society, 1910), under name.

21. The risk was probably well worthwhile financially, given the high prices which booksellers could charge for recusant books. See Alexandra Walsham,

' "Domme Preachers": Post-Reformation English Catholicism and the Culture of Print' (*P&P* 168 (2000), 72–123); and Shell, 'Catholic Texts', p. 44.

22. Published by George Purslowe for Samuel Rand, and dated on the title page: 'Calend. Nouemb. 1618.' This book does not appear in the Stationers' Company register.

23. His son Thomas (Pater Joannes Baptista) became a Franciscan priest and was martyred. His biographer describes how he came of an orthodox family: Mason, *Certamen Seraphicum* (1649), pp. 31–61, comments about parents on pp. 31–32. See also Timothy J. McCann, 'Some Unpublished Accounts of the Martyrdom of Blessed Thomas Bullaker O.S.F. of Chichester in 1642', *Recusant History* 19(2) (1988), 171–182. John Bullokar's dedication of a pamphlet in 1616 to Jane Browne, Viscountess Montague, is some evidence of implication in the Catholic literary culture of early seventeenth-century Sussex. For the Browne family and their Catholicism, see G. E. Cockayne, *The Complete Peerage*, 14 vols (repr. Gloucester: Alan Sutton, 1982), vol. 4, p. 100, under Anthony Maria Browne, Viscount Montague (husband of Jane Browne); Richard Smith, trans. and ed. A. C. Southern, *An Elizabethan Recusant House, comprising the life of the Lady Magdalen Viscountess Montague (1538–1608)* (London: Sands & Co., 1954); Julia Roundell (Mrs Charles Roundell), *Cowdray: the History of a Great English House* (London: Bickers & Son, 1884).

24. An article by Victoria Burke and Sarah Ross of the Perdita Project, Nottingham Trent University, 'Elizabeth Middleton, John Bourchier and the Compilation of Religious Manuscripts', forthcoming in *The Library*, charts the manuscript circulation of a version of Bullokar's poem which includes stanzas by Southwell. Bourchier, its author/compiler, had Calvinist sympathies; the variations between Bullokar and Bourchier, and between different surviving versions of Bourchier's adaptation, are nevertheless not especially significant from the denominational point of view. Bourchier's poem may well have been read by puritans and non-conformists. I am grateful to the authors for allowing me to see this article, and to Elizabeth Clarke for lending me photocopies of relevant manuscripts. See also Clarke's article, 'Elizabeth Middleton, Early Modern Copyist', *N&Q* 240 (1995), 444–5.

25. *O Sacrum Convivium* is the second Antiphon of the second Vespers of the Office of Corpus Christi in the Sarum Breviary (ed. F. Procter and C. Wordsworth (Cambridge: Cambridge University Press, 1879–86), vol. I, cols mlxxiv–v) and the York Breviary, 2 vols (ed. S. W. Lawley (Durham: Surtees Society 71 (1880–3), vol. I, col. 539). It is also translated by the Catholic writer Richard Verstegan in *Odes* (1601: Dubinski 1212.66) It has often been attributed to Aquinas, though authorship is not certain. I am grateful to Ian Doyle for help on this point.

26. For a full text and translation of *Pange, Lingua*, see Joseph Connelly, ed., *Hymns of the Roman Liturgy* (London: Longmans, Green & Co., 1957), pp. 118–21. These lines are translated as 'Let the old types depart and give way to the new rite' (p. 120). Aquinas's hymns would have been available in contemporary copies of the Little Office of the Blessed Sacrament (e.g. in John Wilson, *The Treasury of Devotion*, 1622), primers, and devotional collections drawing on these (e.g. *A Manual of Prayers* (1613, STC 17273)). Verse 13 of *Lauda Sion* may also be being referred to.

27. 'Behold, the bread of angels', line 63 from *Lauda Sion Salvatorem*: see Connelly, ed., *Hymns of the Roman Liturgy*, p. 128.
28. I am grateful to Seán Hughes for his comments on this poem. Throughout the late sixteenth and early/mid-seventeenth centuries, translations of *Lauda Sion Salvatorem* – though often partial – made their way into the mainstream via other, and more Protestant, sources than Southwell: e.g. John Cosin, who translated and adapted verses 2, 5 and 6 for his *Collection of Private Devotions*, ed. P. G. Stanwood (Oxford: Clarendon Press, 1967), pp. 229, 352–3; and the compiler of Folger V a 399, a conformist Royalist miscellany, who translates two verses of Aquinas's *Lauda Zion* (Sub diversis speciebus ... nec sumptus consumitur', f.59a). Kenneth Larsen discusses Crashaw's translations of Aquinas, arguing that they are marked by Anglican eucharistic theology ('The Religious Sources of Crashaw's Sacred Poetry', Ph.D. thesis, Cambridge University, 1969, pp. 181–205).
29. For the effects of Trent on Catholic eucharistic theology, see P. J. FitzPatrick, *In Breaking of Bread: the Eucharist and Ritual* (Cambridge: Cambridge University Press, 1993), esp. ch. 1, and the debate between Fitzpatrick and Herbert McCabe in *God Matters* (London: Mowbray, 1987), part 4. I am grateful to Dr FitzPatrick for his further comments on the eucharistic poetry in this essay.
30. *The Works of George Herbert*, ed. F. E. Hutchinson (Oxford: Clarendon Press, this edn 1959), p. 200. On how the poem addresses the question of the efficacy of the elements, see Elizabeth Clarke, *Theory and Theology in George Herbert's Poetry* (Oxford: Clarendon Press, 1997), pp. 160–1.
31. *Works of George Herbert*, p. 78; cf. comments in Martz, *Poetry of Meditation*, pp. 97–98.
32. 'Original Poems on Several Subjects', MS Rawl.poet.101, f.4a, slip between 4b and 5a. The author was also responsible for MS Lt 50 at the Brotherton Library, University of Leeds, in which a version of this poem appears (ff.43a–44b). The Brotherton catalogue provisionally identifies him as William Tipping. For a Protestant poem on this topic which comes to a different conclusion, see Francis Quarles, *Divine Fancies* (1641), Bk III, no. 49, p. 135: 'On a Crucifixe'.
33. This is one of the central arguments in *Protestant Poetics*.
34. This argument is developed further in Shell, *Catholicism, Controversy*, ch. 2.

7
John Foxe and the Godly Commonwealth, 1563–1641

David Loades

Those who are aware of John Foxe's Great Book today usually think of it as an enormous and extremely successful piece of Protestant polemic, which turned Henry VIII's unfortunate elder daughter into 'Bloody Mary', and set up almost three centuries of violent anti-Catholicism, which was one of the most powerful influences upon the formation of English national consciousness.[1] Some also think of it as a great piece of English narrative prose, second in influence only to the vernacular Bible. While he would undoubtedly have welcomed the revulsion against Catholicism which he had done so much to create, Foxe himself would have been worried by the negative priority which this created, and puzzled by the jingoistic imperialism which sometimes accompanied it.

At the end of the dedicatory epistle to the Queen which introduced the 1583 edition of the *Actes and Monuments*, Foxe wrote:

> Besides other manifolde examples and experiments of Gods great mercies and judgements in preserving his church, in overthrowing tyrauntes, in confounding pride, in altering states & kingdomes, in conserving religion against errors and dissensions, in relieving the Godly, in brideling the wicked, in losing and tying up again of Sathan the disturber of Commonweales, in punishing transgressions as well against the first table as against the second; wherein is to be seen Idolatrie punished, blasphemy plagued, contempt of Gods Holy Name and religion revenged, murder with murder rewarded, adulterers & wedlocke breakers destroyed, periuries, extortions, covetous oppressions and fraudulent counsels come to naught, with other excellent works of the Lord: the observing and noting whereof in histories, minister to the readers thereof wholesome admonitions of life, with experience and wisdom both to know God in his workes, and to worke

the thing that is Godly; especially to seek unto the Son of God for their salvation . . .[2]

His immediate concern, particularly in 1563, may have been to shore up the Elizabethan settlement, but that was a means and not an end. The end was to justify the ways of God to man, and to create in England a Godly Commonwealth which would have been a visible cell of the true church. Foxe never referred to England as an 'Elect Nation', or even as a nation of the Elect, but God had chosen to test his church in England in a particularly rigorous way, and that was a sign of his favour.

The *Actes and Monuments* had originally been conceived during the reign of Edward VI as a general justification of the Protestant Reformation; an answer to the Catholic challenge – where was your church before Luther? It had been intended, in a manner similar that employed by John Bale in *The Image of bothe churches*, to trace the continuities of true and false belief since the days of the early church.[3] The continuity which he had particularly chosen to follow was that of persecution, since it was axiomatic to him that the true church would always suffer persecution, and the false church would always inflict it. This was based upon the first ten persecutions, down to the time of Diocletian, the pagan emperors representing the false church in this context. The victory of the true church under Constantine created something of a problem for him, which he resolved schematically by postulating a thousand-year binding of Satan.[4] During this period persecution properly so-called did not take place within Christendom. However, the loosing of Satan was anticipated when, from the eleventh century onward, Antichrist began to infiltrate the church. Taking advantage of the pride and ambition of unworthy popes, the Enemy took over the pontificate, and as a result the institutional church became corrupt. From some point rather vaguely located in the thirteenth century, persecution began again, the true church being represented by those opponents of its wickedness which the papacy tried to suppress: the Waldensians, the Lollards, and the Hussites. Doctrinally the hallmark of the false church was idolatry, and it was for rejecting transsubstantiation, just as much as for rejecting papal authority, that these Godly victims had been persecuted. For Foxe, therefore, these latter-day victims were the true heirs of the martyrs of the early church, and the late-medieval papacy the true heir of the Pagan Empire.[5]

It was with this plan in mind, therefore, that he began to collect martyr stories of the fourteenth and fifteenth centuries. His search was not confined to England, and he had originally no particular intention of focusing upon his home country, but the Lollard stories were the ones which came first to hand, and were what he had with him when he was forced into exile in 1554. The Catholic restoration which accompanied Mary's accession in 1553, and the persecution which followed it, altered Foxe's whole agenda. The need for a general justification did not disappear, but it was superseded by a life and death struggle for the souls of his fellow countrymen. At the same time, an almost academic detachment was replaced with a burning anger and commitment. Mary's victims were not just his fellow Christians, they were often his personal friends. As with many Protestants who took refuge abroad in this crisis, Foxe had an uneasy conscience. One part of his mind told him that he should have stayed in England and testified with his own blood. However, he consoled himself (and allowed others to console him) with the thought that his vocation was to record the sufferings which God was using in the service of his truth, that the sacrifices might not be in vain.[6] These developments did not take place overnight. Shortly after arriving in Strasburg, and before the Marian persecution had really begun, he published the *Commentarii rerum in Ecclesia Gestarum*. This was the Lollard part of his original plan, and was aimed at a European audience. Exercised as he was about the situation which began to unfold in England in February 1555, for the time being he did no more than collect information, and wait upon events.[7] It was Mary's unexpected death in November 1558 which galvanized him and his fellow exiles into action.

As soon as Elizabeth began to make her intentions clear, Edmund Grindal persuaded Foxe to abandon his original plan, and write a vernacular martyrology, which would spell out for every literate Englishman the lesson which the Protestants wished him to learn from the events of the previous four years. Although he preferred writing in Latin, it is unlikely that Foxe needed much persuading. Not only did he have to justify his own exile, he could see just as clearly as Grindal the enormous opportunities which the new reign was opening up. So he hastily published in Basle a revised version of the *Commentarii*, entitled *Rerum in Ecclesia Gestarum*, adding some notes on the recent martyrs, and then handed over all the European material which he had collected to his friend Henri Panteleon.[8] Later in 1559 he returned to England, to a position in the household of his former pupil the Duke of Norfolk, and began what was to prove his life's work. He was inspired by a passionate conviction that the Roman Catholic priesthood was the incarnation of evil, and was quite prepared to argue that not only Mary but also Philip were lawful rulers seduced by a clerical conspiracy. This, of course, made his task very much easier, because although Elizabeth hated her half-sister, and did everything she could to reverse her policies and undermine her reputation, she would not allow the lawfulness of her authority to be called in question. This was the mistake made by such Protestant writers as Christopher Goodman and John Knox, who argued that ungodly rulers might lawfully be removed by their godly subjects.[9] Elizabeth was only too aware that godliness can be in the eye of the beholder. Foxe was a scrupulous upholder of the royal supremacy; so Mary was unfortunate, misled, even betrayed, but never evil in herself. A godly commonwealth, on the other hand, could only be led by a godly prince, so when the first fruit of his labours, *Actes and Monuments of these latter and perillous days*, was published in 1563, it was dedicated to Elizabeth as the new Constantine.[10]

The tone of this first edition was triumphalist. Antichrist had been defeated, and the new Queen was God's reward to his faithful people for having so resolutely withstood the evil one. The purposes of God might be inscrutable, but here was clear evidence of divine favour. Foxe drew no further conclusions from this. England was not unique in enjoying this favour, and no sense of false security should be encouraged. The main task for the moment was to convince all Englishmen, whatever their previous views, that they had just witnessed a traumatic and successful test of the worthiness of England for God's future purposes. As might be expected, the *Actes and Monuments* was immediately and enormously controversial. The followers and kindred of those who had suffered rejoiced, and often bombarded the author with fresh material of the same sort. Those accused of complicity in the persecution cried foul, and denounced Foxe as a liar in 35 different positions.[11] Most important, however, it was welcomed at court, and among the new episcopate. Edmund Grindal, now bishop of London, was particularly pleased, and so was the powerful Secretary, William Cecil.[12] Within two months of its publication Foxe was installed in the Salisbury Prebend of Shipton-under-Wychood, worth £39 a year. He was in many ways an unworldly man, and never sought further preferments. In 1569 he moved out of Norfolk's household into his own property in London, and although he had the melancholy task of attending his patron to the scaffold in 1572, his material fortunes did not suffer as his pension had been converted into an annuity before the Duke's attainder.[13] This independence protected him against charges of time-serving, both at the time and since, so that although his enemies continued to denounce his accuracy, no one suggested that he had sold his integrity for personal gain.

By 1570 Foxe's optimism had waned. Although he still regarded Elizabeth (more or less) as a Godly Prince, he knew perfectly well that she was personally responsible for obstructing the completion of that reformation for which he pined. Although Catholicism was still formally excluded, it had not been effectively suppressed, either at court or in the country. Abroad the Counter-Reformation was growing in strength, and at home the 1569 rebellion and the fact that Mary Stuart was the nearest heir to the throne, gave cause for constant anxiety. Foxe's insistence on the need to honour the memories of the martyrs acquired a new contemporary resonance.[14] Nor had these anxieties waned when the third edition appeared in 1576. Foxe had carefully weeded out dubious ancedotes, inserted new documents, and generally responded to criticism, but the fear that the Queen might submit to a foreign and Catholic marriage in an attempt to protect the succession was still lurking, in spite of her 43 years.[15] Only with the fourth edition of 1583 did a measure of confidence return. In spite of all its imperfection, the English church was unquestionably reformed, and England had not succumbed to invasion, nor the Queen to conspiracy. On the other hand, the waning of the Catholic threat had produced no noticeable increase in Godliness. If gratitude to God for his mercies was reflected in a zeal to obey his will, then the English were conspicuously ungrateful. Not only did they indulge in every sort of vice, but they also disputed furiously over the very nature of godliness itself:

> In the mean time [Foxe admonished them] let us for our parts with all patient obedience wait upon his gracious leisure, and glorify his holy name, and edifie one another with all humilitie. And if there cannot be an end of our disputing and contending one against another; yet let there be a moderation in our affections.[16]

It was typical of Foxe that he did not require unanimity, but obedience to authority and a rational moderation in debate. 'There is no commonwealth,' he conceded, 'in which nothing is amiss.' If there were, there would be no need for laws. In his youth Foxe, like most Protestants, had argued that the Bible was the self-evident word of God, and made itself clear to the faithful.[17] However, the experience of a Protestant establishment had disillusioned him. Within the bosom of a true church, there was room for many disagreements, but they must be conducted with charity and forbearance. In spite of his hatred of the Catholics Church, Foxe was not an ideologist; indeed it was precisely the intolerance and inflexibility of the traditional priesthood which were for him the brands of Antichrist. In this respect he was unusual. It was normal for both Catholics and Protestants to argue that there was a single inviolable truth, from which deviation was death – either literally or metaphorically. It was also consistent with that position that he should have been one of the few men on either side who rejected the death penalty for heresy. Even Cranmer, from whom Foxe took his position on many issues, had accepted it, and assisted in the inflicting of it from time to time. Foxe did not (as far as I know) comment on the use of the death penalty for secular crimes, but he argued that belief constrained by the fear of death was useless, and that if God wished to kill his enemies, he would find other ways of doing it. His comments on the executions of Catholics under Henry VIII, or of Anabaptists by Protestant governments, tend to be dismissive rather than critical, but he certainly interceded for the life of Edmund Campion.[18] On the other hand, when God himself intervened to punish transgressors, Foxe's descriptions display a relish which does not reflect modern tastes.

By the time of his death in 1587 the *Actes and Monuments* had become a manifesto for the Church of England. It is very unlikely that many people read it from cover to cover; the third edition amounted to some two and a half million words, and at about 15 shillings a copy it was well beyond most people's means. However, in 1570 the Convocation ordered that a copy should be set up in every cathedral church, and in the homes of Deans and other senior clergy.[19] Many better off parishes followed suit, although there was never any requirement for them to do so. Just as the English bible was read aloud for the benefit of those who could not read it for themselves, so was the 'Book of Martyrs'. No doubt, as with the Bible, favourite passages were read over and over again, and many parts neglected altogether. Moreover the *Actes and Monuments* was illustrated, and some of the woodcuts had a raw emotional appeal which can still be impressive.[20] We now know that Foxe did not actually write much of the book himself. Most of it was compiled from other people's narratives, from documentary sources, from letters and from dictated eyewitness accounts. What he added, consistently, was a sharp edge of moral indignation. How typical it was of Bishop Bonner to burn a man's hand with a candle, or to flog another in his orchard! The thought that Bonner, in his rough way, was actually trying to save himself the distasteful task of burning heretics was not allowed to intrude. An idolatrous priesthood was evil by definition, and therefore malice, cruelty and injustice were to be expected. It was a powerful polemical weapon, because there was little defence against it. Even Bonner did not attempt to deny that he had burned, flogged and imprisoned his victims as stated. That he did deny that he had acted out of malice, or even of his own volition, never reached the record. In fact Bonner was constantly harried by the council on the

Queen's orders to 'do his duty', but after 1558 it would have been worse than useless to make such an excuse.[21] The point was that it was the cause that made the martyr, not the death. For Foxe these men and women were martyrs not because they had been cruelly and maliciously put to death, but because they had died in the cause of the true faith. In attacking Foxe, Harpersfield and Persons did not attempt to deny that so many people had died in such a fashion and at such a time; but because they had died in a false cause they were mere malefactors.[22] That within a generation of his death his great work was known as 'Mr. Foxe's Book of Martyrs' is therefore symbolic of his victory. Rightly or wrongly, it was Foxe's account, particularly of the Marian persecution, which entered the national consciousness, and his moral indignation which was transmitted to subsequent generations.

Foxe died before he could witness the defeat of the Spanish Armada, but he would surely have approved of the spirit in which that success was received. 'Flavit deus et dissipati sunt.' The divine approval which this victory reflected embraced the whole English establishment, not only the Godly reformation, such as it was, but also the Queen's proceedings.[23] God clearly liked the way in which the English were managing their affairs, and that not only rebutted criticism from the 'right', but also from the 'left'. Foxe may not have been entirely satisfied with the English church, but he was never prepared to countenance non-conformity, and strongly opposed the Presbyterians. The union of church and commonwealth, set out in the Elizabethan settlement and established by over 20 years of general acceptance, represented God's intention for England. I don't know whether Foxe ever read William Charke's *Answer to a seditious pamphlet*, which appeared in 1580, but the sentiment was substantially the same as his own:

> He that smiteth our religion woundeth our commonwealth; because our blessed estate of policie standeth in defence of religion, and our most blessed religion in maintenance of the commonwealth. Religion and policy are, through God's singular blessings, preserved together in life as with one spirit; he that doth take away the life of the one doth procure the death of the other.[24]

Although it is quite correct to point out that the defeat of the Armada was not the end of the war, and that Elizabeth continued in dread of another attempt for at least 10 years, it was the victory which clinched the argument over the legitimacy of the English church. Neither recusants nor puritan critics went away, but the former began to dispute among themselves, and the latter subsided into a less political stance.

Although he had aimed his work at a wide readership, Foxe had resolutely resisted any suggestion that the *Actes and Monuments* should be abridged. Although it was in a sense an occasional piece designed to discredit the Marian clergy, for him it was always far more than that. It was a sweeping indictment of false religion down the centuries and across the whole of Europe; to pick out a few sensational stories was to miss the point. Nevertheless the argument for a cheaper and more manageable version was very strong, and within two years of Foxe's death an abridgement had appeared.[25] The author, Timothy Bright, got round the opposition of Foxe's literary executors by using a royal patent which had been granted to him for a different purpose, and we must judge that the enterprise was not a great success as it was not repeated for over 20 years.[26] In a sense Bright remained true to Foxe's vision. He reduced the bulk of the work by taking out all the doctrinal digressions and pastoral counselling, and most of the documentary illustrations, but he did not reduce its scope. On the other hand, he introduced a dimension of his own by adding a special note on God's providential plan for England. This ran

> England, the first kingdom that universallie embraced the gospel.
> Constantine, the first Christian Emperor ... an Englishman.
> John Wycliffe, that first manifestly discovered the pope ... an Englishman.
> The most noble prince king Henry VIII, the first king that renounced the pope.
> The worthy prince king Edward VI, the first king that utterlie abolished all popish superstition.
> Her royal majestie, our most gracious soveraigne, the very maul of the pope, and a mother of Christian princes; whom the Almighty long preserve over us.
> England, the first that embraced the Gospel; the only establisher of it throughout the world; the first reformed.[27]

It may be debated (and has been recently debated) whether Bright was here using the reformed faith to bolster national pride, or national pride to bolster the reformed faith.[28] What is clear is that, in 1589, he made a much clearer link between England and the purposes of God than Foxe had ever done. There are hints of this sentiment in Foxe, but the explicit language is Bright's. Foxe was only too aware of the range of Antrichrist's activities, and of the role of the 'best reformed churches' of Germany and

Switzerland. Two of his greatest heroes had been Jan Hus and Jerome of Prague. On the other hand, in this respect it was Bright rather than Foxe who left his fingerprints on the national consciousness; and if you think you can hear echoes of his last sentiment in Rudyard Kipling – I would agree.

There were further full editions of the *Actes and Monuments* in 1596 and 1610, under the auspices of the Stationers' Company, which had acquired the rights.[29] Both added material, mainly arising from the civil wars in France, which brought the work 'up to date', but neither altered the main thrust of the argument. By this time Foxe had become a national institution, routinely praised (but not much read) by Protestant authors, and routinely vilified by the Catholics. By the 1620s the recusants had a real problem with Foxe/Bright, because they were anxious to play down their own Continental connections, and represent themselves as 'good Englishmen'. England should not, they claimed, be treated as a missionary field, like China, because it was one of the oldest jewels in the church's crown. Many of them struggled to find an acceptance oath to the Crown which could express their loyalty in all temporal matters.[30] But the fires of Smithfield burned across their path; to be English was to be Protestant. However Charles I, far more than his father, was sympathetic to their dilemma. He had been converted to that school of thought which regarded the Catholic Church as an erring parent rather than an agency of Antichrist. When John Field and John Whitfit fell out in the 1580s, they vied with each other in praising Foxe, and claiming him for their side; but to Arminians like William Laud, he was something of an embarrassment. Neither Laud nor Charles had the slightest intention of becoming a Catholic; indeed both objected fundamentally to many aspects of contemporary Catholic teaching, but their refusal to regard the papacy as a diabolical institution sowed widespread suspicion.

It was against this background that a further edition of the *Actes and Monuments* appeared in 1632, with a supplement which altered its whole agenda. Although Foxe's work had addressed an ongoing issue in the search for true godliness, it had been primarily a thanksgiving for sufferings successfully endured and now rewarded. In short, it had been a work of prophetic history. However, in 1632 the editors added 'A treatise of afflictions and persecutions of the faithfull, preparing them with patience to suffer martyrdome', which was addressed not to the past, but to the future.[31] The situation anticipated was not some Catholic invasion arising from the Thirty Years' War, but the apostasy of the English Crown. 'It is impossible to live godly and not suffer persecution' quoted the author, from St Paul. The logic of this extension was impeccable, because although Foxe had rejoiced at the triumph of the True Church under Elizabeth, at the back of his mind still lurked the uneasy conviction that the true church must always suffer persecution. 'Whilst corrupt nature lives in us, and brings forth such bitter fruits, God hath and will in all ages, raise up some Tyrant or other as means to mortify and tame the pride and rebellion thereof'.[32] Charles I was fulfilling a deep psychological need among the reformed by allowing himself to be cast as the Tyrant who would demonstrate to the godly the validity of their vocation. It is hardly surprising that William Laud was not amused by this hi-jacking of one of the great pillars of the Anglican establishment. The Archbishop himself was ambivalent about Foxe, not sharing his convictions about the papacy, but respecting his achievement as an historian of the Reformation. However, from this point onward the *Actes and Monuments* became a weapon in the armoury of the puritan opposition, a situation which would probably have horrified the martyrologist himself if he had still been alive. There were no further editions as long as Laud's power lasted, but as soon as it was broken, in 1641, another appeared. This was essentially a repetition of the 1632 book, but there was added to it a memoir of Foxe's life, probably by his son Simeon, who after a distinguished medical career was still living in London. Simeon makes no comment on the circumstances which had prompted this memoir after so many years, but the extent to which he emphasizes his father's unease about the retention of conservative practices within the English church of his day suggests that he was quite happy to acquiesce in the use to which the *Actes and Monuments* was now being put. It was this 1641 edition to which John Bunyan and George Foxe referred when they testified to the effects which Foxe had had upon their own thinking and faith.

Foxe's significant contribution to the Godly Commonwealth of the Interregnum pretty well guaranteed his relegation to the lumber room after the Restoration. The intense didacticism and sheer bulk of the work added to the impression of dustiness and obsolescence. Peter Heylin was not alone among Restoration divines in believing that the *Actes and Monuments* represented a wrong turn in the development of the Anglican church, and was a positive handicap to its healthy development.[33] However, an unfashionable Foxe simply moved downmarket, and his influence remained unimpaired. Bowdlerized extracts began to appear with titles like *The Spirit of the Martyrs is Risen* (1665) and *A Brief Historical Relation* (1676).[34] The horrors of Smithfield became primarily a weapon in the hands of those who, for a variety of reasons, wished to stir up anti-Catholic emotions. The Popish Plot and the Exclusion Crisis provided plenty of scope for such activities, and it is probably significant that 1684 saw the only full edition of the *Actes and Monuments* between the Restoration and the end of the eighteenth century. The association between popery and arbitrary government, which can first be seen in the Divine Right controversies of the 1630s, became a fixture in the English political consciousness from about 1670, and became inextricably entangled with hostility to France. The Test Acts and the settlement of 1689, which permanently excluded the possibility that England might be subjected to a Catholic government by the vagaries of hereditary succession, thus represented the culmination of Foxe's influence on the English commonwealth. However, it seems to me very unlikely that the martyrologist would have been pleased with a church triumphant which justified itself on the grounds of common sense, compatibility with the secular constitution, and the fact that it was good for trade.

The *Actes and Monuments* was never subject to censorship, for several perfectly good reasons. Until the seventh edition it was for all practical purposes a work of government propaganda, and Foxe himself was *persona grata* with the establishment. Moreover, on 11 November 1559 John Day had been given a privilege for seven years to print any books prepared at his own expense, 'so that they be not repugnant to Holy Scripture or the law', and provided that the copy did not belong to someone else.[35] The former condition might, of course, be a matter of opinion, and the usual safeguard was applied. Every book was to be 'perused and allowed before printing, according to the late injunctions ...' These injunctions, which had been issued earlier in the same year, had decreed that:

> no manner of person shall print any manner of book or paper, or what sort, nature, or in what language soever it be, except the same be first licenced by Her Majesty by express words in writing, or by six of her Privy Council, or be perused and licenced by the Archbishops of Canterbury and York, the Bishop of London, the Chancellors of both Universities, the Bishop being Ordinary, and the Archdeacon also of the place where any such shall be printed, or by two of them, whereof the Ordinary of the place to be always one...[36]

In the case of Day, or Foxe, what this grand formula would have boiled down to would have been a quiet word with their friend Edmund Grindal, the Bishop of London, who was one of Foxe's chief backers. Theoretically the 1563 edition should have carried Grindal's imprimatur, but in the circumstances it is not surprising that nobody bothered to insert it. Because of Day's privilege, he did not have to register his copy with the

Stationers' Company, but it was noted as being on sale in his shop 'under the gate' at Aldgate, with the date 20 March 1563, which seems to have been the date of its formal publication.[37]

Day's privilege was renewed in similar terms on 2 June 1567 for 10 years, and then on the 26 August 1577 for life, in survivorship with his son, Richard.[38] He died in 1584, shortly after completing the fourth edition of the *Actes and Monuments*, the rights in which passed first to Richard, and then to his assigns. By 1596, when the fifth edition appeared, they resided with the Stationers' Company itself. First because of the privilege, and then because the Company did not register its own rights, there is no record of any copy, although the appearance of the second and third editions was noted.[39] The ecclesiastical licensing of second and subsequent editions was a grey area, and in the case of an author whose credentials were as well established as Foxe's, it is highly unlikely that anyone bothered to scrutinize the later editions of the *Actes and Monuments*, in spite of the fact that substantial changes were made. This complacency would haven entirely justified until the appearance of the sixth edition in 1610, because the changes were innocuous from the government's point of view. However the seventh edition, as we have seen, was a different matter entirely. It is most unlikely that Laud, as Bishop of London, would have sanctioned the 'Treatise of afflictions', if he had been aware of it, and it is hard to avoid the conclusion that the Stationers' Company exploited a loophole in the regulations. Laud as Archbishop is alleged to have declared that he would not countenance any further editions of this once-revered work, and it may have been knowledge of that determination which deterred any further attempt until it was safe to do so.

Foxe himself did not make a major issue out of censorship. For him it was axiomatic, and worth no more than a passing gibe, that the false church would seek to destroy the truth wherever, and in whatever form, it found it. Mary's draconian attempts to suppress Protestant propaganda were therefore to be expected, and deplored, but had nothing like the emotional impact of live burnings. Elizabeth's censorship, on the other hand, was the responsible stewardship of a Godly Prince, protecting a true church still fragile and vulnerable. Foxe never had to face a situation in which his own vision of the truth was seriously at odds with that of an authority which he recognized and accepted. By the time that something like that situation arose, the martyrologist had been dead for a generation. The participation of Simeon in the eighth edition seems to indicate that he, at least, believed that his father would have approved of the use to which his great work was then being put, but that is mere conjecture. After the restoration, while the Anglican establishment was still jittery and a proposal for a fresh edition might well have been rejected, as far as I am aware none was made. Like virtually all men of his generation, Foxe saw no particular virtue in free speech. During the Protestant ascendancy of Edward VI's reign Hugh Latimer had declared that 'the gainsayers' must 'have their mouths stopped', a sentiment from which neither Stephen Gardiner nor William Laud would have dissented.[40] Censorship was far more than a device to protect civil or ecclesiastical order against disruption. Godly Princes and magistrates had a duty to protect the truth and suppress falsehood. So Foxe's concept of the Godly Commonwealth could not afford to take the relaxed view that the truth would triumph by its own virtue, and in the event the church which his efforts had helped to create turned out to be stronger than the monarchy upon which it had originally depended.

Notes

1. It was not actually Foxe who coined the phrase 'Bloody Mary', although he might well have done. He was careful not to describe the Queen as evil, but did not attempt to disguise her responsibility for what was done, and called her reign a 'dreadful and bloody regiment'. William Haller, *Foxe's Book of Martyrs and the Elect Nation* (London: Cape, 1963), p. 187.
2. John Foxe, *Actes and Monuments of matters most speciall and memorable* ... (1583), 'To the Queenes Maiestie'. sig. *1.
3. John Bale, *The Image of bothe churches* (Antwerp, ca. 1545; London, ca. 1548).
4. For Foxe, consequently, the millennium was already in the past, which was not the commonly held view at the time. His eschatology therefore looked forward to a Second Coming which would immediately proceed the Day of Judgement. There was no room for a Kingdom of Christ on earth, or a 'rule of the saints'.
5. Foxe deliberately introduced many *topoi* to link his martyrs with their early predecessors, and likened (for example) John Hooper to Polycarp.
6. J. F. Mozley, *John Foxe and his Book* (London: SPCK, 1940), pp. 59–60.
7. Ibid., pp. 37–61.
8. Who published much of it in his *Martyrum Historia. Hoc est, Maximarum per Europam Persecutionum ac Sanctorum Dei Martyrum ... Commentarii* (Basle, 1563).
9. Christopher Goodman, *How Superior Powers ought to be obeyed* (Geneva, 1558); John Knox, *The First Blast of the Trumpet against the monstrous regiment of women* (Geneva, 1558).
10. *STC* 11222, sig. *1.
11. Notably Nicholas Harpesfield, the former Archdeacon of Canterbury, in *Dialogi Sex contra Summi Pontificatus, Monasticae vitae, Sanctorum, Sacrarum Imaginum Opugnatores, et Pseudomartyres* (Antwerp, 1566).
12. For Foxe's supporters at all levels in London, see Brett Usher, 'Backing Protestantism: the London Godly, the Exchequer and the Foxe Circle', in

David Loades, ed., *John Foxe: an Historical Perspective* (Aldershot: Ashgate, 1999), pp. 105–34.

13. Mozley, *John Foxe and his Book*, p. 84.

14. Thomas Betteridge, 'From Prophetic to Apocalyptic: John Foxe and the writing of History', in Loades, ed., *John Foxe and the English Reformation* (Aldershot: Ashgate, 1997), pp. 210–32.

15. For a recent examination of these fears, and the impact which they had upon contemporary politics, see M. A. R. Graves, *Thomas Norton: the Parliament Man* (Oxford: Blackwell, 1994). Norton was one of the council's 'men of business', who were attempting to use parliament to persuade the queen of the dangers of the course which she was pursuing.

16. *Actes and Monuments* (1583): 'A protestation to the whole church of England'.

17. On this see particularly Norskov Olsen, *John Foxe and the Elizabethan Church* (Berkeley: University of California Press, 1973), pp. 123–51.

18. In his memoir of his father's life, published in the 1641 edition, Simeon wrote, 'I could produce letters of his wherein he persuadeth the lords and others who then held the places of chiefest authority, not to suffer Edmund Campion and his fellow conspirators to be put to death, nor to let that custom continue longer in the kingdom that death rather than some other punishment should be inflicted on the papist offenders.'

19. Edward Cardwell, *Synadolia* (Oxford, 1842), I, pp. 115, 117.

20. Margaret Aston and Elizabeth Ingram, 'The Iconography of the *Acts and Monuments*', in Loades, ed., *John Foxe and the English Reformation*, pp. 66–142.

21. G. Alexander, 'Bonner and the Marian Persecutions', *History* 60 (1975), 374–92.

22. Harpesfield, *Dialogi Sex*; Robert Persons, *A Treatise of Three Conversions of England* (St Omer, 1603–4). Ceri Sullivan, ' "Oppressed by the Force of Truth": Robert Persons Edits John Foxe', in Loades, ed., *John Foxe: an Historical Perspective*, pp. 154–66.

23. 'God blew and they were scattered' was the motto engraved on the commemorative medal. Felipe Fernandez Armesto, *The Spanish Armada: the Experience of War in 1588* (Oxford: Oxford University Press, 1988).

24. *STC* 5005, sig. C1r & qv.

25. T. Bright, *An Abridgement of the Booke of Actes and Monuments of the Church* (London, 1589); *STC* 11229.

26. Bright was the inventor of a system of shorthand writing, for which the patent was originally intended. Damian Nussbaum, 'Whitgift's Book of Martyrs: Archbishop Whitift, Timothy Bright and the Elizabethan Struggle over John Foxe's Legacy', in Loades, ed., *John Foxe: an Historical Perspective*, pp. 135–53.

27. Bright, *An Abridgement*, sig. *8b.

28. Nussbaum, 'Whitgift's Book of Martyrs'.

29. *STC* 11226 ('assigns of R. Day'); 11227 (Stationers' Company).

30. Michael Questier, ' "Like Locusts all Over the World": Conversion, Indoctrination and the Society of Jesus in late Elizabethan and Jacobean England', in T. M. McCoog, SJ, ed., *The Reckoned Expense: Edmund Campion and the Early English Jesuits* (Woodbridge: Boydell, 1996), pp. 281–2.

31. Damian Nussbaum, 'Appropriating Martyrdom: Fears of Renewed Persecution and the 1632 Edition of *Acts and Monuments*', in Loades, ed., *John Foxe and the English Reformation*, pp. 178–91.

32. *Actes and Monuments* (1632), *STC* 11228, sig. A2b.

33. Peter Heylin, *Ecclesia vindicata; or the Church of England justified* (London, 1657).
34. *Wing* S2663, 2037. For a full discussion of this 'sub-Foxeian' literature, see Eirwen Nicholson, 'Eighteenth Century Foxe', in Loades, ed., *John Foxe and the English Reformation*, pp. 143–77.
35. *Calendar of the Patent Rolls*, Elizabeth, I, p. 4.
36. Royal Injunctions of Queen Elizabeth, 1559, 51: W. H. Frere, *Visitation Articles and Injunctions of the Periods of the Reformation* (London: Alcuin Club, 1910), III, p. 24.
37. Edward Arber, *A Transcript of the Registers of the Company of Stationers of London, 1554–1640* (London, 1875–94), V, p. 45.
38. *Calendar of the Patent Rolls*, Elizabeth, IV, p. 108; VII, p. 230.
39. Arber, *Transcript*, V, pp. 73, 99.
40. Such sentiments are scattered throughout Latimer's surviving writings, but see particularly *The Sermons and Remains of Bishop Latimer*, ed. G. E. Gorrie (Cambridge: Parker Society, 1845), pp. 6–7.

8
Licensing and Religious Censorship in Early Modern England

Arnold Hunt

Effective censorship is invisible. In saying this, I am not merely referring to censorship as understood by new-historicist critics – censorship as a hermeneutic code, invisible because all pervasive. I am also referring to censorship as understood by historians and bibliographers – censorship as part of the routine process of getting a book into print, invisible precisely because it is so routine, and because the evidence of its operation is not deemed sufficiently remarkable to be worth preserving. This, of course, poses a methodological problem, in that the best-documented cases of censorship may be the ones that are least representative. The high-profile acts of suppression – book burnings at Paul's Cross, and so forth – tell us very little about the normal mechanism of censorship as it functioned at other times.

In this essay, I want to try and get behind that cloak of invisibility. I want to do this in two ways: first, in general, by looking at the system of licensing books for the press, and trying to draw a few conclusions about the way it operated; secondly, in particular, by looking at two books that went through the licensing system in the mid-1630s, and trying to reconstruct the policies and priorities of the licensers in those years. Some historians, such as Nicholas Tyacke, have argued that there was a systematic attempt to alter the established doctrine of the Church of England by means of the licensing system; others, such as Sheila Lambert and Peter White, have argued that the extent of government control of the press has been greatly exaggerated; while Anthony Milton has recently taken the debate a stage further, arguing that censorship did exist but that it operated in more subtle and sophisticated ways than has often been supposed. In this paper, I want to offer a further contribution to this ongoing debate, by arguing that it is impossible to understand the nature of censorship in the early modern period without looking at the mechanics of the licensing system, and the way that system changed over time. I want to present the period 1560–1640 as a period of gradually tightening controls over the press, leading to qualitative as well as quantitative changes in the licensing system.

I

The royal Injunctions of 1559, issued only a few months after Elizabeth I had come to the throne, provide a convenient starting-point for our discussion. The Injunctions were principally concerned with the government and worship of the newly reformed Church of England, but also included, among a host of other regulations governing various aspects of parish life – the preaching of sermons, the distribution of alms, the placing of the communion table, the shape of the sacramental bread, and so forth – a clause 'against heretical and seditious books', establishing the basic parameters of the licensing system that remained in force for the next 80 years. It laid down two main methods for licensing books. In special cases, a licence could be granted by the Queen herself ('by expresse wordes in writynge') or by six members of her Privy Council. In more routine cases, books were to be licensed by a group of ecclesiastical dignitaries consisting of the archbishops of Canterbury and York, the Bishop of London, the chancellors of Oxford and Cambridge, and the diocesan bishop and archdeacon of the place where the book was printed, two signatures being required before a licence could be granted. Since most printing was done in London, this meant that the responsibility for licensing books rested chiefly with the Archbishop of Canterbury and the Bishop of London. The Injunctions also laid down special rules for 'pampheletes, playes and balletes', which were to be licensed by the commissioners for ecclesiastical causes; and for school and university textbooks, which were exempted from these provisions.[1]

The Injunctions established a pre-publication licensing system which should, in theory, have applied to all new printed matter. In practice, however, the rules were interpreted very flexibly – and it is not hard to see why. The express purpose of the licensing system was to prevent 'heretical and seditious' texts from getting into print; and unless the system was conspicuously failing in this regard, there was no reason why all texts should be subjected to detailed scrutiny. The vast majority of new books, after all, contained no objectionable material, and in such cases the approval of the licenser was merely a formality. As a result, the system was routinely disregarded: as the stationer Felix Kingston explained to Sir John Lambe in 1636, 'the Master and Wardens [of the Stationers' Company] licensed all, and ... when they had any divinity book of much importance they would take the advice of some two or three ministers of this town'.[2] This rough-and-ready distinction between religious and secular books is corroborated by the Elizabethan scribe and hack writer Richard Robinson, whose autobiographical treatise *Eupolemia* lists all his published works, together with the names of their licensers. R. B. McKerrow, writing in 1930, was the first to point out that Robinson's works were licensed in two different ways, depending on their subject-matter: his theological and devotional writings were all licensed by an ecclesiastical authority, whereas his secular writings were licensed only by the wardens of the Stationers' Company.[3]

The 1580s saw several attempts to tighten up the licensing system. The first of these was the parliamentary bill drafted by William Lambarde in 1580 'to restrain the licentious printing, selling and uttering of unprofitable and hurtful English books', which would have placed the licensing system under the control of a committee known as the Governors of the English Print, consisting of the Dean of St Paul's, the Dean of Westminster, the Dean of the Arches, the Recorder of London, and two lawyers from each of the four principal Inns of Court.[4] There are several interesting features about this proposal. To begin with, it would have taken the licensing system out of ecclesiastical control, and placed it in the hands of a committee on which clerics were heavily outnumbered by lawyers. It would also have removed it from the direct control of central government, recognizing the increasingly London-based nature of the book trade by entrusting the licensing system to a committee drawn exclusively from London and Westminster. In both these respects, Lambarde's proposal was a remarkably radical one, and had it passed into law it would have changed the whole basis on which press control was conducted. In the event, however, official policy moved in the opposite direction, towards tighter and more centralized ecclesiastical control. In 1583 the bishops petitioned the Queen 'that no bookes be printed beeing not before perused and allowed under the hande of the Archebishopp of Canterbury or Bishopp of London for the tyme being', and in 1586, as part of the Star Chamber decree regulating the book trade, the licensing process was formally placed under the control of the Archbishop of Canterbury and Bishop of London.[5]

However, this concentration and centralization of authority brought its own problems. It rapidly became clear that the work was far too time-consuming for the two prelates to perform unaided, and in 1588 Whitgift nominated a panel of 12 London clergymen to assist in the licensing of books. In fact, the old system of informal approbation persisted long after

1588, despite the new regulations, and a recommendation by any reputable London minister, whether or not he was a member of Whitgift's panel of correctors, seems to have been accepted as a licence. As a result, works of questionable orthodoxy still managed to find their way into print. One of the most striking examples of this is a work by the French Reformed minister Matthieu Virel, *La Religion Chrestienne declarée par dialogue*, first printed in Paris in 1586, and published in London in 1594 in an English translation by the London puritan minister Stephen Egerton, under the title *A Learned and Excellent Treatise containing all the principall grounds of Christian Religion*. This is an overtly presbyterian treatise, which declares quite explicitly that 'the office of a Bishop [is] the same with the office of a Pastor'. Remarkably, the presbyterian content was left almost entirely untouched in the English edition – the only alteration made by the English translator was the omission of a marginal note describing episcopacy as 'humanum ac sathanicum', a human and devilish invention – and the book does not appear to have run into any kind of trouble, as it went through 14 editions in the next 40 years.[6]

What this example strikingly illustrates is the religious consensus which existed in the late Elizabethan and Jacobean church, in which disagreements over matters of discipline – church government, ceremonies, and so on – were accommodated within a broad framework of agreement on key doctrinal issues. As historians of the Elizabethan church have shown, the existence of this doctrinal consensus enabled the majority of the puritan clergy to remain within the established church, despite their opposition to certain aspects of the Book of Common Prayer.[7] It is reflected in many of the religious publications of the Elizabethan period – from the official defences of the Church of England written by conformist divines like Whitgift and Bridges, to the sermons preached under official auspices at Paul's Cross in London – and it is no surprise to find it reflected in the licensing system as well. But by the late sixteenth century, this consensus was becoming increasingly strained; and it is possible to relate this to a change in the nature of the licensing process. As long as the licensing system was directed towards the suppression of marginal and oppositional texts, it was unlikely to have much impact on the religious mainstream. But when it was used to shape and define an emerging Anglican orthodoxy, it began to uncover tensions within the religious mainstream which had previously been glossed over or ignored – and as we shall see, this is precisely what began to happen in the early seventeenth century.

In the late Elizabethan period the licensing system was tightened up again, and the task of licensing religious books was delegated to the episcopal and archiepiscopal chaplains. The advantage of this system was that the chaplains usually resided in their master's household, and could thus be supervised more closely. Several of Richard Robinson's publications were 'perused and allowed' by one of Bishop John Aylmer's chaplains but were then entered in the Stationers' Register on Aylmer's own authority, suggesting that the chaplains were required to pass manuscripts to their superior for final approval.[8] Similarly, when Samuel Harsnett got into trouble in 1599 for having licensed John Hayward's *First Part of the Reign of King Henry the Fourth*, he argued that the ultimate responsibility for licensing the book rested with his superior, Bishop Bancroft. In Harsnett's own words, 'my approbation of any booke whatsoever is but a leading and inducement to my Lord of London my Master to passe his further approbation to the same, without which ... [my] allowance is no sufficient warrant for the Author to prynt his booke'. This was a somewhat disingenuous excuse, but, as Sir Walter Greg pointed out in his discussion of the case, Harsnett was legally in the right: 'all that a corrector had the right to do was to advise his superior, and if his advice was accepted, that was the superior's responsibility'. In theory, the episcopal and archiepiscopal chaplains acted solely on behalf of their superiors, and their authority to license books immediately lapsed if their superior died or if they themselves were dismissed.[9]

In practice, however, things were not so clear-cut. In most cases the licence was simply a matter of routine, and for much of the time the chaplains acted as independent agents, licensing books on their own authority without consulting their superiors. As a result, the boundaries of orthodoxy were still quite fluid: much depended on the attitude of the particular individual to whom a manuscript was submitted, and it was still possible for works of doubtful orthodoxy to get into print with the help of a sympathetic licenser. The books licensed by Daniel Featley, who served as one of Archbishop Abbot's chaplains from 1617 to 1625, illustrate this point particularly well. Featley was an extremely prolific licenser, for whom the task of reading and correcting manuscripts for the press must have been virtually a full-time occupation. Although a Prayer Book conformist in his own religious practice, he was widely regarded as being sympathetic to puritan non-conformity: his opponent Richard Montagu referred caustically to 'Dr Featley and his Puritans', and, as one modern historian has commented, 'the impression is that Featley remained sympathetic to puritan publishing and would not make unnecessary difficulties'.[10] Featley's activities as a licenser are thus of considerable interest: not only do they serve as a useful case study of the practical operation of the licensing system, they also show how far the envelope of orthodoxy could be stretched in order to accommodate puritan texts.

Featley seems to have interpreted his duties very widely, to include informal advice to prospective authors as well as the formal process of correcting and licensing manuscripts. One of his surviving letters, addressed to a 'Mr Vicars' (probably the Somerset clergyman Thomas Vicars), offers advice on a 'catechism and table' which Vicars had sent him to read. Featley praised it as 'the best I have seene in that kinde', but went on to offer a number of detailed suggestions for its improvement, pointing out, for example, that the division of the catechism into 52 sections ('as I conceive, to furnish every Sabbath with a convenient portion') had led to considerable repetition, a problem which could be solved by adopting a slightly different arrangement, 'first appointing the general declaration in the Catechisme to be handled, and thereafter particularly and more exactly allotting every article in the creede and petition in the Lords prayer and commandment in the decalogue to be explicated upon several sundays, according to your Method.'[11] This kind of informal contact between author and licenser is rarely documented, but was probably quite commonplace. Featley apparently regarded himself not merely as a censor but also as a collaborator, helping to ease the passage of books into print, and acting almost as a sort of literary agent; his own excursion into practical divinity, *Ancilla Pietatis* (1626), expresses the hope that the Church of England 'will be hereafter as fruitfull' as the Church of Rome in the publication of religious books, and he evidently did all he could to encourage this through his activities as a licenser.[12]

Vicars' catechism was a fairly straightforward case, in which the principal alterations were merely stylistic; but there were other occasions when Featley needed to make alterations for reasons of religious or political expediency. William Hart's translation of an anti-Catholic work by the French writer Francis de Croy was licensed by Featley and published in 1620 as *The Three Conformities: that is, the harmony and agreement of the Romish Church with Gentilisme, Judaisme and auncient heresies.* It was typical of many works of anti-Catholic controversy published in the 1620s; the problem, for Featley, was to find a way of preserving the anti-Catholic polemic while removing any criticisms of the Catholic ceremonies retained in the Church of England. One whole chapter on 'Archbishoprickes, Bishoprickes and other Popish dignities' was cut, but other passages on religious ceremonies were allowed to stand, with the addition of a few phrases inserted by Featley himself. One passage, for example, attacks Roman Catholic vestments and claims that they are pagan in origin, derived from the white robes worn by the pagan priests of ancient Rome. This obviously reflects on the use of the surplice in the Church of England, and Featley might well have cut it out completely; instead, he simply inserted a qualifying phrase in brackets: '(we except not against the colour or garment, if it be not made a part of Gods worship, and applied to a mysticall sense, as it is in the Church of Rome)'.[13]

William Crompton's book *Saint Austins Summes*, licensed by Featley and published in 1625, was censored in a similar way. Featley cut three chapters on the parity of ministers, remarriage after divorce, and the unlawfulness of marriage between Protestants and Catholics, but left the remarks on religious ceremonies practically untouched. In one passage, Crompton declared that the sign of the cross had been introduced into the Church by the heretic Valentinian, as late as 160 AD, and 'could be to no good end, coming from so bad an Author'. This could obviously be applied to the Church of England's use of the sign of the cross in baptism, and Featley might well have decided to cut the whole passage. The only alteration he made, however, was to insert the words '(*as some report*)', 'thereby' – as he later explained – 'giving the Reader to understand, that I avowed not the thing there reported, but branded it with suspition'.[14] Taken together, these two cases are highly revealing of Featley's priorities as a licenser. He did not hesitate to cut passages which favoured presbyterianism – in this respect, the licensing system had evidently been tightened up since the 1590s – but where ceremonial conformity was concerned, he was only prepared to make the minimum amount of correction necessary to render a work suitable for publication. In retrospect, he admitted that instead of correcting Crompton's work, 'I might have wholly rejected the book'.

Once we know what to look for, we can spot traces of Featley's handiwork elsewhere. Several books licensed by him contain marginal notes clarifying or correcting ambiguous passages in the main text. Paul Bayne's commentary on the first chapter of Ephesians, licensed by Featley and published in 1618, is arguably too extreme in emphasizing that God's decree of election is absolute rather than conditional: 'God cannot have such a conditional decree: *I will elect all, if they will believe.*' However, a marginal note is inserted at this point, explaining that the divine decree can be regarded as conditional, even though the condition is impossible to fulfil: 'He decreeth on this condition, though he seeth that neither they can do it of themselves, neither is he minded to worke it in them.'[15] George Throgmorton's *Treatise of Faith*, licensed by Featley and published in 1624, contains a carelessly worded passage declaring that when a true heart is 'purged and sanctified . . . then followes assurance of faith', which could be taken to imply that sanctification is the cause of assurance. Again, a marginal note is inserted to correct any misunderstanding, making it clear that the cause of assurance is not sanctification but faith itself: 'Faith first purgeth the heart, and by that purgation after increaseth its own assurance in the heart.'[16] In each of these cases, one is struck by the fact that the main text does not obviously bear the interpretation imposed on it by the marginal note; and it seems likely that the notes were added by Featley in the course of the licensing process.

In an important article on press control in early Stuart England, Anthony Milton has characterized Featley's activities as a form of 'benign censorship' designed to expedite the publication of puritan works; he argues that Featley used his position as licenser 'to massage texts with which he was in broad agreement, by removing radical or unnecessarily provocative passages in order to secure their acceptance'.[17] This is essentially correct, but it would be wrong to assume that Featley took a different approach to texts with which he was not in broad agreement; in fact, his understanding of his role as licenser seems to have remained remarkably consistent, even when he was faced with works that were not to his own taste. In the case of Edward Maie's crypto-Catholic *Sermon of the Communion of Saints* (1620), for example, Milton argues that Featley 'sought to censor and tamper with the text of a work which he found offensive and doctrinally suspect'. Yet even here, Featley followed his usual practice of inserting qualifying phrases to render contentious passages more acceptable. Where Maie had described the clergy as 'the Makers of Christ his body', Featley inserted the words '(to wit, in a sacramentall and mysticall sense)', and where Maie declared that lay-preaching had no power to convert, Featley added the saving clause '(setting aside the efficacie of inspired Scripture)'. As in the other cases we have been discussing, Featley chose to gloss the author's words rather than delete them altogether.

Why was Featley so restrained in his alterations to Maie's sermon? The answer is that he was surprisingly respectful of what we would now term 'authorial intention', and very reluctant to make changes without the author's consent. In the case of Edward Elton's controversial sermon collection *Gods Holy Mind* (1624), he claimed that he had stopped correcting the manuscript as soon as he heard that the author had died. He had read and licensed the first 52 pages of Elton's book, 'in which I was confident that there was nothing contrary to the discipline or doctrine of the Church of England', but then 'made a stop, because I then understood the Author had made a period of his life. Whilst he lived I might and did alter with his consent, what we thought fit: but after his decease I left off intermedling in such a worke wherein I could not suffer all things to passe as they were in that copy, *bona conscientia*, nor yet change or mend any thing *bona fide*.' Featley evidently preferred to work in collaboration with the author, and it was only as a last resort, if this method of collaboration failed, that he exercised his right to impose changes against the author's wishes. Collaboration first, compulsion second: even Richard Montagu, no friend to Featley, acknowledged this obliquely when he recalled that Featley had 'told me once, if I did not correct my booke voluntarily, I should be forced'. This, surely, explains why Featley's alterations to Maie's sermon were so restrained: they were part of a compromise deal worked out in consultation with the author.

Putting all this evidence together, we can see the outlines of a coherent licensing policy beginning to emerge: clarify or qualify where necessary, cut only as a last resort, and never rewrite an author's words without prior consultation. Clearly, this fitted in very well with a policy of 'benign censorship' designed to get puritan texts into print with minimal alterations; but it did not merely provide the rationale for a tolerant attitude towards puritan non-conformity, it also reflected a distinctive understanding of the licensing process itself. In effect, it was a minimalist interpretation of the licenser's role, in which the licence was viewed as a form of *nihil obstat*, a declaration that there was nothing to prevent a book being published. As we shall see, however, this understanding of the licensing process began to change during the reign of Charles I, under the pressure of increasing religious polarization.

II

The operation of the licensing system in the 1630s is extremely well documented, largely as a result of the evidence presented at Archbishop Laud's trial in 1644, where the issue of press censorship was given great prominence. On his appointment as Archbishop of Canterbury in 1633, Laud was alleged to have engineered a dramatic change in licensing policy, in which new works of Protestant theology had either been refused a licence or, at the very least, purged of all anti-Catholic material before being published. In the words of the prosecuting counsel, 'most of the principall passages in severall bookes and sermons tendered to the press against popery, popes, priests, Jesuits and Arminians in generall, and against the principall erroneous tenets of papists and Arminians in particular, have been expunged and altered, and the very authors meanings in some places perverted.'[18] Laud's involvement with the licensing system formed a major part of the evidence against him, partly to compensate for the lack of documentary evidence in other areas, and Laud himself commented on the great importance that the prosecution attached to it, remarking with some irritation that 'this and the like passages about expunging some things out of books makes such a great noise, as if nothing concerning popery might be printed'.[19] In the remainder of this chapter, I want to discuss two of the books produced in evidence at Laud's trial, Daniel Featley's *Clavis Mystica* (1636) and Richard Clerke's *Sermons* (1637), and use them to illustrate the reasoning behind the Laudian licensing policy.

We have already encountered Featley as one of Archbishop Abbot's licensers in the 1620s. In the 1630s, however, he himself became the victim of censorship, when a volume of his collected sermons, published under the title *Clavis Mystica: a Key opening divers difficult and mysterious Texts of Holy Scripture*, was expurgated by Laud's chaplain William Bray. According to Featley's later account, the book was already going through the press when he was summoned to an interview with Laud at Lambeth Palace. Laud asked him 'whether his Sermons were licensed, and whether any of his Chaplaines had perused them or not', to which Featley replied 'that they were licensed long since, when himselfe had power to license books, and printed by vertue of that license'. This was not entirely accurate: six of the sermons had indeed been licensed and entered in the Stationers' Register in 1625, apparently in preparation for an edition that never appeared, but there is no evidence that the remainder were ever licensed, and some had been preached in the 1630s when Featley no longer had the authority to license them. Certainly this excuse failed to satisfy Laud, who then 'commanded him, before he published these Sermons, to carry them to Doctor Bray his Chaplaine to peruse, to see if there were any offensive or unfitting passages in them, to the end, that if any such were, they might be corrected, or expunged'. Featley accordingly took the sermons to Bray, who 'gelt them exceedingly, and purged out all the smart and masculine passages against both the Papists, Jesuits and Arminians', with the result that 17 sheets were cancelled and reprinted before the book was published.[20]

The importance of Featley's testimony was that it served to implicate Laud personally in the licensing process. In his own defence, Laud had argued that he could not be held responsible for the work of his chaplains, for 'though it be the place and office of the Archbishop of Canterbury to have a care what Books are Licensed, yet Doctor Featly himselfe (who hath been a Chaplain and Licenser of Books under my Predecessor) can attest, that the Archbishop himselfe did seldome or never use to peruse or licence Books in person'. This was a fair point, especially since Bray had already been held personally responsible for another work licensed in the same year. Featley's evidence, however, showed that Laud had been directly involved in the licensing process, and implied that the alterations to *Clavis Mystica* had been made with his approval. Indeed, Featley recalled Sir Edmund Scot telling him 'that he conceived it would be to no purpose to complain, for he thought the Arch-bishop's Chaplaines had directions from their Lord for what they did, and that his Grace would not alter any thing of this kind done by his Chaplaines; whereupon he submitted and complained no further'. Sir Edward Dering made the same point in more colourful language, remarking that Laud would hardly have appointed Bray as his chaplain if he had not approved of his views. 'I must call the Chaplains *imprimatur*, the Bishops *imperatur*. I may know his Lordships dyet by his Cook. His Chaplaine durst not dish forth these Romane *quelque choses*, if he had not the right temper of his masters tast.'[21]

The subject of our second case-study, Richard Clerke, was one of the translators of the Authorized Version and, for the last 30 years of his life, one of the Six Preachers attached to Canterbury Cathedral.[22] He published nothing during his lifetime, but when he died in 1634 he left his unpublished sermon manuscripts to his friend Charles White, another Canterbury preacher, with instructions to get them 'carefully printed for the publike good'. According to his later testimony, White took the sermons to Laud's chaplain William Haywood, 'who receiving no lesse than forty shillings for his fee for perusing and licensing them, expunged all the chiefe passages in them against the Pope, Popery, Priests, Jesuits, Arminianisme', and so forth, 'at which Master White being very much discontented, to see his deceased friend's Sermons so abused, demanded his intire copy and moneys again, but could procure neither of them, but the copy thus altered and expunged, which must either be totally suppressed or printed as he had castrated it.' White then took some more of the sermons to Bishop Juxon's chaplains, but with exactly the same result: they 'made the like alterations and purgations in them, as Doctor Haywood had made in the rest', and the book was eventually published in 1637 in a heavily expurgated version.[23] This account is corroborated by bibliographical evidence. The entry in the Stationers' Register covers only 27 sermons and names Haywood as the licenser, but the book itself contains over 70 sermons, with an imprimatur signed by Juxon's chaplain Thomas Wykes, from which it appears that the sermons were licensed in two separate batches by two different individuals.

There are several points of interest about this narrative. First, there is the reference to the licenser's fee, an aspect of the licensing process not mentioned elsewhere. Even for a book of the size of Clerke's *Sermons* –

over 500 pages in folio – 40 shillings seems a remarkably large amount, and it would be interesting to know what effect the licenser's fee may have had on the economics of publishing.[24] Secondly, there is the clear implication that White was shopping around for a sympathetic licenser. The four licensers at this period – Laud's chaplains William Bray and William Haywood; Juxon's chaplains Samuel Baker and Thomas Wykes – were not entirely uniform in their approach, a fact which did not go unnoticed by contemporaries: Sir Edward Dering, for example, later wrote that in comparison with Baker, 'I ever held Dr Bray the more moderate man'.[25] Of the two licensers of Clerke's *Sermons*, Haywood was something of a maverick, who was prepared to license a translation of St Francis de Sales' *An Introduction to a Devout Life* (1637) with only minimal concessions to Protestant sensibilities, whereas Wykes was more of a moderate, whose immense popularity as a licenser (particularly in the later 1630s, when he was by far the most active of the four licensers), suggests that he was regarded as a more lenient individual who was less likely to make radical cuts.[26] Indeed, this lack of uniformity may even have been deliberate, as a way of introducing a measure of flexibility into the licensing system; the moderation of Bray and Wykes, in other words, may have helped to make the extremism of Baker and Haywood more tolerable.

The principal significance of these two case-histories, however, is that they enable us to test the accuracy of William Prynne's account of Laud's trial, *Canterburies Doome* (1646). Prynne's book contains a mass of information on the workings of the licensing system – as well as reporting the testimony of Featley, White and other witnesses, it also prints many of the passages deleted by the licensers – and is an invaluable source of evidence, not just on ecclesiastical censorship but on the seventeenth-century book trade in general. Prynne's quotations are usually accurate, but his account needs to be used with caution, as it does not always put the censored passages in their proper context and tends to ignore the revised versions of these passages that were inserted to fill the gaps in the text. This is where our two case-histories come in useful – for in both cases, a record of the uncensored text has survived and can be used as an independent check on Prynne's account. In the case of Featley's *Clavis Mystica*, the survival of some copies of the original sheets, printed before the book was submitted for licensing, makes it possible to compare the two versions of the text – before and after censorship – and see exactly what changes the licenser made.[27] In the case of Clerke's *Sermons*, the survival of the 'exact catalogue' compiled by White for use at Laud's trial, 'amounting to 210 corruptions and purgations ... which were afterwards made use of and reduced under several heads', enables us to reconstruct the original text in more detail than is possible from Prynne's very selective list of the censored passages.[28]

So what does this evidence reveal about licensing policy in the 1630s? The principal charge against Laud, as we have seen, was that he had systematically deleted, or caused to be deleted, all the strongest passages of anti-Catholic polemic – and many of the licensers' alterations do indeed seem to bear this out. In revising Clerke's sermons, the licensers tried to moderate some of the more purple passages of anti-papal invective: the term 'Popeling', for example, was altered to the less offensive 'Romanist', and a description of the papacy as 'this Babylonian whore' was replaced by a neutral reference to 'that See [of Rome]'.[29] Some of the more polemical passages in Featley's sermons were also toned down, as in the following example, one of several occasions when the licenser removed a passage specifically identifying the Pope as Antichrist:

[Before:] the *Panders of Antichrist*, who goe about to entice you … to spirituall whoredome …
[After:] the agents of Rome, who goe about to withdraw you from the love of your Country, your allegiance to your Prince, and … from the true and pure worship of God …[30]

These alterations illustrate the Laudian aversion to the use of harsh or violent anti-Catholic language, 'even though,' as Anthony Milton has pointed out, 'such language had been the staple fare of English Protestantism since the Reformation.' The conspicuous absence of anti-Catholic polemic, Milton concludes, was symptomatic of a 'reversal of polemical priorities' in which Catholicism was no longer regarded as a major threat to the English church.[31]

But not all the anti-Catholic passages were removed. Commenting on the alterations to Featley's sermons, Laud himself observed that 'though some few smart Passages of this kinde are expunged, mitigated, and left out; yet there are in his Sermons, yea in those very Pages complained of, many sharpe passages against Popery left in', and an examination of the text shows that he was quite right.[32] One of Featley's sermons unequivocally declares that the Pope is Antichrist: 'in the Pope all or the principall marks of Antichrist are to be found: Ergo the Pope is the Antichrist … Babylon is figuratively Rome, and Rome is mystically Babylon'. One of Clerke's sermons, drawing on the same vein of apocalyptic imagery, declares that as the Papacy 'was first bred of bloud, so it ever fed of bloud … It breathed first by murder, and it breathes murders still'.[33] These and many other passages of strong anti-papal polemic were left entirely untouched by the licensers. In his report of the trial, Prynne dismissed this as an oversight, commenting that if any anti-Catholic passages had been allowed to remain, it was doubtless because 'the Booke being large, they passed undiscerned till after its publication'. But it is hard to believe that the retention of these passages was merely accidental. In some cases, the licenser made changes to the text while allowing anti-Catholic material to remain, while in other cases, new anti-Catholic material was actually inserted to fill a gap in the text. Thus, for example, the licenser deleted Clerke's prediction of the imminent fall of the papacy, but substituted a new passage declaring that the Gunpowder Plot 'may justly provoke the loathing of so bloody a religion'.[34]

At first glance, this pattern of alterations may seem utterly inconsistent, but on closer examination it is possible to discern the outlines of a coherent licensing policy. The tone of the sermons remained fiercely anti-Catholic; but by drawing attention to the diversity of Catholic beliefs and practices, the licensers made it clear that the errors of some Catholics were not shared by all. Attacks on specific abuses in the Roman church were retained, whereas attacks on Catholicism in general, such as Clerke's claim that 'all Romes Religion is almost lyes', were generally cancelled. Other doctrinal errors were reattributed as the opinion not of 'all Papists', but merely of 'some of them'; not of 'Rome' in general, but of 'some Romanists'; not of 'the schoolemen', but of 'some schoolemen'; and not of 'the Pope', but of 'some in the Pope's behalf'.[35] The licensers were also willing to acknowledge the presence of some sincere Christians within the Roman communion: thus Clerke's statement that 'Rome had in it in Saint Pauls time many good Christians; but few now' was softened slightly to read: 'Rome had in it in Saint Pauls time, and long after, many good Christians; but not so many now.' Similarly, a passage in one of Featley's sermons comparing popery to paganism – a staple of Jacobean anti-Catholic polemic, as we have already seen – was qualified by the insertion of a new passage, warning the reader that this should not be misinterpreted 'as if I put no difference between a Heathen and a Papist . . . All that I intend to shew herein is that in some practices of theirs, they may bee rightly compared to the Heathen'.[36]

This passage from Featley's sermons provides a particularly clear illustration of the way that the licensers' alterations were deliberately misinterpreted by Prynne. Prynne pointed out, quite correctly, that the licenser had deleted a long quotation from the Homily Against the Peril of Idolatry, in which the Catholic practice of 'bowing downe, and praying before Images and Pictures' was denounced as idolatrous. The omission of this quotation, he argued, was clear evidence of a pro-Catholic licensing policy designed 'to subvert the established doctrine of our Church, against the setting up and adoration of Images'.[37] However, it is highly unlikely that the licenser intended to gloss over the anti-Catholic sentiments of the Homily, as the censored text still cites the Homily in a marginal note and continues to affirm its authoritative status as part of the Church of England's official formularies. On further examination, it becomes clear that the quotation from the Homily was omitted in order to make way for a new passage on the possibility of salvation in the Church of Rome, which declared that in spite of the errors of the Roman church, it was still possible for its members to be saved, 'though not as Papists, that is, not by their Popish additions and superstitions, but as Protestants, that is, by those common grounds of Christianity which they hold with us'. The effect of this alteration was not to relax the basic anti-Catholic stance – which remained fairly uncompromising, with the Roman church attacked as 'very corrupt and unsound' – but simply to put forward anti-Catholic arguments in a slightly more moderate and persuasive way, consistent with Laud's expressed wish to appeal to the 'understanding Papist' who might be deterred by gratuitous abuse.

This, however, was not the only reason why anti-Catholic passages were removed or revised. One of the most interesting and significant of the licensers' alterations occurs elsewhere in Featley's sermons, in a passage attacking 'our adversaries' (the Papists) for beautifying their churches rather than their souls. Here it is clear that the problem lay not in the attack on the Church of Rome, but in its potential application to the Church of England, and particularly to the Laudian reordering of church interiors in the 1630s:

> Their rood-lofts they paint, their pillars they engrave, their timbers they carve, their images they cloath, their pictures they cover, their stone altars they gild, their crosses they adorn with jewels and pretious stones ... If we speake of the true adorning of the Church, it is not with the beauty of pictures, but with holinesse...[38]

The passage can be read as an attempt to reappropriate that favourite Laudian slogan, 'the beauty of holiness', as referring to spiritual rather than physical beauty; and when Featley's words were quoted at Laud's trial they stung Laud into replying, rather testily, that it was 'a point that might well be left out. Little necessity, God knows, to preach or print against too much adorning of churches among us, where yet so many churches lie very nastily in many places of the kingdom, and no one too much adorned to be found.'[39]

What makes this passage particularly interesting is the very selective
way that it was revised. The licenser retained the general point about the
over-ornamentation of churches, but qualified it by making it conditional,
and removing the specific attacks on images, pictures and stone altars.
'True adorning' was altered to 'chief adorning', thus avoiding the
implication that these decorations were a false form of religious worship;
and 'the beauty of pictures' became 'the beauty of colours', thus deflecting
the criticism of religious imagery:

> It will little make for the glory of their Church to paint their rood-lofts,
> to engrave their pillars, to carve their timber, to gild their altars, to set
> forth their crosses with jewels and precious stones, if they want that
> precious pearle [of the Gospel] ... The chief adorning of Churches is
> not with the beauty of colours, but of holinesse ...[40]

These changes are slight, but their cumulative effect is considerable. The
Catholic use of religious art is no longer perceived as a form of idolatry,
but merely as a misguided over-reliance on material objects, thus
depriving Featley's anti-Catholic polemic of its essential justification.
Nevertheless, some traces of Featley's original intentions do survive, albeit
in a somewhat muted form, in the remarks on rood-lofts, altars and
crosses; and it is significant that the licenser did not take the opportunity
to delete the passage altogether. The purpose of the revision, it seems, was
not to abolish the difference between Catholicism and Protestantism, but
simply to redefine it so as to permit the partial toleration of religious
imagery.

What, then, should we make of these changes? First and foremost, they
serve as a warning against underestimating the severity of censorship in
the 1630s. The Laudian licensing system shows little sign of the
'arbitrariness' attributed to it by one recent historian: on the contrary,
the sermons of Featley and Clerke were censored very extensively and
with minute attention to detail, and these cannot be regarded as isolated
examples.[41] Anthony Milton has identified well over 30 religious books
that were censored or stopped at the press between 1625 and 1640;
moreover, as he observes, 'further examples continue to emerge ... and it
is quite possible that our current knowledge only represents the tip of an
iceberg of petty intrusiveness by licensers'.[42] A glance down the list of
books published immediately after the collapse of episcopal censorship in
1641 (aptly described by Sheila Lambert as 'the books that came in from
the cold') reveals other examples of books that were refused a licence in
the 1630s. The preface to William Hinde's biography of the puritan

gentleman John Bruen, licensed on 16 January 1641, states that the work had languished unpublished for over a decade, 'suffering more than an Ostracisme, before it could be admitted to speake in the language of the Presse'; while the editor of another godly biography, *The Last Conflicts and Death of Mr Thomas Peacock*, licensed on 14 March 1641, informs us that the work had been submitted for licence in 1637, but that the licenser 'kept it long in his hands, and at last refused it, as too precise for those times'.[43] These and other examples leave no doubt that religious censorship had a marked effect on the output of the London printing presses, significantly narrowing the range of opinions allowed into print.

But while there can be no doubt that censorship did exist, explaining why it operated in the way it did is more problematic. Anthony Milton interprets it in terms of a 'conflict between different clerical factions ... each of which sought to use the mechanisms of licensing and censorship in order to outlaw the works of their theological opponents'. On this reading, there was very little difference between censorship in the 1620s and censorship in the 1630s: the mechanism of the licensing system remained the same; all that had changed was the clerical faction in control of the system, and the type of orthodoxy being promoted.[44] However, a comparison of the two decades suggests that there was a significant difference, not simply in religious orthodoxy but in the nature of the licensing system itself. In 1624, Featley had been reluctant to make any corrections to the text of Elton's sermons once he heard that the author had died, yet his successors in the 1630s seem to have had no qualms about censoring Clerke's sermons – and very heavily at that – despite the fact that the work was being published posthumously. Censorship in the 1630s seems to have been more interventionist, with licensers more ready to interfere with the texts of the books they licensed, regardless of the author's own intentions.

What is happening here, I think, is not simply the redefinition of orthodoxy by means of the licensing system, but also the redefinition of the licensing system itself. In the 1620s, as I argued earlier, we can see a minimalist interpretation of the licensing system in operation, in which the licence is regarded as a *nihil obstat*, a declaration that there is nothing to prevent a book being published. This, in effect, legitimizes a large body of doctrine that is, by the standards of the Church of England, neither unquestionably orthodox nor positively erroneous but merely indifferent. But in the 1630s, for the first time, the licence started to be used as an *imprimatur* rather than a *nihil obstat* – in other words, a positive recommendation of a book's orthodoxy, printed with the book and often declaring that its publication will be to the public benefit, 'cum utilitate publica'. This 'positive' rather than 'negative' interpretation of licensing permitted the licensers to intervene far more radically to alter the meaning of texts.

Notes

1. The text of the Injunctions can be found in W. H. Frere, ed., *Visitation Articles and Injunctions of the Period of the Reformation*, vol. 3, 1559–1575 (London: Alcuin Club, 1910), pp. 8–29; the clauses relating to the book trade are printed in Edward Arber, ed., A *Transcript of the Registers of the Company of Stationers in London*, 1554–1640 (London: privately printed, 1875), I: xxxviii. On the significance of the Injunctions, see W. W. Greg, *Some Aspects and Problems of London Publishing between 1550 and 1650* (Oxford: Clarendon Press, 1956), p. 5, and Cyndia Clegg, *Press Censorship in Elizabethan England* (Cambridge: Cambridge University Press, 1997), pp. 37–40.
2. Greg, *Aspects and Problems*, p. 47.
3. R. B. McKerrow, 'Richard Robinson's *Eupolemia* and the Licensers', *The Library*, 4th series, vol. 11 (1930–1), pp. 173–8, p. 177. The original manuscript of *Eupolemia* is now BL MS Royal 18.A.66; it is printed in George McGill Vogt, 'Richard Robinson's *Eupolemia* (1603)', *SP* 21 (1924), 629–48. See also W. W. Greg, 'Richard Robinson and the Stationers' Register', *MLR* 50 (1955), 407–13, and, for the most recent and authoritative account of Robinson's career, H. R. Woudhuysen, *Sir Philip Sidney and the Circulation of Manuscripts 1558–1640* (Oxford: Clarendon Press, 1996), pp. 195–203.
4. Greg, *Aspects and Problems*, p. 7.
5. Ibid., pp. 8–9; Clegg, *Press Censorship*, pp. 58–63.
6. Matthieu Virel, A *Learned and Excellent Treatise containing all the principall grounds of Christian Religion* (1594). I have compared this with the Latin edition, *Religionis Christianae Compendium* (Geneva, 1587); the offending note appears on sig. v2v (f. 154v) of the Latin edition, and is omitted at sig. P5r (p. 225) of the English edition.
7. See, among others, Peter Lake, *Anglicans and Puritans?: Presbyterianism and English Conformist Thought from Whitgift to Hooker* (London: Allen and Unwin, 1988), and Nicholas Tyacke, *Anti-Calvinists: the Rise of English Arminianism c. 1590–1640* (Oxford: Clarendon Press, 1987).
8. Greg, 'Richard Robinson and the Stationers' Register', p. 412.
9. Greg, *Aspects and Problems*, p. 62. Thomas Buckner, one of Archbishop Abbot's chaplains, was in the process of licensing a manuscript in 1633 when the Archbishop's death prevented him from doing so: see W. W. Greg, A *Companion to Arber* (Oxford: Clarendon Press, 1967), p. 287.
10. Nicholas Tyacke, *The Fortunes of English Puritanism, 1603–1640* (London: Dr. Williams Trust, 1990), p. 9.
11. Bodleian Library, MS Rawlinson D. 47 (Daniel Featley's letter-book), f. 22.
12. Daniel Featley, *Ancilla Pietatis: or, the hand-maid to private devotion* (1626), A6r. Featley was echoing the sentiments of earlier writers, notably Richard Rogers in his *Seven Treatises* (1603), A6v, who had also expressed concern at the lack of Protestant practical divinity.

13. Francis de Croy, *The Three Conformities: that is, the harmony and agreement of the Romish Church with Gentilisme, Judaisme, and auncient heresies* (1620); a pre-publication manuscript of the work, including the passages omitted by Featley, is in the Beinecke Library at Yale, Osborn MS b. 280.

14. Daniel Featley, *Cygnea Cantio* (London, 1629), D3v.

15. Paul Bayne, *A Commentarie upon the First Chapter of the Epistle of Saint Paul, written to the Ephesians* (1618), H3v.

16. George Throgmorton, *A Treatise of Faith* (London, 1624), F3v.

17. Anthony Milton, 'Licensing, Censorship and Religious Orthodoxy in Early Stuart England', *HJ* 41 (1998), 629.

18. PRO, SP 16/499/3.

19. Laud, *Works*, vol. 4 (Oxford, 1854), p. 241.

20. William Prynne, *Canterburies Doome* (1646), 211v. See also Lambert B. Larking, ed., *Proceedings, Principally in the County of Kent* (Camden Society, 1862), pp. 80, 84, 85, for Featley's evidence to the parliamentary subcommittee on religion in 1640.

21. Sir Edward Dering, *A Discourse of Proper Sacrifice* (London, 1644), c3v.

22. On Clerke's career, see Patrick Collinson, Nigel Ramsay and Margaret Sparks, eds, *A History of Canterbury Cathedral* (Oxford: Oxford University Press, 1995), p. 183.

23. Prynne, *Canterburies Doome*, 2L1v.

24. Dering's notes on the licensing and publication of William Jones's *Commentary upon the Epistles to Philemon and to the Hebrewes* (1635) provide some useful comparative figures. According to Dering, the stationer Robert Allot paid £40 for the copyright, printed 1700 copies at a cost of almost £400, but was unable to sell them when it became known that the work had been censored: see Lambeth Palace Library, MS 943, p. 735.

25. Dering, *Discourse*, d4r. This is corroborated by Robert Porter, *The Life of Mr John Hieron* (London, 1691), D3v, which describes how a group of Derbyshire puritans were summoned to Lambeth to face charges of non-conformity: no prosecutor appeared, and they applied to have the charges struck out; Baker refused to dismiss them, but they then went to Bray, 'who courteously received them … and obtained their discharge'.

26. On Haywood's licensing of de Sales, see *The Petition and Articles … against Dr Heywood* (1641), R.M., *An Answer to a Lawless Pamphlet* (1641), Peter Blayney, *The Texts of King Lear and their Origins* (Cambridge: Cambridge University Press, 1982), pp. 305–8, and N. W. Bawcutt, 'A Crisis of Laudian Censorship: Nicholas and John Okes and the Publication of Sales's *An Introduction to a Devout Life*', *The Library* (7th ser., 1:4 (Dec. 2000), pp. 403–38). On Wykes, see Greg, *Licensers for the Press*, pp. 101–6. Greg describes Wykes as 'much the most active of all licensers'; he licensed over 600 titles, and was one of only two licensers to retain their posts under the Long Parliament.

27. The entry in the *Short Title Catalogue* (*STC* 10730) draws attention to two cancelled sheets, but in fact there are 17 (C2.5, C3.4, I3.4, V2.5, X1.6, Y1.6, Z3.4, 2P1.6, 2S2.5, 2T3.4, 2V2.5, 3F2.5, 3V1.6, 3X3.4, 3Y2.5, 4G2.5, 4H1.4). Censored copies can easily be recognized by the list of errata on the final page (p. 907, sig. 4H4v), which does not appear in uncensored copies.

28. 'A note of the severall variations, additions, and expunctions in Dr Clerkes sermons, by the Lycensers Dr Heywood Chaplaine to the Lord Archbishop of Canterbury and Dr Wykes Chaplaine to the Lord Bishop of London', PRO, SP 16/339/56 (cited below as 'PRO list'). See Prynne, *Canterburies Doome*, 2L1v, for its use at the trial.
29. Clerke, *Sermons*, K3v, X1r; PRO list, nos 31, 94.
30. Featley, *Clavis Mystica*, 3Y2v (p. 796).
31. Anthony Milton, *Catholic and Reformed: the Roman and Protestant Churches in English Protestant Thought, 1600–1640* (Cambridge: Cambridge University Press, 1995), p. 66.
32. Prynne, *Canterburies Doome*, 3Y2v.
33. Featley, *Clavis Mystica*, 3Z2v. Clerke, *Sermons*, X1r; PRO list, no. 93.
34. Clerke, *Sermons*, X5v; PRO list, no. 117.
35. Clerke, *Sermons*, 2F6v, 2B4r, C3r; PRO list, nos 148, 123, 5.
36. Clerke, Sermons, 2G6r; PRO list, no. 155. Featley, *Clavis Mystica*, 3X4r (p. 787).
37. Prynne, *Canterburies Doome*, P2v (p. 788).
38. Featley, *Clavis Mystica*, V5r (p. 225).
39. Laud, *Works*, vol. 4, p. 282. Laud seems to have assumed that the whole passage had been deleted.
40. On the installation of stone altars and religious images in English churches in the 1620s and 1630s, see Nicholas Tyacke, *Anti-Calvinists: the Rise of English Arminianism* (Oxford: Clarendon Press, 1987), pp. 118 (the altar at Durham Cathedral), p. 194 (paintings of Christ in Peterhouse chapel).
41. On the alleged 'arbitrariness' of early modern censorship, see Glenn Burgess, *Absolute Monarchy and the Stuart Constitution* (New Haven and London: Yale University Press, 1996), p. 7.
42. Milton, 'Licensing, Censorship and Religious Orthodoxy', pp. 644–5.
43. William Hinde, *A Faithfull Remonstrance of the Holy Life and Happy Death of John Bruen* (1641), A6r. *The Last Conflicts and Death of Mr Thomas Peacock* (1646; *Wing* B3514), D4r.
44. Milton, 'Licensing, Censorship and Religious Orthodoxy', p. 633.

Part III
Political Censorship

9
Censoring Ireland in Elizabethan England, 1580–1600

Andrew Hadfield

Soon after he ascended to the English throne, James I visited the records held in the Palace of Whitehall and remarked: 'We had more ado with Ireland than all the world besides.'[1] James's comment on the wealth of the official material collected in London is borne out by the extensive deposits in the state papers where Ireland has warranted its own extensive calendar. Such profusion stands in marked contrast to the paucity of material available in printed form for the more general reader. Very few texts on Ireland were published between 1580 and 1603, the period now characterized as the second reign of Elizabeth when the Queen began to clamp down on the various forms of political opposition to her reign which were developing in response to her increasingly autocratic government.[2] What was the reason for this discrepancy? Was material on Ireland routinely censored? If so, was this because Ireland was already 'turning into the official English unconscious', and exposing the brutal foundations on which the English/British state was built?[3] Or were there more immediate practical reasons for putting the lid on discussion given the importance of the Anglo-Irish conflict in the latter stages of Elizabeth's reign?[4] The alternatives are tantalizing, the evidence hard to interpret with any certainty, and central to the concerns of this collection. In this chapter I will try to provide an overview of the subject and weigh up the evidence, examining a series of important examples and cases.

General descriptions and histories of Ireland were available to interested readers.[5] The first edition of Holinshed's *Chronicles* (1577) contained a 'History of Ireland' by Richard Stanihurst. The second edition (1587) contained a translation of Gerald of Wales, *Expugnatio Hibernica* (1188), by John Hooker, who also contributed a 'History of Ireland' up to 1587. Both editions were subject to government intervention and, ultimately, censorship.[6] The Privy Council wrote to the Bishop of London, John Aylmer, on 5 December 1577, claiming that key events from ancient Irish history had been falsely represented by Stanihurst, and ordered that he summon the printer, find out how many copies of the chronicle had been sold and stop further copies being printed and distributed. Another letter was sent to Gerald Fitzgerald, Earl of Kildare, demanding that he send his servant, Richard Stanihurst, to London to answer the charges. The Acts of the Privy Council note that in January 1578 the matter had been cleared up and the work could be printed with the offending passages cancelled.[7]

Annabel Patterson has shown that greatest concern was generated over recent events recorded in the *Chronicles*, and it is likely that some of the cancelled passages were designed to remove hostile references to Archbishop Alen.[8] The second edition, entered into the Stationers' Register in 1584, also caused anxiety due to its representation of recent events, and the delay in its publication is probably explained by the need for careful checking of contemporary material. When the second edition finally appeared in 1587, various cuts had been demanded and made. The omissions included a number of references to recent events in Ireland, and Stanihurst's enthusiastic biography of Henry Sidney, who had subsequently fallen from grace, was truncated.[9] Government sensitivity was not exclusively directed towards Ireland, but it was clearly singled out as an area of potential concern. It is noticeable that the historians Holinshed employed to write the Irish material appear to have been especially sensitive to the delicate balancing act that their task required. In his dedication to Henry Sidney, Stanihurst laments 'How cumbersome . . . and dangerous a taske it is to ingrosse and divulge the dooings of others, especiallie when the parties registed or their issue are living.'[10] Elsewhere Stanihurst writes of the difficulty of including and excluding historical detail, in words that can be applied to the problems of writing a historical narrative, but which also seem to hint at the extra problem of writing under fear of punishment: 'as for the passing over in silence of diverse events (albeit the law or rather the libertie of an historie requireth that all should be related . . .) yet I must confesse, that I was not able, upon so little leasure, to know all that was said or doone'.[11] Ireland, it seems, was always an area of concern for English authorities and instilled a nervous reaction in writers.

John Derricke's poem, *The Image of Irelande, with a Discoverie of Woodkarne*, a text which appears not to have suffered any unwelcome attention from the central authorities, contains the most vivid account of life in Ireland in the period. It was published in 1581, having been entered into the Register of the Stationers' Company in 1580. The text was accompanied by 12 woodcuts which survive in very few copies. Presumably owners tore out the plates 'for use as wall-decorations'.[12] Derricke's work celebrates the campaigns of Sir Henry Sidney in the 1560s and 1570s, especially his success against Rory Oge O'More, as well as presenting a hostile perception of the Irish as uncivilized, violent brutes, culminating in the often-reproduced woodcut of the Irish Lords, the MacSweynes, feasting in the open air (woodcut 3).[13] Derricke's text would seem to be an exemplary case of Elizabethan publishing, having been entered through the correct channels, clearly responding to demand, and so enjoying relatively wide circulation and readership.

However, it should be noted that *The Image of Irelande* appeared at a time when it looked as if the English conquest of Ireland would proceed to a relatively smooth conclusion, despite the rebellion in Munster which necessitated a series of bloody campaigns.[14] In the 1580s the English still felt confident enough to proceed with plans to establish colonies of English settlers throughout Munster as a means of making sure that such resistance was never repeated.[15] Henry Sidney was a governor who had been lionized by his entourage before, notably in Edmund Campion's *History of Ireland* (1570–1), when he had argued that Sidney's victories had paved the way for civilizing the recalcitrant Irish, a message parallel in substance, if not in style, to that of Derricke. Campion's work formed the basis of Stanihurst's 'History of Ireland' reproduced in the first edition of Holinshed's *Chronicles*, and was later published alongside Spenser's *View of the Present State of Ireland* in Sir James Ware's *Ancient Irish Histories* (1633).[16]

The English situation in Ireland took a serious turn for the worse in the 1590s and it is perhaps no accident that not one serious treatise on or history of Ireland was published in that decade, apart from the peculiar case of Richard Beacon's *Solon his Follie* (1594) (see below). The outbreak of the Nine Years' War precipitated by the rebellion of Hugh O'Neill, Earl of Tyrone, in 1594, coupled with England's continuing conflict with Spain, led to legitimate English fears that Ireland was a crucial theatre of war which could become a bulwark for Spanish European domination, especially when O'Neill himself began to see the conflict he had started in terms of a holy Catholic crusade against the heretic English Protestants.[17] Numerous treatises and thoughts on the ways and means of solving the crisis were written, most arguing, unsurprisingly, that huge military aid was required, and looking back with nostalgia to the brutal Deputy-ship of Lord Grey De Wilton.[18] None of these made their way into print, but clearly circulated in manuscript among officials and other interested parties, as had generally been the case with such material throughout the century.[19]

Manuscript circulation was a common form of disseminating ideas in early modern England. As Henry Woudhuysen has observed, scribal publication had key advantages over printing, even if the argument that many aristocrats thought that there was a stigma involved in entering noble ideas into the vulgar marketplace of books is left aside.[20] Circulating a manuscript gave the author greater control over who actually read the work, so that 'author and scribes could reach precisely the audience they wanted to address'.[21] Moreover, manuscripts 'allowed a certain freedom of expression, especially about political, religious, and personal names, which printed books might not ... Numerous works which were liable to attract official displeasure circulated in manuscript.'[22] It is significant that manuscript circulation did not die out with the emergence of the printing press, but was clearly modified by the development of commercial publishing. Works which were not designed for a larger audience, or which had to be kept hidden from prying eyes, invariably remained in manuscript. Given that manuscripts were generally produced by or on behalf of aristocrats, many closely involved in court politics, it is often hard to determine whether material remained in manuscript because authors wished to keep their thoughts within a closed circle for fear of hostile action, whether they were simply following a common practice, or whether they felt there was no point in trying to broadcast them further via the printing press. The medium might not *be* the message, but the message cannot be read without a knowledge of the medium.

This issue is central, it seems to me, to the most notorious case of 'censorship', the non-appearance of Edmund Spenser's *A View of the Present State of Ireland*.[23] Spenser's text was entered into the Stationers' Register – as *The Image of Irelande* had been nearly 20 years earlier – by the printer Matthew Lownes on 14 April 1598 'uppon Condition that hee gett further authoritie before yt be prynted'.[24] The text appeared in print for the first time in 1633 when the Dublin scholar, Sir James Ware, published it as one of the four works in his *Ancient Irish Histories*. Ware suggested in the preface that had Spenser 'lived to see these times, and the good effects which the last 30 yeares peace have produced in this land ... he would have omitted those passages which may seeme to lay either any aspersion upon some families, or generall upon the Nation'.[25] Readers have inferred that what seemed offensive to one early modern reader would also have seemed offensive to the authorities in 1598, especially given the contingent and specific nature of Ware's criticisms of Spenser.[26]

However, such straightforward links between a text and its non-appearance may disguise a whole host of problems and questions. First, it does not necessarily follow that the proviso attached to the entry advising the publisher to 'gett further authoritie' before proceeding to print, means that the work had aroused the hostile attention of the censors. Entries in the Register were really required to establish the authority of the publisher to print the work, an early form of copyright law policed by the stationers themselves. As Jean Brink has pointed out, approximately 15 per cent of entries between January and June 1598 'contain some kind of conditional note'.[27] Some of these, it is true, were probably subject to censorship, but many were arguments over publishing rights. It is quite possible that the *View* failed to appear because of a dispute with Matthew Lownes, who had just pirated a copy of Sidney's *Astrophil and Stella* (1597), a year ahead of the authorized edition of William Ponsonby, who was Spenser's normal publisher. Furthermore, Ponsonby was made a warden of the Stationers' Company in 1598, so would have possessed the power to halt any devious move on Lownes' part.[28]

More striking still, is the fact that Spenser's text was the only analytic political text dealing with Ireland entered into the Stationers' Register in the 1590s. By 1598, the Nine Years' War had reached a critical stage, and it is clear that the *View* was written in response to the gathering crisis (even if it had been largely completed by 1596).[29] Serious defeats in Ulster had undermined English confidence and there had been a startling number of changes in military personnel and leadership. On 14 August 1598, Marshal Bagenal's army was defeated at the Yellow Ford, and on 12 March 1599, the Earl of Essex was appointed lieutenant and made overall military commander. When Essex's campaigns did nothing to improve the situation it was forbidden 'on pain of death, to write or speak of Irish affairs'.[30] On 21 July 1599, Francis Cordale wrote to Humphrey Galdelli in Venice that he could 'send no news of the Irish wars, all advertisments thence being prohibited, and such news as comes to Council carefully concealed. I fear our part has had little success, lost many captains and whole companies, and has little hope of prevailing.'[31]

If it was problematic to try and publish the *View* in the spring/summer of 1598, it would appear that any chance it might have had of appearing in print disappeared within the following year as the Irish crisis became even more intense. Authorities were extremely unlikely to look favourably on a work which wrote so openly about military tactics, gave a clear sense of where the author thought the strengths and weaknesses of English policy in Ireland lay, provided a definite sense of exactly what should be done, down to geographical details concerning the location of garrisons.[32]

The point to be made is that there were certainly *sufficient* reasons for the *View* to be censored; but this does not mean that it *necessarily* was. We do not usually know how carefully censors read texts. The only substantial notes which do survive are those of the Master of the Revels who annotated play texts, and there is considerable disagreement over his exact role in the process: whether he was effectively a policeman, or whether he was a mediator between writers and the authorities.[33] Given the number of works published, it would have been an impossible feat had the meagre resources assigned to the Herculean task of reading scandalous and dangerous material – after 1586 the Archbishop of Canterbury and the Bishop of London – accomplished even a small part of their mission.[34] The most spectacular cases of censorship were actually cases on 'non-censorship', recalling offensive and subversive works after they had entered the public domain. Less than a year after the *View* was entered into the Stationers' Register, John Hayward's *The First part of the life and raigne of king Henrie the IIII* was published (Feb. 1599), a work which appeared to compare Elizabeth's reign to that of the deposed Richard II. The work was dedicated to Essex, and became an important piece of evidence in Essex's treason trial after his rebellion. But what is significant is that 'Hayward's work did not receive much attention from the Queen or her Councillors until *after* Essex's catastrophic return from Ireland and subsequent fall from royal favour.'[35] Dangerous and subversive works did find their way into print. In fact, they only became the targets of hostile attention from the authorities when events conspired to make them so, as was the case with the unfortunate John Stubbes, author of *The Discovery of a Gaping Gulf* (1579).[36]

Such evidence would appear to suggest that censors rarely read works with close scrutiny, probably owing to pressures of time. Only when events focused attention on a problematic or offensive work did the wheels of repression start to turn. The most perplexing aspect of the *View*'s entry in the Stationers' Register is that it ever appeared there at all. There is a considerable number of surviving copies, one of which appears to have been owned by the Earl of Essex, indicating that the work circulated widely in manuscript and reached precisely the audience that authors of such manuscripts generally desired them to reach.[37] It is odd that anyone wanted such a work to reach a wider audience, unless it was a case of a publisher attempting to cash in on the considerable selling power of a major author at the height of his fame. Lownes' behaviour over *Astrophil and Stella* would suggest that this is a plausible explanation of events.

However, this does not, of course, rule out the possibility that the *View* was actually censored, or was a candidate for suppression. 1598 and 1599 were years when desperate English inhabitants in Ireland would most have wanted to publicise their plight as their homes and livelihoods were destroyed as Tyrone's rebellion reached the Munster Plantation (Spenser was one of the high-profile casualties).[38] Equally, these were years when such works were least likely to appear. It is quite plausible that the *View* was withdrawn from the process of publication after it was entered into the Stationers' Register – although there is no evidence that this was the case – preventing any hostile attention.[39]

Spenser's tract has often been compared to the one serious work on Ireland which did make its way into print in the 1590s, Richard Beacon's *Solon His Follie* (1594).[40] The books do share many features in common and are serious works of political science which try to offer an in-depth analysis of the situation the English were facing in Ireland, and provide a clear and manageable solution. Both try to provide a context to enable non-specialists in England to understand exactly what is going on; both are dialogues based on contemporary humanist and classical models; both are happy to recommend violent solutions and military conquest (although Spenser places far greater emphasis on the need for a systematic invasion); both owe a considerable debt to Machiavelli.[41] As Clare Carroll notes, Spenser constructs an elaborate 'ethnography of the Irish', tracing their genealogy from Scots, Gauls and Scythians, 'deployed to justify his rejection of the common law in Ireland'. Beacon's approach has a similar purpose but is 'political, historical, and legal' (*Solon his Follie*, p. xxviii).

The question that needs to be asked is why Beacon's dialogue made its way into print when Spenser's did not. Some initial points can be made. First, *Solon his Follie* appeared at the start of the Nine Years' War, when tension was high but nowhere near being at the same level as in 1598, just before the destruction of the Munster Plantation. Second, Beacon's text was published in Oxford, at the university press, not London, where regulations appear to have been much more lax. The Royal Charters which established the monopoly of printing for the Stationers' Company in 1557 and 1559 allowed the presses set up in Oxford and Cambridge to remain outside the jurisdiction of the Company and, hence, free from its injunctions.[42] Beacon was educated at Cambridge and appears to have had no direct link with Oxford or its university. Could he have had *Solon his Follie* published surreptitiously? Although the dedication to Elizabeth praises her reform of Ireland, there is no reference to Ireland in the title or subtitle, and the text itself tells the story of Solon's attempt to capture the island of Salminia for his native Athens. Of course, the work is a transparent allegory of English attempts to assert control over Ireland, which even the most casual reader would have realized a short way into the narrative when the speakers start making direct references to Irish laws, customs and figures (coyne and livery (p. 21); Lord Grey (p. 22), Sir Richard Bingham (p. 23)). But, the text would have had to have been read by a censor for this to have been realized, another indication that circumventing control and placing material in the public sphere might have been a comparatively easy task.

Arguably, however, it is the differences between *Solon his Follie* and the *View* which serve to explain their contemporary significance and fate. The *View* is clearly a work targeted at a specific problem at a particular time, and can be read as a desperate plea that a huge, well-supplied and well-supported army be sent to cure Ireland's ills. *Solon his Follie* does not have such a clear, narrow focus, but appropriates the example of Ireland to reflect on the question of contemporary government. Its use of republican political theory – whatever the purpose of this language – suggests that the work is as much about England and the rest of Europe as Ireland.[43] Its subtitle, *A Politique Discourse touching the Refomation of common-weales conquered, declined or corrupted*, gives an accurate indication of the contents and the purpose of the work, precluding a simple reading of the dialogue as a treatise on Ireland *per se*. The key authors on whom Beacon bases his ideas – in addition to Machiavelli – are Jean Bodin, Francesco Guicciardini and Justus Lipsius, as well as the apocalyptic emphasis of the Geneva Bible (pp. xxxviii–xliii). Spenser's text is also informed by such authorities, but they are not so prominently or widely discussed. The *View* relentlessly targets its questions and answers to the task in hand, so that when Irenius seems to be straying from the point in describing the genealogy of the Irish, Eudoxus upbraids him for it: 'but yet from that (meseemes) ye have much swarved in all this long discourse, of the first inhabiting of Ireland; for what is that to your purpose?' Irenius has to explain that his extensive commentary has not been a digression: 'for if you marked the course of all that speech well, it was to shew, by what meanes the customes, that now are in Ireland, being some of them indeede very strange and almost hethenish, were first brought in'. Eudoxus draws attention to the problem and the reader is left to decide the relevance of the information: 'You bring your self Iren. Very well into the way againe, notwithstanding that it seemeth that you were never out of the way.'[44] In *Solon his Follie*, questions and statements invariably open out onto wider political perspectives. Two examples chosen at random will give a sense of the content of the work; 'Epimenides: but where the manners of the people be not corrupted, there a milde course of government doth worke his office, and carrieth with it allowance and commendations' (p. 83); 'Solon: It must be confessed that in common-weles gained by conquest, you shall advance your government more assuredly by the favoure of the people, then by the might of the nobilitie' (p. 105). Beacon's work bears a strong resemblance to contemporary histories based on Roman historians (most notably, Tacitus), which were widely produced in the 1590s and early 1600s, and aphoristic works of political advice, often based on Guicciardini.[45]

The point is that Spenser's *View*, as Ciaran Brady has argued in a slightly different context, marks a departure from the type of works written about Ireland before it, while remaining within an easily identified tradition.[46] *Solon his Follie* cannot be compared to the *View* in a straightforward manner because they are really works which belong to different generic categories. The *View* can be seen to stand as the end of a tradition of 'reform thought' in Ireland, works written by English and Anglo-Irish politicians, which were designed to provide a solution to the variety of ills which beset Ireland under the Tudors.[47] Such works always circulated in manuscript, because there was no purpose in making them public. *Solon his Follie*, in contrast, belongs to a tradition of works of political theory and philosophy, such as Jean Bodin's *Les Six Livres de la Republique* (1576), or Justus Lipsius's *Six Bookes of Politickes or Civil Discourse* (1589, trans. 1594), that grew out of and were responses to a specific situation or crisis, but which reflected on wider political issues.[48] Of course, it would be wrong to claim that such works are discrete categories or mutually exclusive: all texts contain generic markers of other texts within them, as any reading of a *View* alongside previous manuscripts on the ways and means of reforming Ireland, or *Solon his Follie*, will demonstrate: 'all genres are inescapably mixed'.[49] Nevertheless, certain generic characteristics and marks demand that the reader read the work in question in a particular way.

Solon his Follie, I would suggest, is better read alongside an earlier work, William Herbert's Latin treatise, *Croftus Sive De Hibernia Liber* (ca. 1591).[50] Herbert's work, like *Solon his Follie*, uses the example of Ireland to reflect on wider issues of politics and government. Herbert adopts a consciously Ciceronian style and refers to ancient and modern authorities – Plato, Livy, Tacitus, Pliny, Suetonius, Machiavelli, Lipsius – throughout the text to support and conclude his arguments. For example, a discussion of government starts with a citation from Aristotle's *Politics*, leads on to the statement that 'Tyranny exercised by a prince or supreme magistrate can be ended or punished by God alone. All other remedies are either unholy or foolish' (p. 67), and concludes with comments from Thucydides, Cicero and the Book of Exodus. Herbert's work was not printed, but the state of the manuscript, prepared by a professional scribe, would suggest that the author was interested in having the manuscript published. As his modern editors point out, while this cannot be proved, the evidence of author and text would seem to support such an inference. Herbert had already had one work published so is unlikely to have been averse to seeing another in print. The text seems to have been designed for a wider readership, which it deliberately addresses. Early on, Herbert 'expresses the hope that his work will be of use not only to his sovereign and his fellow citizens but to all men'. The use of Latin further marks *Croftus* out as an unusual work, suggesting that 'Herbert was looking beyond his immediate audience in England to Europe' (p. xviii). Other writers, like Beacon and Spenser, wrote in English. In the absence of further evidence, we will probably never know why *Croftus* was not published. It may be another sign of the difficulty of getting books on Ireland into print, a consequence of the busy author changing his mind, or a realization that he had misjudged the potential audience for his work. But it may help to explain why *Solon his Follie* was published and why Spenser's *View* was not.

Cyndia Clegg argues in Chapter 10 below that James I took a personal interest in the problem of censorship. While he was often prepared not to intervene, despite his obvious disapproval of particular works, he was happy to perform spectacular public acts of censorship when he felt he had much to gain. I want to conclude this essay with an example of James's sense of the significance of censorship, which occurred before his assumption of the English crown, and points to the relevance of Ireland as a dangerous subject and also a location where subversive material was produced.

When Edmund Spenser published the second edition of *The Faerie Queene* in 1596, he included a number of thinly veiled references to relatively recent historical events, concentrated mainly in Book V. Canto ix, for example, included a detailed account of the trial of Mary Queen of Scots, which ended with the establishment of her guilt and execution pending. This passage angered her son, James VI, so much that he refused to have the poem sold in Scotland, demanded that the remaining copies of the poem be impounded, and insisted that 'Spenser for his fault may be duly tried and punished'.[51] The English secretary in Scotland, Robert Bowes, tried to smooth over the problem by answering James's allegation that 'this book was passed with privilege of Her Majesty's Commissioners for the view and allowance of all writings to be received into print'. Bowes wrote to Lord Burghley that he thought he had satisfied James that 'it is not given out with such privilege', a reference to the fact that entering a work in the Stationers' Register, as the second edition of *The Faerie Queene* had been (20 January 1596), did not imply royal approval. Bowes' words further indicate the lack of centralized control over books or careful censorship of them in Elizabeth's reign.[52]

James was clearly angered by a literary work which he thought might undermine his claim to the English throne, as a later entry in the state papers makes clear. George Nicholson, a servant of Bowes, wrote to Robert Cecil on 25 February 1598, to let him know that one Walter Quinn, at St Andrews University, was 'answering Spencer's book whereat the King was offended'. James had also instructed the royal printer to publish a book by Quinn which would prove his right to the English throne.[53] It is clear that had Spenser survived James's accession he would have had much to fear. Indeed, it is likely that James's hostility to Sir Walter Raleigh may have been intensified by his very public allegiance to Spenser in the 1590s (the second edition of *The Faerie Queene* makes an impassioned defence of Raleigh, after his fall from grace).[54] It is noticeable that the specific historical events represented in *The Faerie Queene*, Books IV–VI, are mainly ones from the previous decade – the trial of Mary, the Dutch Wars, the French Civil Wars, the defeat of the Spanish Armada.[55] This suggests that Spenser had taken the recent action against the representation of contemporary events in historical chronicles and plays to heart.[56]

After Spenser died, Matthew Lownes, who had inherited William Ponsonby's papers, published the first folio edition of *The Faerie Queene* (1609).[57] This included 'Two Cantos of Mutabilitie', a fragment of an apparently uncompleted seventh book of the poem. The cantos reflect directly on the problem of the succession in a manner that would appear to have gone beyond even what was acceptable in the 1590s.[58] Elizabeth is represented as cruelly subject to the ravages of time and the brutal effects of Mutability, as she ages beyond her usefulness as a ruler and hastens towards her death:

> Even you, faire *Cynthia*, whom so much ye make
> *Joves* dearest darling, she was bred and nurst
> On *Cynthus* hill, whence she her name did take:
> Then is she mortall borne, how-so ye crake;
> Besides, her face and countenance every day
> We changed see, and sundry forms partake,
> Now hornd, now round, now bright, now brown and gray:
> So that *as changefull as the Moone* men use to say.
> (*FQ*, VII.vii.50.)

The stanza is also an explicit attack on Elizabeth as a fickle and foolish ruler who has put her own caprices and vacillations before the long-term needs of her subjects. The figure of Mutabilitie can be seen to stand for the forces which will assume government after Elizabeth has died. The poem has warned repeatedly that the chaos enveloping Ireland in the 1590s can easily spread to England if firm action is not undertaken to stop it.[59] Mutabilitie, on one allegorical level, clearly stands for the Stuart claim through Mary Queen of Scots. *The Faerie Queene*, significantly enough, does not actually show her execution, implying that her threat had not been extinguished, undoubtedly through the continuing claims of her son.

All of which would suggest that James was an astute reader of *The Faerie Queene*. Spenser, for his part, ended the version of his epic poem published in his lifetime with a distinct allusion to censorship, when he feared that his verses would undoubtedly be savaged by the Blatant Beast and possibly suppressed just as his earlier poem, *Mother Hubberds Tale*, had fallen foul of Lord Burghley:

> Ne spareth he most learned wits to rate,
> Ne spareth he the gentle Poets rime,
> But rends without regard of person or of time.
>
> Ne may this homely verse, of many meanest,
> Hope to escape his venemous writs, all were they clearest
> From blamefull blot, and free from all that wite,
> With which some wicked tongues did it backbite,
> And bring into a mighty Peres displeasure,
> That never so deserved to endite.
>
> (*FQ*, VI.xii.40–1)[60]

The published version of *The Faerie Queene* clearly sailed pretty close to the wind. 'Two Cantos of Mutabilitie', which show Diana (Elizabeth) abandoning Ireland to chaos, and make it clear that England's fate will be the same if the succession passes to the Stuarts, probably indicate what Spenser thought he could not write as the 1590s drew to an end. Barnaby Rich later remarked (1615) that 'thos wordes that in Englande would be brought wythin the compasse of treason, they are accounted wyth us in Ireland for ordynary table taulke'.[61] Spenser's posthumously published verses give a further reason why English authorities were so wary of Irish matters.

Notes

1. Cited in J. H. Andrews, 'Appendix: the Beginnings of the Surveying Profession in Ireland – Abstract', in Sarah Tyacke, ed., *English Map-Making, 1500–1650* (London: British Library, 1983), p. 20.

2. John Guy, 'The 1590s: the Second Reign of Elizabeth I?', in John Guy, ed., *The Reign of Elizabeth I: Court and Culture in the Last Decade* (Cambridge: Cambridge University Press, 1995), pp. 1–19.
3. Declan Kiberd, *Inventing Ireland: the Literature of the Modern Nation* (London: Cape, 1995), p. 656. See also Willy Maley, *Salvaging Spenser: Colonialism, Culture and Identity* (Basingstoke: Macmillan, 1997), p. 1.
4. See Steven G. Ellis, *Tudor Ireland: Crown, Community and the Conflict of Cultures, 1470–1603* (Harlow: Longman, 1985), ch. 9; Colm Lennon, *Sixteenth-Century Ireland: the Incomplete Conquest* (Dublin: Gill and Macmillan, 1995), ch. 10.
5. A list of works published with Ireland in the title is given in Andrew Hadfield, *Spenser's Irish Experience: Wilde Fruyt and Salvage Soyl* (Oxford: Clarendon Press, 1997), appendix.
6. Cyndia Susan Clegg, *Press Censorship in Elizabethan England* (Cambridge: Cambridge University Press, 1997), ch. 7.
7. Annabel Patterson, *Reading Holinshed's Chronicles* (Chicago: University of Chicago Press, 1994), pp. 11–12. My account of Holinshed is heavily indebted to Patterson's excellent analysis.
8. Ibid., p. 12.
9. Ibid., p. 11; Janet Clare, *'Art Made Tongue-tied by Authority': Elizabethan and Jacobean Dramatic Censorship* (Manchester: Manchester University Press, 2nd edn, 1999), pp. 38, 47.
10. Cited in Patterson, *Reading Holinshed's Chronicles*, p. 12.
11. Cited in Ibid., p. 13.
12. John Derricke, *The Image of Irelande*, ed. David Beers Quinn (Belfast: Blackstaff, 1985), p. xvii. Subsequent references to this edition in parentheses in the text.
13. On Rory Oge O'More, see Lennon, *Sixteenth-Century Ireland*, pp. 185–200. Useful recent articles on the work include Maryclaire Moroney, 'Apocalypse, Ethnography, and Empire in John Derricke's *Image of Irelande* (1581) and Spenser's *View of the Present State of Ireland* (1596)', *ELR* 29 (1999), 355–74; Vincent Carey, 'John Derricke's *Image of Irelande*, Sir Henry Sidney, and the Massacre at Mullaghmast, 1578', *IHS* 123 (May, 1999), 305–27. For a claim that Shakespeare may have made use of *The Image of Irelande*, see Andrew Hadfield, 'Shakespeare, John Derricke and Ireland: *The Comedy of Errors*, III.ii.105–6', *N&Q* 242 (March, 1997), 53–4.
14. For details, see Lennon, *Sixteenth-Century Ireland*, ch. 8.
15. Michael MacCarthy-Morrogh, *The Munster Plantation: English Migration to Southern Ireland, 1583–1641* (Oxford: Clarendon Press, 1986).
16. Edmund Campion, *Two Bokes of the Histories of Ireland*, ed. A. F. Vossen (Assen: Van Gorcum, 1963), Introduction.
17. Hiram Morgan, *Tyrone's Rebellion: the Outbreak of the Nine Years' War in Ireland* (Woodbridge: Royal Historical Society/Boydell, 1993).
18. Hadfield, *Spenser's Irish Experience*, ch. 1.
19. Ciaran Brady, *The Chief Governors: the Rise and Fall of Reform Government in Tudor Ireland, 1536–1588* (Cambridge: Cambridge University Press, 1994). See also Hiram Morgan, 'Beyond Spenser? A Historiographical Introduction to the Study of Political Ideas in Early Modern Ireland', in Hiram Morgan, ed., *Political Ideology in Ireland, 1541–1641* (Dublin: Four Courts Press, 1999), pp. 9–21. An example of a later work produced at the time of the worst crisis of English rule when many similar works appeared is 'The Supplication of the blood of the English, most

lamentably murdred in Ireland, Cryeng out of the Yearth for Revenge (1598)', introduced and transcribed by Willy Maley, *Analecta Hibernica*, 36 (1994), 3–91.

20. J. W. Saunders, 'The Stigma of Print: a Note on the Social Base of Tudor Poetry', *EC* 1 (1951), 139–64.

21. H. W. Woudhuysen, *Sir Philip Sidney and the Circulation of Manuscripts, 1558– 1640* (Oxford: Clarendon Press, 1996), p. 12. See also Harold Love, *Scribal Publication in Seventeenth-Century England* (Oxford: Clarendon Press, 1993).

22. Woudhuysen, *Sidney*, p. 12.

23. There are a number of explanations as to why Spenser's text did not appear. Arguments are summarized and debated in Jean R. Brink, 'Constructing the *View of the Present State of Ireland*', *Sp.St.* XI (1990) [1994], 203–28, at pp. 204–9; Andrew Hadfield, 'Was Spenser's *A View of the Present State of Ireland* Censored? A Review of the Evidence', *N&Q* 239 (Dec. 1994), 459–63. See also Andrew Hadfield, 'Certainties and Uncertainties: By Way of Response to Jean Brink', *Sp.St.* XII (1991) [1998], 197–202; Jean Brink, 'Spenser and the Irish Question: Reply to Andrew Hadfield', Sp.St. XIII (1992) [1999], 265–6.

24. Edward Arber, ed., *A Transcript of the Register of the Stationers' Company, 1554–1640*, 5 vols (London and Birmingham: privately printed, 1875–94), III, p. 34.

25. Edmund Spenser, *A View of the State of Ireland*, eds Andrew Hadfield and Willy Maley (Oxford: Blackwell, 1997), p. 6.

26. Ware's omissions are listed in ibid., appendix 2.

27. Brink, 'Constructing the *View*', p. 208.

28. Hadfield, 'Was Spenser's *View* Censored?', p. 461.

29. David Edwards, 'Ideology and Experience: Spenser's *View* and Martial Law in Ireland', in Morgan, ed., *Political Ideology in Ireland*, pp. 127–57.

30. Clare, '*Art Made Tongue-tied by Authority*', p. 62.

31. *CSPD, 1596–1601*, p. 251.

32. See Bruce Avery, 'Mapping the Irish Other: Spenser's *A View of the Present State of Ireland*', *ELH* 57 (1990), 263–79; John Breen, '"Imaginative Groundplot": a Vewe of the Present State of Ireland', *Sp.St.* XII (1991) [1998], 151–68.

33. Opposing assessments are offered in Clare, '*Art Made Tongue-tied by Authority*'; and Richard Dutton, *Mastering the Revels: the Regulation and Censorship of English Renaissance Drama* (Basingstoke: Macmillan, 1991). See also Richard Burt's provocative and thoughtful essay, '(Un)censoring in Detail: the Fetish of Censorship in the Early Modern Past and the Postmodern Present', in Robert C. Post, ed., *Censorship and Silence: Practices of Cultural Regulation* (Los Angeles: Getty Research Institute, 1998), pp. 17–41.

34. For details see Clegg, *Press Censorship*, part 1.

35. Ibid. p. 204.

36. Ibid., ch. 6.

37. See *Spenser's Prose Works*, ed. Rudolf Gottfried (Baltimore: Johns Hopkins Press, 1949), appendix 3.

38. See A. J. Sheehan, 'The Overthrow of the Plantation of Munster in October 1598', *The Irish Sword* 15 (1982–3), 11–22; McCarthy-Morrogh, *Munster Plantation*, ch. 4.

39. It should be made clear that authors who produced books which drew hostile attention from the authorities did not necessarily damage their subsequent careers, as the examples of John Stubbes, Ben Jonson and Joseph Hall indicate (see Clegg, *Press Censorship*, *passim*, for details). Matthew Lownes appears to

have enjoyed a successful publishing career in the early seventeenth century, whatever the truth behind the affair over the *View*'s non-appearance (for details, see *STC*, III, pp. 109–10).

40. See, for example, Brendan Bradshaw, 'Robe and Sword in the Conquest of Ireland', in Claire Cross, David Loades and J. J. Scarisbrick, eds, *Law and Government under the Tudors: Essays Presented to Sir Geoffrey Elton on his Retirement* (Cambridge: Cambridge University Press, 1988), pp. 139–62; Richard Beacon, *Solon His Follie, or A Politique Discourse Touching the Reformation of common-weales conquered, declined or corrupted*, eds Clare Carroll and Vincent Carey (Binghampton, NY: MRTS, 1996), Introduction, *passim*. Subsequent references to this edition in parentheses in the text.

41. On this past point, see Sydney Anglo, 'A Machiavellian Solution to the Irish Problem: Richard Beacon's *Solon His Follie*', in Edward Chaney and Peter Mack, eds, *England and the Continental Renaissance* (Woodbridge: Boydell Press, 1990), pp. 153–64; Edwin Greenlaw, 'The Influence of Machiavelli on Spenser', *MP* 7 (1909), 187–202; Richard McCabe, 'The Fate of Irena: Spenser and Political Violence', in Patricia Coughlan, ed., *Spenser and Ireland: an Interdisciplinary Perspective* (Cork: Cork University Press, 1989), pp. 109–25.

42. W. W. Greg, *Some Aspects and Problems of London Publishing between 1550 and 1650* (Oxford: Clarendon Press, 1956), ch. 1.

43. Compare Markku Peltonen, *Classical Humanism and Republicanism in English Political Thought, 1570–1640* (Cambridge: Cambridge University Press, 1995), pp. 76–102; Vincent Carey, 'The Irish Face of Machiavelli: Richard Beacon's *Solon his Follie* and Republican Ideology in the Conquest of Ireland', in Morgan, ed., *Political Ideology in Ireland*, pp. 83–109.

44. Spenser, *A View of the State of Ireland*, eds Hadfield and Maley, p. 54.

45. J. H. M. Salmon, 'Stoicism and Roman Empire: Seneca and Tacitus in Jacobean England', *JHI* 50 (1989), 199–225; John Hayward, *The First and Second Parts of John Hayward's The Life and Raigne of King Henrie IIII*, ed. John J. Manning (London: Royal Historical Society, 1991; Camden Society, 4th series, vol. 42); Sir Robert Dallington, *Aphorismes civill and militarie, amplified with authorities* (1613).

46. Ciaran Brady, 'Spenser's Irish Crisis: Humanism and Experience in the 1590s', *P&P* 111 (1986), 17–49; *Chief Governors*, p. 300.

47. Ciaran Brady, 'The Road to the *View*: On the Decline of Reform Thought in Tudor Ireland', in Coughlan, ed., *Spenser and Ireland*, pp. 25–45.

48. For a discussion of these texts, see Richard Tuck, *Philosophy and Government, 1572–1651* (Cambridge: Cambridge University Press, 1993), pp. 26–9, 45–63.

49. Deborah L. Madsen, *Rereading Allegory: a Narrative Approach to Genre* (Basingstoke: Macmillan, 1995), p. 26.

50. William Herbert, *Croftus Sive De Hibernia Liber*, eds Arthur Keaveney and John A. Madden (Dublin: IMC, 1992). All subsequent references to this edition in parentheses in the text.

51. Willy Maley, *A Spenser Chronology* (Basingstoke: Macmillan, 1994), pp. 67–8. The best analysis of the episode is Richard A. McCabe, 'The Masks of Duessa: Spenser, Mary Queen of Scots, and James VI', *ELR* 17 (1987), 224–42.

52. Maley, *Spenser Chronology*, p. 68. The best account of the mechanisms of censorship and their significance is Clegg, *Press Censorship*, part 1.

53. Maley, *Spenser Chronology*, p. 71.

54. For details see Walter Oakshott, *The Queen and the Poet* (London: Faber, 1960).
55. On the historical events in *The Faerie Queene*, Book V, see Michael O'Connell, '*The Faerie Queene*, Book V', in A. C. Hamilton, ed., *The Spenser Encyclopedia* (Toronto: University of Toronto Press, 1990), pp. 280–3.
56. See Clare, '*Art Made Tongue-tied by Authority*', ch. 3, although, of course, Spenser's poem was composed over a number of years and reincorporated earlier material. The best work on the composition of *The Faerie Queene* remains J. W. Bennett, *The Evolution of 'The Faerie Queene'* (Chicago: University of Chicago Press, 1942).
57. Colin Burrow, *Edmund Spenser* (Plymouth: Northcote House, 1996), p. 41. Lownes' inheritance of Ponsonby's papers suggests that either the two men never really fell out, or that the quarrel over Spenser's works had been patched up.
58. On the hostile representations of Elizabeth in the 1590s see Helen Hackett, *Virgin Mother, Maiden Queen: Elizabeth I and the Cult of the Virgin Mary* (Basingstoke: Macmillan, 1995), ch. 6.
59. For further details see Hadfield, *Spenser's Irish Experience*, chs 6–7.
60. On the censorship of *Mother Hubberds Tale*, see Richard S. Peterson, 'Laurel Crown and Ape's Tail: New Light on Spenser's Career from Sir Thomas Tresham', *Sp.St.* XII (1991) [1998], 1–35.
61. E. M. Hinton, 'Rich's "Anatomy of Ireland", with an Account of the Author', *PMLA* 55 (1940), 73–101, p. 91.

10
Burning Books as Propaganda in Jacobean England

Cyndia Susan Clegg

Curiously absent from the accounts of press control in the early seventeenth century is the figure of James I, a king more astute in his personal use of the press than perhaps any other English monarch. James wrote personally and prolifically with the clear intent that his published writings would mould domestic and international policy. For a king who possessed such faith in print to take a personal interest in censorship is unremarkable. That James in 1604 would write to the Stationers telling them of personally choosing three individuals to peruse and allow all books, except those relating to law, divinity and medicine, is as consistent with his conception of print as his extension of the authority of the High Commission in 1611 'to enquire and search for all heretical, schismatical and seditious books' and to seize the presses that printed them. Although these actions perhaps expressed a more lively personal interest in the printed word than had been taken by his immediate predecessor, they were well within the legal precedents that had been established for press control. James, however, did engage in some acts of personal censorship that were extraordinary – in particular, the public burning of books at Paul's Cross and equally public squares at Oxford and Cambridge.

Exploring the personal censorship of James I necessarily leads onto the rough sea of Jacobean historiography and biography – one unsettled by the crossing currents of Whigs, revisionists, political philosophers and New Historicists. The two versions of James most useful for understanding the book burnings at Paul's Cross – that of New Historicist Jonathan Goldberg and that of ecclesiastical historians Kenneth Fincham and Peter Lake – stand in curious polarity to each other. Jonathan Goldberg discovers in James's writings, primarily *Basilikon Doron* and *Trew Lawe of Free Monarchy*, a ruler who embraced, on the one hand, the trope of himself as an actor transparently displayed, and on the other, that of the *arcana imperii*, 'a rhetoric of power that covers the secret pleasures and shrouds the body in the image of the state'.[1] The *arcana*, according to Goldberg, became to James,

> an illusionary but comforting idealization that allowed him simulta-
> neously to display authority and withdraw from monarchy's public
> demands. James's inability to heed the demands of his times, his
> refusal to pay attention to details of his administration, his loathing of
> public appearances, and his retirement to the country ... are parts of
> this pattern.[2]

Alternatively, Kenneth Fincham and Peter Lake view 'personal contact and management' as 'central' to James's monarchic style. Until the outbreak of the Thirty Years' War, in both the domestic and international arenas, James managed what Fincham and Lake identify as a 'consistent ecclesiastical policy' through his 'detailed grasp of abstract theory' and 'native political shrewdness'.[3] He accomplished this domestically by 'defusing "radical" Puritanism and rabid anti-popery through the incorporation of evangelical Calvinism into the Jacobean establishment', which also counted several 'cryptopapists' among its members.[4] Outside Britain's borders, James sought the reunification of christendom through an 'irenic rhetoric' that emphasized a common profession of faith in the Trinity and the Incarnation, 'played down' other doctrinal differences, and criticized papal pretensions to supremacy and the power to depose secular rulers.[5]

Although these two versions of James differ markedly in their assessment of what today would be called his 'management style', both draw attention to the self-consciousness with which James stepped to centre stage in his use of the printed word. James's intent, from Goldberg's perspective, was to speak *'verbum dei'*.[6] While Goldberg sees James ascending the dais to speak 'in the sayle of Gods', Fincham and Lake remind us that James viewed print as a means to exercise his royal responsibility to defend the faith. In 1609 James wrote, 'my care for the Lord's spiritual kingdom is so well known, both at home and abroad, as well as by my daily actions as by my printed books'.[7] Since James's attitude towards print and his care for the Lord's kingdom inform the Paul's Cross book burnings, both deserve a fuller consideration here.

In his preface to the 1603 edition of *Basilikon Doron*, James tells a curious story about the printing of the first edition. According to James, the book and its printing were a private affair. He wrote 'for exercise of [his] ... owne ingyne' and the instruction of his son, Prince Henry, and 'therefore for the more secret and close keeping of them', he 'onely permitted seuen of them to be printed, the Printer being first sworne for secrecie'.[8] These seven he distributed among his 'trustiest Seruants . . . lest in case by the iniquitie, or wearing of time, any of them might haue been lose, yet some of them might haue remained after me, as witnesses to my Sonne . . .'[9] James here shows he believes that words and writing, even his, are ensured a legacy only in print. *A Remonstrance for the Right of Kings* reiterates James's faith in print's longevity when he consoles himself that although the tract might not affect current affairs in France, 'at least many millions of children and people yet vnborne, shall beare me witnesse, that in these dangers of the highest nature and straine, I haue not been defectiue: and that neither the subuersions of States, nor the murthers of Kings, which may vnhappily betide hereafter, shall haue so free passage in the world for want of timely aduertisement before.'[10]

This last passage betrays the subtext present in so many of James's published writings – that the printed word may vindicate its speaker in a way that other language does not. James repeatedly returns in his writing to the 'golden sentence, which Christ our Sauiour vttered to his Apostle' that opens the preface to *Basilikon Doron*, 'that ther is nothing so couered, that shall not be reuealed, neither so hidde, that shall not be knowen and whatsoeuer they haue spoken in darknesse, should be herd in the light'.[11] While this transparency becomes the *raison d'être* for James's prolific publication, it is rarely divorced from the concomitant purpose of 'clearing these mists and cloudes of calumnies, which were iniustly heaped vpon me'.[12]

In his consideration of *Basilikon Doron*, Goldberg contends that monarchy's public stage produced in James a 'fear of being misunderstood' – a fear that his 'inward intention' could not be read rightly – and this, in turn, provoked his retreat behind the rhetoric of the *arcana imperii*.[13] While this may be true of *Basilikon Doron* and *Trew Lawe* (the texts most often sounded for James's political theory), *A Premonition to all Most Mightie Monarches, Kings, Free Princes, and States of Christendome; A Remonstrance for the Right of Kings, and the Independance of their Crownes*; and *A Declaration concerning the Proceedings with the States Generall of the Vnited Prouinces of the Low Countreys, In the cause of D. Conradvs Vorstivs* reveal a man prominently and confidently mounting the enduring stage of the printed word to offer his own defence as a beacon of truth. Neither the zeal with which he approached this task nor his personal presence in these works went unnoticed by his contemporaries. In December 1607, the Venetian Ambassador, Zorzi Giustinian, reported to the Doge and Senate in Venice that James, with 'the plea of the chase' was living 'in almost absolute retirement in the company of one man, a Dean, very learned' to prepare an answer to Catholic objections to the Oath of Allegiance.[14] A few years later, Isaac Casaubon, the great classical scholar whom James sought out for his ecumenical interests, wrote in a letter that James, 'great and learned as he is, is now so entirely taken up with one sort of book, that he keeps his own mind and the mind of all about him occupied exclusively on the one topic'.[15]

James, of course, recruited some of the finest minds to his polemical pursuits. Casaubon, James Mountague, Lancelot Andrewes, John Donne, John Barclay, Thomas Preston, and Marcus Antonius de Dominis (the Archbishop of Spalato) were joined by a host of lesser-known writers and theologians.[16] Given the scale of this literary assistance and the seriousness of their enterprise, James's personal presence in these texts, uncloaked, as it were, in the *arcana imperii*, seems extraordinary. His personal voice in *A Premonition* did not escape the Venetian ambassador, who wrote,

> In it the King complains of being nine times insulted, accused and given the lie, and seven times charged with falsehood by Cardinal Bellarmine in his reply ... The King is biting and free in speech and makes frequent use of jokes. He declares that he had great cause to write the 'Apology' in defence of the oath of Allegiance in reply to numerous Pontifical Breves and to save his life from the machinations of the Catholics.[17]

One part of *A Premonition* that displays the characteristic style noted by the Venetian ambassador, James's creed, is particularly personal and, indeed, makes him vulnerable to subsequent *ad hominem* attacks. In this he affirms his faith in the tenets of the church universal, but he also attacks Roman practices he finds objectionable. Of one of these, in particular the veneration of the true cross, James speaks with remarkable candour:

> Except then they could first prooue that CHRIST had resouled to blesse that tree of the Crosse whereupon hee was nailed; they can neuer proue that his touching it could giue it any vertue. And put the case it had a vertue of doing miracles, as Peters shadow had; yet doeth it not follow, that it is lawful to worship it ... Surely the Prophets that in so many places curse those that worship Images, that haue eyes and see not, that haue eares and heare not, would much more haue cursed them that worship a piece of a sticke, that hath not so much as any resemblance or representacion of eyes or eares.[18]

Another passage in *A Premonition* responding to Cardinal Bellarmine's defence of purgatory reflects how truly 'free' James could be in his style: 'Onely I would pray him to tell me; If that faire greene Meadow that is in Purgatorie, haue a brooke running thorow it; that in case I come there, I may haue hawking vpon it.'[19] While all James's writing is not so derisive as this, the prevailing use throughout of the personal 'I' rather than the royal 'we' underscores his confidence in print as an enduring and transparent vehicle for his personal ecumenical vision.

The theology that grounded this vision has often proved particularly perplexing, in part, I believe, because the Arminian current of Caroline Anglicanism (Archbishop William Laud's 'Catholic' ceremonialism) has been associated with James's distrust of 'Puritans'. To identify James with Arminianism is to see James as anti-Puritan, and hence as anti-Calvinist. (Similarly, to see James as anti-Puritan is to make him a pro-Catholic Arminian.) The English Church under James acknowledged the monarch's role as nurturer and governor of the church but clearly distinguished this from power to minister God's word or sacraments. It recognized a monarchy and an episcopacy, both of which governed *de jure divino*.[20] The mainstream of this episcopacy was Calvinist. According to Patrick Collinson, 'Calvinism can be regarded as the theological cement of the Jacobean Church, in Nicholas Tyacke's phrase "a common and ameliorating bond" uniting conformists and moderate puritans.'[21]

James's domestic ecclesiastical policy, begun at the 1604 Hampton Court Conference, as Fincham and Lake demonstrate, was to 'detach the moderate from the radical Puritans' and to bring moderate Puritans into the church's mainstream. This was accomplished, in part, by appointing Calvinist bishops.[22] The mark of the radical Puritan became opposition to the King's government of the church and adherence to separatism, but such views, according to Fincham and Lake, largely disappeared during the middle years of James's reign.[23] It is important to remember, however, that although the mainstream may have been Calvinist, James also brought into his *via media* divines whose views differed from the majority. Most of these have been identified as Arminians, but as Tyacke makes clear, in the Jacobean church this was identifiable by their views on grace rather than the kind of Laudian ceremonialism which marked latter Arminians.[24]

James's policy toward English Catholics corresponded to his treatment of Puritans. To English Catholics James offered tolerance rather than toleration. Those Catholics who were prepared to conform received royal preferments, but even those who could not conform but could demonstrate their loyalty by signing the Oath of Allegiance, received a measure of 'de facto tolerance'. Catholics who subscribed to the deposing power of the Pope – in short, who adhered to the views of the Jesuits, the 'Puritan-Papists' – were subject to the harshest sanctions of English recusancy laws.[25]

James's commitment to peace in the church beyond Britain's borders is well known. During his reign he repeatedly appealed to the Pope for a council to mend the tears in the church's body. His support for the Synod of Dort to heal differences in the Dutch churches derived from the same motivation. At the end of *A Premontion* James's appeal to his fellow rulers to commit to 'spreading of the trew worship of God, according to his reuealed will ... and not following the vaine, corrupt and changeable traditions of men'[26] springs from his ecumenical interest. This ecumenicism conjoined with James's domestic religious policy – appointing Calvinist bishops and preferring conforming Catholics – seems to require that James simultaneously embrace radically contradictory theological perspectives – Roman Catholicism, Calvinism and a more moderate Protestantism. This explains why, when considered out of context, accounts of James's religious views often appear contradictory. If one turns, however, to James's statement of personal belief in *A Premonition*, a much clearer and consistent rationale for his ecumenicism emerges.

James defends himself in *A Premonition* as 'a Catholike Christian, as beleeveth the three Creeds'.[27] By this, he affirms his belief in the Holy Trinity; the Incarnation; Jesus's crucifixion, death and resurrection; the Apostles' establishment of the Church; and baptism. When James uses the word 'Catholike', he refers to the universal church established by the apostles, what he later refers to as 'the Primitiue Church'. In doing so, he aligns himself with the language of Calvinism. While he here claims kinship with both the Church of Rome and fellow Protestants, he clearly discriminates between those practices which belong to the Primitive Church acceptable to Protestants, and those Romanist practices ('Nouelties') added since 'Primitive' times that Protestants disdain: prayers to saints, transubstantiation, works of supererogation, the veneration of saints' relics and images. Of his rejection of these, James remarks:

> If my faith bee weake in these, I confesse I had rather beleeue too little then too much: And yet since I beleeue as much as the Scriptures doe warrant, the Creeds doe perswade, and the ancient Councels decreed: I may well be a Schismatike from Rome, but I am sure I am no Heretike.[28]

These essential tenets of faith were for James the bonds between Christians – Romanists, Lutherans and Calvinists alike – by which he could forge reunification of the church. Everything else was secondary – arguable, yes – but not essential to salvation.

The stumbling-block to James's plan was what he regarded as the biggest novelty of all – papal supremacy and the Roman church's claim 'that the Pope may lawfully depose Hereticall Princes and free their Subiects from yeelding obedience vnto them'. In June 1606 James confided in the Venetian ambassador Zorzi Giustinian his chagrin with the Pope:

> This Pope holds me and my crown for the most abominable thing in the world; but I claim to be a better servant of God then he is. To his Divine Majesty and before mankind I protest that I have no greater desire than to see the Church of God reformed of those abuses introduced by the Church of Rome. There is nothing I am more desirous of than the convocation of a legitimate Counsel.[29]

Giustinian goes on to tell the Venetian Council that James is most upset by the 'usurpation of supreme and absolute power by the Pope' and has taken considerable interest in Bellarmine's writings related to the controversy about papal authority in Venice. The Powder Treason served to reify the matter in James's mind, and the Oath of Allegiance that followed was the means James devised to protect his royal authority from the Pope's efforts to assert his 'absolute power'. That James took such interest in Venice and Bellarmine before he wrote in defence of the Oath helps to explain why James's assault on papal authority continued long after he wrote *The Apology*. From its inception, James's confrontation with the Pope was as much about the former's ecumenical vision as it was about the Pope's assault on James's authority. James accepted the Pope's contempt for his crown as an invitation to lead a challenge that could build political solidarity that could, in turn, pave the way for ecclesiastical reunification.

James's comments to the Venetian ambassador epitomize the manner in which he proceeded in all of his ecclesiastical policy; they underscore the self-consciousness of his leadership and the vulnerability of that 'self' to opposition and criticism. In a sense, this goes back to what Goldberg discovered in the *Basilikon Doron* – James envisioned himself as always on a stage and was always anxious about how others viewed him. James's writings participate in a relentless effort to assure that both his position and his words are clearly and correctly received. The Paul's Cross book burnings, as we shall see, essentially extend this effort.

Burning books in England, of course, was nothing new. Deriving from Roman canon law's prescribed mode of execution for the confirmed heretic, Henrician statutory law extended from the heretical body to the heretical book the sentence that they 'be utterlie abolished, extinguished and forbidden to be kept'.[30] In June 1555 a Marian proclamation consigned to the fires prepared for Protestant martyrs 'any works by any protestants'; bishops and local civic officials were called to 'enter into the house or houses, closets, and secret places of every person whatsoever degree' to discover these writings.[31] Burning heretical books, however, was largely associated with Romanist practice as the accounts in Foxe's *Book of Martyrs* make clear. While Henry VIII and Mary burned books to 'utterlie' abolish their false doctrines, the books burned under Elizabeth were perceived to endanger the exercise of civil authority – indeed Elizabethan propaganda consistently argued that the state's enemies were not those who differed with England's religion but those who opposed Elizabeth's rule.[32] The books burned at Paul's Cross during the reign of James bear as little resemblance to those burned by his predecessors as the public means of their destruction bears to the earlier acts of utter annihilation.

In 1609 Marc Antonio Correr, the Venetian ambassador, described to the Doge and Senate the burning of *Prurit-anus*, a scurrilous book that had offended James by using scripture to attack Henry VIII and Elizabeth for usurping papal authority. Correr reported that following the Sunday sermon at Paul's Cross in which the 'preacher inveighed against the author, who, not content with insulting the King, had blasphemed the Deity and shamefully treated the meaning of Scriptures', the books were 'publicly burned'.[33] On 25 November 1613, John Chamberlain wrote that 'On Sonday divers positions of Jesuites (specially Suárez the Spaniard) were read and discussed at Paules Crosse, very derogatorie to the authoritie of Princes, and after the Sermon a goode number of his bookes were there publikely burnt'.[34] In June 1622 similar ceremonies sur-rounded the burning of the works of David Pareus, not only at Paul's Cross but at public squares in Oxford and Cambridge, following a declaration by the Archbishop of Canterbury and 12 other bishops, made at the King's request, that Pareus's books were 'contrary to Scripture and the Church of England'.[35] Chamberlain describes the Paul's Cross occasion:

On the first Sonday of this terme the bishop of London preached at Paules Crosse, where there was a great assemblie but a small auditorie, for his voyce was so low that I thincke scant the third part was within hearing. The chiefe points of his sermon were touching the benevolence ... another part was about the repayring of Paules, and the largest in confuting Paraeus opinions touching the peoples authorities in some cases over unruly and tirannicall Princes, for which heresie of state his bookes were publickely burnt there toward the end of the sermon.[36]

Other books joined these – the works of the Dutch Arminian, Conrad Vorstius, in 1611; Caspar Schoppe's *Ecclesiasticus*, probably in 1613; the Racovian Catechism, in 1614; and Edward Elton's *God's Holy Mind*, in 1625. Unidentified 'Popish' books were twice burned at Paul's Cross, in 1605 and again in 1620.[37]

Of the motivation for these conflagrations, C. R. Gillett observes, 'there does not seem to be a single thread upon which the story of the books burned during the reign of James can be strung'.[38] If one looks only to the books' contents, their diverse religious perspectives tend to support Gillett. The accounts of the burnings at Paul's Cross, however, tell a common story. Books were brought before one of the most public audiences in London, their contents described and refuted, and then they were burned. The remarks about Francisco Suárez's book, a Jesuit articulation of the Pope's authority to depose monarchs that was condemned in France and England, are particularly telling – only a 'goode number' were burned. The Paul's Cross book burnings were ceremonies designed to call public attention to the book's status as officially censured – as condemned by King James. The impetus for this derives more from contemporary French practice than from the historic canon law sentence for heretics that had influenced Henrician and Marian censorship. When in 1610 the Parliament of Paris condemned Cardinal Bellarmine's book, *Tractatus de potestate Summi Pontificis in rebus temporalibus* (1610), it decided that to avoid public uproar it would simply prohibit it rather than treat it as they had Mariana's book on papal authority. Mariana's 1599 *De rege et regis institutione, libri tres*, which justified killing monarchs, was sent 'round the town in the car of infamy' and then burned 'by the hands of the common executioner' in 1610 following the assassination of Henry IV.[39] James's principal motivation in burning a particular book – or group of books – at Paul's Cross at a particular time was publicly to align himself with or to oppose a given ideological perspective, and by doing so, enhance his own reputation.

The focus of James's concern about his reputation and public image relates directly to those enterprises he undertook in issuing the Oath of Allegiance and in his writings – reunifying the church universal by identifying in creedal Christianity the common ground among Protestants and Papists and by opposing papal claims to temporal supremacy. To keep the high ground in this required that he always be perceived as 'a catholike Christian' tied to the primitive church and untainted by latter-day heresies. Furthermore, the position of self-appointed spokesman for all Christian princes required an undaunted armour of personal moral authority. When Catholic resistance to James's enterprises emerged and became focused on the Oath of Allegiance, James appears to have been totally unprepared for what he perceived a personal response. In describing letters and breves by Bellarmine and the Pope opposing the Oath, the Venetian ambassador Guistinian observed that they contained 'many passages which touch the King's *amour propre* (*propria essistemazione*) and he is deeply affected'.[40] Jesuit responses to James's defence of the Oath seem to have affected him even more. Instead of the kind of ideological and theological debate James appears to have expected, James perceived in the Catholic response personal attacks. According to the English Ambassador, answers to the Apology 'greatly disturbed the King because of the defamation and calumnies in which they abounded. His Majesty is styled "apostate", "heretic", "persecutor."'[41] Catholic responses to James's *Premonition* were even less favourable. Taking personal interest in the book, the Pope had prepared a list of James's heretical positions, which he gave to ambassadors at the Vatican to encourage them to seek the book's suppression in their states.[42] Papal nuncios were sent to Paris and Venice and throughout christendom to appeal to rulers to refuse James's gift and cause their names to be removed from the book's frontispiece.[43] In August 1609 when the Venetian ambassador in Rome met with the Pope to report that Venice would not permit the book to be 'seen, circulated or published', the Pope responded that this did not go far enough. According to the Pope, 'The book ... was really full of most vicious heresies and it must be admitted that it was the work of a grand heretic' and so should have been 'prohibited'.[44] A few days later, the Pope told the ambassador that 'he thought it not only right but necessary that it should be prohibited in such a way that everyone should know it'.[45] By October, the Inquisition had issued orders to all booksellers not to sell the book.[46] The sentence for violating orders like these, in Rome at least, was excommunication, and in some cases death.[47]

Suppression was not the Papists' only response; beginning in 1609 numerous books made their way to England from the Continent opposing James's positions. Some of them, like Bellarmine's *Apologia Roberto Bellarmino pro responsione sua ad librum Jacobi Magnae Brittanniae* (1610), seriously engaged the controversy; others libelled James. The libels ranged from mere 'contempt and derision'[48] to 'lies and impudent slanders' such as the one that 'stated that from his earliest days the King ate frogs and that he was accomplice in his mother's death', and further, that the Republic of Venice was 'a corpse and the King of england a crow that settled on it'.[49] In his reports to the Doge and Senate, the Venetian ambassador's reports chronicle James's growing indignation. What started as annoyance grew to rage:

> After this last book, printed in Prussia (Pruscia), came into the King's hands, and after the death of the King of France, his Majesty is so furious against the Catholics that, contrary to his habit, he is considering how to abase and annihilate them if possible in this Kingdom. He has had several conferences with members of Parliament on this matter and displayed such heat that people marvel to see him so intent upon this point while he is embarked on other important affairs...[50]

Despite James's anger at these responses, the two book burnings at Paul's Cross in these years were only tangential to the controversy. *Prurit-anus*, burned in July 1609, disputed the legitimacy of the English reformation by attacking Henry VIII, 'the one who usurped pontifical authority' as 'Anti-Christ', Elizabeth I and James.[51] *Prurit-anus* appeared at the very moment that James's ambassadors were presenting gift copies of *A Premonition* to the crown princes of Europe. A few years later, by burning the writings of Conrad Vorstius which articulated anti-Trinitarian positions consistent with the Pelagian and Arian heresies, James demonstrated his utter contempt for two central positions taken by his Catholic opponents – that the English church, rather than being a reformed version of the ancient church, was the innovation of two heretics; and that James himself supported heretical teachings.

On 23 August 1609, barely a month after the English ambassador had presented the Doge with James's gift of *A Premonition* bound in crimson velvet, he appeared again to report on *Prurit-anus*. Wooton's account reflects James's anxiety about his reputation among his Venetian allies:

> I am ordered by his Majesty to give your Excellencies an account of this affair. A certain book under an assumed name was written, published and brought to England. A copy came into the King's hands and seeing that it was full of blasphemies and tended only to render his Majesty odious he caused inquiry to be made as to who was selling it. Your Excellencies must know that no book is prohibited in England even if it touch on controversy with Rome – the works of Cardinal Bellarmine

are better known in England than in Italy; provided books do not endeavour to destroy loyalty they are not prohibited. But this book, as I have said, has no other tendency than to render his Majesty's name odious ... The object of the devilish author is to hold up to hatred, not merely the present King, but the memory of deceased Sovreigns. His method is the most hideous, horrid, infamous that was ever invented, it consists in taking passages of the Scriptures and wresting them into phrases of defamation, derision and vilipending of their Majesties. I have marked some passages to read to your Excellencies.[52]

Wooton continues, drawing attention to the obnoxious passages. In doing so he seeks to ally the Venetians to the King's contempt for his opponents, and thereby strengthen the ties between England and Venice, a strategy not unlike that of *A Premonition*. According to an observer in the Cabinet:

The Ambassador then read the passages marked, which in substance were as follows: talking of Queen Elizabeth, who styled herself Head of the Anglican Church and Virgin, the writer accuses her of immodesty, of having given birth to sons and daughters, of having prostituted her body to many different nationalities, of having slept with blackamoors; of Henry VIII. that he gave out that Anna Boleyn was his wife whereas she was his daughter. Laughing at the reigning King he is styled 'a foreigner,' hailing from a 'barbarous land' ... 'All,' said the Ambassador, 'for the purpose of rendering the name of his Majesty odious.'[53]

When before the book was burned at Paul's Cross the preacher 'inveighed against the author, who, not content with insulting the King, had blasphemed the Deity and shamefully treated the meaning of Scriptures', he conveyed James's righteous indignation. Thus, both the preacher and the English ambassador recast James as a most Christian King in response to his vile detractor.

James's interest in the Dutch theologian, Conrad Vorstius, was doubly motivated by his concern that the Protestant front appear unified and that his own beliefs be received as orthodox. In *A Declaration concerning the Proceedings with the States Generall of the Vnited Prouinces of the Low Countreys, In the cause of D. Conradvs Vorstivs*, James tells of the 'horrour and detestation' he felt upon receiving Vorstius's books, *Tractatus Theologicus de Deo* (1610) and *Exegesis Apologetica* (1611), which were so filled with 'monstrous blasphemie, and horrible Atheisme' that they were 'worthy to be burnt' and 'the Author himselfe to be most seuerely punished'.[54] In response to this, he sought to have Vorstius barred from his professorship in theology at Leiden, but before he received a response from the Dutch, another book came into his hands, *De Apostasia Sanctorum*, by 'one Bertius, a scholler of the late Arminius, (who was the first in our age that infected Leyden with Heresie)'. Along with his book, Bertius had sent a letter to the Archbishop of Canterbury, maintaining 'that the doctrine conteined in his Booke, was agreeable with the doctrine of the Church of England'.[55] James's fear that Arminianism might infect the Church of England fed his persistent opposition to Vorstius's professorship and presented a motivation for burning his books. As James makes clear in his declaration on the Vorstius affair,

> Let the Church of Christ then iudge, whether it was not high time for vs to bestir our selues, when as this Gangrene had not only taken hold amongst our neerest neighbours; so *as Non Solùm paries proximus iam ardebat*: not onely the next house was on fire, but did also begin to creepe into the bowels of our owne Kingdom; For which cause hauing first giuen order, that the said bookes of Vorstius should be publikely burnt, as well in Paules Church-yard, as in bothe the Vniversites of this Kingdome, we thought good to renew our former request vnto the States, for the banishment of *Vorstius* . . .[56]

The danger James feared to the English church was not the only threat posed. According to Frederick Shriver, a Jesuit controversialist whose works appeared throughout Europe linked James personally with the heresies of Vorstius. In the *Refutatio Apologiae* (1610), Becanus cited Vorstius in arguing the Arianism of James's position in *A Premonition* that the Holy Spirit rather than the Pope is the vicar of Christ. (The Arian and Pelagian heresies asserted the independence rather than the consubstantiality of the persons of the Trinity.) In *Examen Plagae Regiae*, Becanus listed the heretical and atheistic teachings found in Vorstius, implying that James shared them.[57] James's conversations with the Venetian ambassador reflect his desire to clear himself from charges of heresy. In March 1612 Foscarini reported that James maintained,

> that he was doing all that lay in him to imitate the primitive Church, and complained of being called heretical . . . He blamed Jesuit interference in matters of State, and then turning to the discourse he had recently published against Vorstius, he said that he had defended therein the faith this is called Roman quite as much as any other creed of Christians . . .[58]

James's effort to distance himself from Arianism extended beyond seeking to unseat Vorstius at Leiden and ceremonially burning Vorstius's books. In 1612 the King insisted on the execution of Bartholomew Legate for heresy, 'for the position of this man is very similar to that of Vorstius'.[59] James continued his opposition to Arminianism by appointing Calvinists to represent England at the synod of reformed churches that met at Dort in 1618–19 to resolve and finally renounce the challenge to Protestantism posed by the Arminian party in Holland, the Remonstrants, and immediately after Dort, James is recorded as denouncing the Remonstrants as 'mere Pelagians'.[60] As late as 1625, James expressed offence at being in any way identified with Arianism. In *Cygnea Cantio*, Daniel Featley, the Archbishop's chaplain who licensed books for the press, tells of his meeting with James to discuss the licensing of William Crompton's *St Austins Religion*:

> The first thing to my remembrance questioned touching M. Cromptons booke, was a clause in my written defence, that I was rather induced to licence the booke out of a respect to my Lord D. his Grace, to whome the booke is dedicated by his Chaplaine. What a reason is this, (said his Majestie?) Is it an honour to my Lord D. to bee a patron of errors? Is it any honour to me that the Arians in Polonia have dedicated one of their books to me, containing damnable heresies? I account it rather a dishonour, and cannot with patience looke upon their dedication to mee.[61]

Links of James to Arianism did not mark the only limits to the King's 'patience' that led to the fires at Paul's Cross. The other intolerable position, whether from Jesuit or Protestant writers, was that kings might be deposed for religion. While the Jesuit response to James's writings on the Oath from the beginning assumed this resistance theory, the matter became more than hypothetical when Henry IV was assassinated in 1610. What followed was a movement of both France and Spain towards James's position on papal authority. On 8 June 1610 the Parliament of Paris burned Mariana's book, *De rege et regis institutione, libri tres*. When the General of the Jesuits attempted to exonerate the Society to the French ambassador by promising that Jesuits would neither speak nor write further about the persons of sovereigns, the Spanish were displeased and told the Jesuits that 'the King of Spain was at present engaged in expelling the Moriscoes, but that when he had done he would turn his attention to expelling the Jesuits'.[62] In September 1610, the University of Paris published a remonstrance addressed to the Queen Regent and the

Council. Citing the Gunpowder Plot, it condemned the assassination of Sovereigns 'under the plea of piety', and repudiated the 'Jesuit doctrine of Papal authority'.[63] In 1612, an Arrêt of the French Parliament dictated that *Ecclesiasticus* by Caspar Schoppe be burned by the public executioner because it contained passages which attacked the King of England and the memory of Henry IV.[64] It is against this backdrop that James ordered the burning of Suárez's book at Paul's Cross in 1613.[65] Just as he employed the destruction of *Prurit-anus* to reinforce ties with the Venetians, James displayed solidarity with France and Spain by burning Suárez's books. Conveniently, both book burnings allowed him to show his contempt for texts that attacked him personally.

James's public positioning shows throughout a kind of dogged determination. Once he had publicly adopted a stance, James would not relent regardless of the inconsistencies into which his position might lead him. The consequences of this can be seen in what Fincham and Lake, among many other historians, have identified as the perilous foreign policy James adopted at the outbreak of the Thirty Years' War in 1618. When war broke out in the Palatinate between the Catholic Archduke Ferdinand and James's Protestant son-in-law, Frederick, James delayed lending support to Frederick in part because he feared a religious war and in part because Frederick's succession to the crown of Bohemia involved the kind of deposition of a monarch that James detested. In 1619 the Venetian ambassador, Girlamo Lando, described the English response to affairs in the Palatine:

They still persist here in procrastinating about the affairs of the Palatine ... The ministers say that his Majesty is proceeding with great prudence in this affair ... The king seems to fear that the Bohemian war will become one of religion ... All the people here seem infuriated at this long delay, as they naturally detest the Spanish name and power ... His Majesty, though he listens to everything, does not yet seem persuaded by any single argument or by all together ... Being naturally inclined to peace he tries every means to secure its continuation. He lets it be understood that he cannot countenance the practice of deposing kings, and risings and tumults among the people displease him more than anything, as his published books clearly show. He has maintained with weighty arguments how damnable are such doctrines supported more particularly by the Jesuits ...[66]

It may have been this natural inclination towards peace that led James to seek an alliance with Spain and negotiate an end to the disturbances, but he also pursued the Spanish marriage because it would allow him 'to make an example of his son-in-law' and 'keep under the spirits he hates so thoroughly, who want to make targets of crowns and depose kings'.[67] Such consistent adherence to his publicly articulated principles led James to what Peter Lake describes as a 'failure of royal policy'. English Protestants viewed the refusal to enter the war as England's failure to 'align itself on the side of the godly in the international struggle with Antichrist and Spain'.[68] James's policy provoked the antipathy and censure of the English people. Lando describes the conditions that had developed by 1622:

> In this generation his people have been smitten to the heart about their religion, being troubled without in every quarter by the peril of the nation and the grave situation of the king's daughter, while they saw him joined to the Spaniards in hateful negotiations, even suspecting a change in religion ... The preachers daily exhort the people to obedience, although recently some have expressed seditious and most dangerous opinions, offering the strongest opposition to the Spanish marriage, both privately and publicly, with supplication, advice and prediction.[69]

Amidst this climate of criticism, James enacted his most deliberate and sustained campaign of censorship, directed not only at the press but also at parliament and the pulpit.

In December 1620 and in July 1621 James issued proclamations against 'the excess of lavish and licentious speech of matters of state' in which he cautioned his subjects 'to take heede, how they intermeddle by Penne, or Speech, with causes of state, and secrets of Empire, either at home or abroad'.[70] In December 1620 the King ordered the Bishop of London to summon the clergie 'to charge them from the King not to meddle in their sermons with the Spanish match nor any other matter of State'.[71] And while Fincham and Lake have concluded that these efforts had little effect,[72] several preachers were arrested. Furthermore, several members of parliament were detained, ostensibly for their support of Southampton, who opposed Buckingham. More was probably at stake than parliamentary faction, however, for as the Venetian ambassador observed, members of the imprisoned party happened 'to be also the supporters of the King of Bohemia and those most zealous for the honour, safety and religion of this kingdom, in fact they maintain these alone while they favour the interests of friendly princes'.[73] Amidst this, John Knight committed the folly of preaching a sermon at Oxford that not only alluded to current political events but, according to Chamberlain, went 'so far as to say that yf kings grow unruly and tirannical they may be corrected and brought into order by their subjects, which doctrine is so extravagant that the King thretens to have the copie of yt publikely burnt by the hangman as hereticall'.[74] Rather than burning Knight's sermon, however, the King called upon a council of 12 bishops to confer and render judgement on the source of Knight's teachings – a book by David Pareus, a German Protestant theologian. The bishops concluded that 'the doctrine in the book of David Pareus on the Epistle to the Romans, that subordinate magistrates may rise against their Prince if he interfere with religion, is most dangerous and seditious'.[75] While Chamberlain concluded that he knew 'not what good yt can do to burne a few bookes here when they are current in all Christendome',[76] copies of Pareus's book were burned at Paul's Cross at the end of the sermon for their 'heresie of state'.

By burning Pareus's book James afforded himself the opportunity to underscore his objection to doctrines of resistance generally, and more particularly to rationalize his failure to intervene on Frederick's behalf in Bohemia. The action did little to silence critics of the Spanish marriage negotiations. Such a host of books, pamphlets and libels hostile to the Spanish marriage appeared – among them *Vox Populi* and *Vox Coeli* – that in September 1623 James issued another proclamation, this time requiring strict compliance to the pre-print authorization requirements of decrees governing the Company of Stationers.

These final years of James's reign, marked as they were by dissolution of the consensus James had built between Calvinists and 'crypto-Catholics', saw an increased militancy of what now were being described as 'Puritans'. In 1624 Richard Mountagu answered critics of James's religious policy by writing *A New Gagg for an Old Goose?* in which he defended the catholicity James envisioned in the English church. The point of departure from earlier works was his branding of Calvinist views of grace, free will and predestination as 'Puritan' and therefore schismatic. A year later Mountagu's *Appello Caesarem* more explicitly engaged in abrasive anti-Puritanism and anti-Calvinism. According to Fincham and Lake, Mountagu offered James a rationale for opposing 'Puritans' that would allow him to sustain his own rhetoric of catholicity. The further proliferation of anti-Catholic, anti-Spanish writings in 1624 provided James with the opportunity to exercise this rhetoric. In 1624 John Gee's *A foot out of the Snare*, an anti-Jesuit work that listed 150 objectionable papist writings sold in the two prior years, led to an Address of Grievances from the parliament to James calling for him to suppress Catholic writing.[77] James agreed to issue a proclamation against 'Seditious' and 'Popish' books but insisted that it also be directed against 'Puritanicall Bookes and Pamphlets'. In the final Paul's Cross book burning of his reign, James could once again reaffirm the unity of Christianity, aligning himself with true 'catholicism' by repudiating schism – only this time the schismatics were the Puritans and the book, Edward Elton's *Gods Holy Minde*.

Following a sermon that recounted and rebutted its objectionable uncatholic doctrine, Elton's book was burned at Paul's Cross. That evening a pageant was 'made' and an emblem produced to accompany it. The emblem's iconography fixes the oppositional climate in which the book was censored. Daniel Featley described this in *Cygnea Canto*, 'because the Embleme and Motto devised upon this occasion discovereth the affections of many that were there present':

> Saint Pauls Crosse is drawne at large, and a number of men, partly running away that they might not see such a spectacle, partly weeping, and wiping their eies to see a booke so full (as they conceived) of heavenly zeale and holy fire, sacrificed in earthly and unhallowed flames: their Motto was
>   *Ardebant sancti scelaratis ignibus ignes,*
>   *Et mist a est flamma flamma profana pie.*
>   [Their holy fires burned in sinful fires
>   and profane flame was mixed with pious flame.]
> In the middest of the area there is described a huge pile of bookes burning, and on the one side the Author casting his bookes into the fire, with this Motto:
>   *Sancte (ned invideo) sine me liber ibis in igne.*
>   [Holy book, go into the fire without me, nor do I envy you.]
> And on the other side a Popish shaveling Priest answering him with this moot in the next verse:
>   *Hei mihi quod domino non licet ire tuo*
>   [Woe is me that it is not allowed for you to go with your master.][78]

The emblem, which recalls woodcuts of Marian book burnings in Foxe's *Book of Martyrs*, represents the intense polarization that re-emerged between Puritans and Papists at the end of James's reign. The fact that the events at Paul's Cross were 'made' into a pageant underscores the degree to which the culture had absorbed the performativity of the Paul's Cross book burnings. As for Elton's book – it is singularly indistinguishable in its doctrine from countless books that had come before – indeed, books that had been licensed for the press by the Calvinist, Daniel Featley. The doctrines had not changed, but the politics had.[79]

In conclusion, I would like to turn to what might be deemed a 'puzzling incident of non-censorship',[80] if you will, that offers negative evidence for the ceremonial and propagandistic purpose of burning books at Paul's Cross. No record exists to suggest that *Corona Regia* (1615), a book whose suppression James relentlessly sought throughout Europe, was burned. This book offers a stinging mock encomium of James, not only for his pretensions to wisdom and devoutness but for his sexual prowess with members of both sexes, especially the young male favourites he showered with honours. James's agents relentlessly sought to discover the book's author and printer across northern Europe, and once they were found, James demanded that the Belgian Archduke punish the book's makers. The Archduke's refusal reportedly led to an international incident when an English ship seized one of the Archduke's. One observer noted that some were 'inclined to suspect that this is His Majesty's way of showing his resentment at the reluctance of the Archdukes to punish the authors and printers of *Corona Regia*'.[81] James's motivation for not burning this incredibly offensive libel can be found in two parallel events. In 1610 when Wooton discussed with the Venetian Cabinet the libel that had referred to Venice as a 'corpse' and James as 'a crow that settled on it', he told them that he did not wish the book suppressed 'so as not to give it importance or cause it to be sought'.[82] In 1621 parliament sentenced an obscure lawyer named Floyd to 'ride with his face to the horsetale' and then stand in the stocks 'for lewde and contemptuous words against the King and Quene of Bohemia and their children spoken in the Fleet where he was prisoner'. James commuted the sentence, and the received opinion why he did so was that 'the King thincks it better to suppresse such scandalous speaches then by his punishment to blase them further abroade'.[83] These two incidents inform the Paul's Cross book burnings, where, when James burned books, he did so not to control public access to the ideas censored writers expressed, but to attract attention to how distant their ideas were from his own. These public book burnings, which participated as much in the construction of the King's public persona as the works he published, affirmed the monarchical sovereignty of James and other princes, denied papal claims to temporal superiority, confirmed the continuity of Protestantism with the primitive church, and vindicated James from charges of apostasy. Burning books was for James an act of personal propaganda.

Notes

1. Jonathan Goldberg, *James I and the Politics of Literature* (Baltimore: Johns Hopkins University Press, 1983), p. 84.

2. Ibid., p. 140.
3. Kenneth Fincham and Peter Lake, 'The Ecclesiastical Policy of James I', *JBS* 24 (1985), 206.
4. Ibid., p. 207.
5. Ibid., p. 183.
6. Goldberg, *James I and the Politics of Literature*, p. 260.
7. James I, *An humble supplication for toleration & libertie to enjoy & observe the ordinance of Christ Iesus in th'administation of his churches in lieu of humane constitutions* (1609), quoted in Fincham and Lake, 'Ecclesiastical Policy of James I', pp. 169–70.
8. James Mountague, ed., *The Workes of James … King of Great Britaine* (1616), p. 142. All citations from the writings of James I are from this edition. Subsequent citation will be by individual titles and page numbers.
9. Mountague, ed., *Basilikon Doron*, p. 142.
10. Mountague, ed., *A Remonstrance for the Right of Kings*, p. 382.
11. Mountague, ed., *Basilikon Doron*, p. 141.
12. Mountague, ed., *An Apology for the Oath of Allegiance*, p. 286.
13. Goldberg, *James I and the Politics of Literature*, pp. 115–16.
14. *Calendar of State Papers and Manuscripts relating to English Affairs, existing in the Archives and collections of Venice*, vol. XI (London: His Majesty's Stationery Office, 1904), no. 131. Herafter cited as *CSPV*.
15. Isaac Casaubon to Charles Labbe, quoted in Mark Pattison, *Isaac Casaubon* (Oxford: Clarendon Press, 1892), p. 286.
16. See Davis Harris Willson, 'James I's Literary Assistants', *HLQ* 8 (1944–5), 35–57.
17. *CSPV*, XI, no. 484.
18. Mountague, ed., *A Remonstrance*, pp. 304–5.
19. Mountague, ed., *A Premonition*, p. 305.
20. Patrick Collinson, *The Religion of Protestants: the Church in English Society 1559–1525* (Oxford: Clarendon Press, 1982), pp. 10–19.
21. Ibid., p. 82.
22. Ibid., p. 188.
23. Fincham and Lake, 'Ecclesiastical Policy of James I', p. 182.
24. What those who during the reign of James became identified with Arminianism shared was opposition to the Calvinist position that grace was available only to those elect God predestined to salvation.
25. Fincham and Lake, 'Ecclesiastical Policy of James I', p. 185.
26. Mountague, ed., *A Premonition*, p. 342.
27. Ibid., p. 302.
28. Ibid., p. 303.
29. *CSPV*, XI, no. 532.
30. 31 Henry VIII, c. 14 and 34; 35 Henry VIII, c. 1. Statutes of the Realm, III (London, 1810). It is important to note that these statutes followed the fall of the Cromwellian reformation and reflected a return to dogmatic Catholic orthodoxy.
31. Paul L. Hughes and James F. Larkin, eds., *Tudor Royal Proclamations* (New Haven: Yale University Press, 1964–9), vol. II, p. 59.
32. Under Elizabeth, the Archbishop of Canterbury, John Whitgift, ordered burnt in the Stationers' Hall *A Commission sent to the pope and Convenres of freres by Sathen* in 1587 and five foreign books containing doctrines of Catholic resistance in 1595. Among these were 'Thesaurus Principium', 'Ministromachia'

[Cardinal Stanislaus Rescius, Cologne, 1592], 'Rosseus de republica' [William Rainolds, *De just Republicae Chrestianae*, Douay, 1590; Antwerp, 1592], 'Little French bookes in 8 and Surius Chronicle' [Laurentius Surius, probably his hagiographical history, Cologne, 1572] (Edward Arber, *Transcript of the Registers of the London Company of Stationers* (Birmingham, 1874), II, p. 40). Religio-political interests probably motivated this censorship since the Rosseus book addressed the English succession. Whitgift also burned nine books of epigrams and satires (five in 1599 and two in 1600). (See Cyndia Susan Clegg, *Press Censorship in Elizabethan England* (Cambridge: Cambridge University Press, 1997), ch. 7, for a detailed discussion of the censorship of Holinshed's Chronicles and ch. 9 for a discussion of the satires.) Additionally, the Bishop of London, John Hayward, burned at his house the second edition of John Hayward's *The first parte of the raign of King Henry IIII*.

33. *CSPV*, XI, no. 588.
34. Norman Egbert McClure, ed., *The Letters of John Chamberlain* (Philadelphia: American Philosophical Society, 1939), vol. I, p. 488.
35. Domestic State Papers, 14/130/106, London Public Record Office.
36. McClure, ed., *Letters of John Chamberlain*, vol. II, pp. 442–3.
37. Ibid., vol. I, p. 205; II, p. 313.
38. C. R. Gillett, *Burned Books* (New York: Columbia University Press, 1933), vol. I, p. 242,
39. *CSPV*, XII, no.127.
40. *CSPV*, XI, no. 340.
41. *CSPV*, XI, no. 562.
42. *CSPV*, XI, no. 549.
43. *CSPV*, XI, no. 560.
44. *CSPV*, XI, no. 566.
45. *CSPV*, XI, no. 577.
46. *CSPV*, XI, no. 659.
47. When Roger Widdrington's book opposing the Pope's temporal authority appeared in Rome in 1614, it was prohibited and those who read it excommunicated. The same year a man was executed for possessing a similar work, *Homenovus* (*CSPV*, XII, no. 378).
48. *CSPV*, XI, no. 588.
49. *CSPV*, XI, no. 907.
50. *CSPV*, XI, no. 937.
51. *CSPV*, XI, no. 536.
52. *CSPV*, XII, no. 592.
53. Ibid.
54. Mountague, ed., *A. Declaration ... in the cause of D. Conradvs Vorstivs*, p. 350.
55. Ibid., p. 354.
56. Ibid., p. 354.
57. Frederick Shriver, 'James I and the Vorstius Affair', *EHR* 85 (1970), 455.
58. *CSPV*, II, no. 453.
59. McClure, ed., *The Letters of John Chamberlain*, vol. I, p. 336.
60. Fincham and Lake, 'Ecclesiastical Policy of James I', p. 191.
61. Daniel Featley, *Cygnea Cantio* (London, 1629), pp. 10–11. James is here referring to the dedication of the Racovian Catechism to him in the 1614 edn (dated 1609).

62. *CSPV*, XII, no. 20.
63. *CSPV*, XII, no. 62.
64. *CSPV*, XII, no. 715.
65. When Chamberlain describes the burning of Francisco Suárez's books, he mentions the burning of works of other Jesuits. It is likely that Caspar Schoppe's *Ecclesiasticus* was also burned at this time.
66. *CSPV*, XVI.
67. *CSPV*, XVI, no. 603.
68. P. G. Lake, 'Constitutional Consensus and the Puritan Opposition in the 1620s: Thomas Scott and the Spanish Match', *HJ* 25 (1982), 813.
69. *CSPV*, XVI, no. 603.
70. James F. Larkin and Paul L. Hughes, eds, *Stuart Royal Proclamations*, vol. I (Oxford: Clarendon Press, 1973), pp. 497, 520.
71. McClure, ed., *Letters of John Chamberlain*, vol. II, p. 330.
72. Fincham and Lake, 'Ecclesiastical Policy of James I', p. 199.
73. *CSPV*, XVI, no. 83. Among those submitted to custody or questioned were Lord Scroop, Earl of Oxford, Sir John Leedes and Sir Christopher Nevil.
74. McClure, ed., *Letters of John Chamberlain*, vol. II, p. 434.
75. Domestic State Papers 14/130/106. London Public Record Office.
76. McClure, ed., *Letters of John Chamberlain*, vol. II, p. 439.
77. Domestic State Papers, 14/165/53. London Public Record Office.
78. Featley, *Cygnea Cantio*, p. 5.
79. In 1625 in an attempt to embarrass the Calvinist Archbishop George Abbot, Richard Neile, a strong opponent of Calvinism, informed King James that Featley, Abbot's chaplain, had licensed a 'schismatic' book. By publicly burning the book, James could both placate Neile and show his vigilance for carrying out the spirit of his proclamation. (In private, James admonished Featly to take greater care in licensing theological tracts.) See Fincham and Lake, 'Ecclesiastical Policy of James I', p. 197.
80. Annabel Patterson, *Censorship and Interpretation* (Madison: University of Wisconsin Press, 1984), p. 17.
81. Quoted in Winfred Schleiner, '"A Plott to Have his Nose and Ears Cutt Of": Schoppe as Seen by the Archbishop of Canterbury', *R & R* 19 (1995), 183.
82. *CSPV*, XI, no. 909.
83. Domestic State Papers, 14/121/252. London Public Record Office.

11
Andrew Marvell: Living with Censorship

Annabel Patterson

Andrew Marvell wrote all his life under the shadow of political censorship. I do not mean to present him as a victim. Censorship was the kind of shade in which he peculiarly flourished. One of the first poems he wrote (and published) was the commendatory lyric for Richard Lovelace's *Lucasta*, finally released with a licence in 1649 after having been held up for nearly a year, presumably, Marvell implies, because its author has been under indictment as an active Royalist and his estate sequestered by the Long Parliament. The occasion encouraged him to meditate about the relationship between literature, the civil values and an open, non-partisan press. One of the last things he wrote was a letter to his nephew William Popple (later the translator of Locke's *Letter concerning Toleration*) describing how the Restoration licenser, Sir Roger L'Estrange, was attempting to hunt down the printer and author of Marvell's own *Account of the Growth of Popery and Arbitrary Government*, published illegally and anonymously in 1677:

> There have been great Rewards offered in private, and considerable in the Gazette, to any who could inform of the Author or Printer, but not yet discovered. Three or four printed Books since have described, as near as it was proper to go, the Man being a Member of Parliament, Mr. Marvell to have been the author; but if he had, surely he should not have escaped being questioned in Parliament, or some other Place.[1]

The tone of this letter is far from paranoid. To my ear it sounds primarily amused, playing with the parliamentary privilege which supposedly protected an MP from arrest while the Houses were in session.

During the nearly 30 years between these two events, and especially during the decade between 1667 and 1677, Marvell danced around the system, often outmanoeuvring L'Estrange, and gradually extending and complicating his views of what an open press culture could and should be. Though he never wrote a statement as resonant for the future as Milton's *Areopagitica*, he surely provided more evidence for subsequent historians of the press and of parliament that censorship was a cruel fact and not a bogeyman invented by modern liberals. Milton's *Areopagitica*, of course, was written to reproach the Long Parliament, supposedly reformers, for trying to stem the flood of publishing released by the abolition of the Star Chamber and hence of the licensing apparatus of Charles I. Given their other commitments, Milton had some reasonable hope (unrealized in the event) that his audience might think better of their strategy and recall the 1643 Licensing Act. Marvell wrote most of his critique of censorship during the reign of Charles II, when a parliament consisting mainly of cavaliers and high churchmen did their best to undo everything the Long Parliament had done – except its Licensing Act, which was re-enacted in a more rigorous formulation. Both reformers and reactionaries needed censorship; but the Restoration regime was, all in all, significantly more repressive of political and religious dissent.

This was the period governed by the restrictive and intolerant legislation known as the Clarendon Code: the Corporation Act of December 1661, the 1662 Press Act, the 1662 Act of Uniformity, resulting in the expulsion of the non-conforming ministers from their pulpits, the 1664 Conventicles Act and the 1665 Five Mile Act, which prohibited non-conformists from living and working in the city of London. Despite the claims often made for Charles II that he was much more tolerant than his parliament, and some evidence that he actually was, the third Stuart regime defended itself against criticism by simply excluding its critics from a hearing. Occasionally they were imprisoned or even executed.

Perhaps for that reason, perhaps by reason of temperament, more likely because of a combination of the two, Marvell never published a grand rhetorical speech in favour of freedom of the press and freedom of conscience. Instead he continually fenced with the system, sometimes using a rapier without a guard, but always wearing a mask; most of his writing was published anonymously. Even when writing under Oliver Cromwell's patronage, he chose to publish his long panegyric on the Protectorate, the *First Anniversary*, without putting his name to it. The poem commending Lovelace's *Lucasta* was one exception; the *Rehearsal Transpros'd: The Second Part* was another; unlicensed but published over Marvell's name as if to flaunt the fact that the king himself had intervened, via Arthur Annesley, Earl of Anglesey, to prevent L'Estrange from suppressing the first part.

Because the remarkable narrative of Marvell's defeat of the censor in the case of the *Rehearsal Tranpros'd* is comparatively well known,[2] this essay focuses instead on a story hitherto untold, and on two much less read works, the twinned pamphlets, *Mr. Smirke; or, the Divine in Mode* and *A Short Historical Essay Concerning General Councils, Creeds, and Impositions, in Matters of Religion*, which appeared anonymously in 1676. It would only be slightly a distortion to define the first as a satire on the failures and follies of state censorship, and the second as an entirely serious essay on the historical and theoretical need for freedom of conscience in religion; that is to say, on the two branches of what Henry Vane had in the 1640s defined as the Good Old Cause – civil and religious liberty. Marvell did not himself highlight the state–church dichotomy nor comment on the levity–gravity contrast of which he had made so much in the *Rehearsal Tranpros'd*. As his comic subtitle to the first pamphlet, *The Divine in Mode*, makes evident, he was well aware that in Restoration culture it was virtually impossible to separate the church from the world of public legislation, intrigue and intellectual fashion. Indeed, that was part of his point. The divine in mode was Francis Turner, an ambitious young cleric, chaplain to the King's brother, James, Duke of York. Turner, in Marvell's view, had set his heart on a bishopric, and was going about his goal by attacking one of the current champions of principles to which Marvell was himself committed.

That champion was Herbert Croft, Bishop of Hereford. Croft, having begun as a Roman Catholic, and converted back in the 1630s to ardent Anglicanism, had by the early 1670s become one of the spokesmen for compromise; not for religious toleration, or the removal of penalties for those who could not join the national church, but for comprehension within it of as many Protestants as possible by stressing what they had in common rather than the ceremonial points that divided them. In 1668 he had worked with Colonel Birch to introduce a Bill for Comprehension,[3] and he and Sir Edward Harley, Marvell's friend and correspondent, opposed the new and more rigorous Conventicles Act of 1670. At that time he resigned as royal chaplain. In May 1675, as the Commons floundered about with bills, on the one hand, to prevent 'Papists' from sitting in parliament, and on the other to abolish the medieval statue *de heretico comburendo*, he and five other bishops attended a meeting of Anglican divines who supported some sort of comprehension, and Croft was nominated to write a pamphlet arguing this position. The result was *The Naked Truth: or, the True State of the Primitive Church*.[4]

Croft must have written it in something of a hurry, trying to reach the parliament before the summer recess. The result was a flouting of the Press

Act. Marvell tells us in *Mr. Smirke* that Croft arranged for 400 copies of *The Naked Truth* to be printed, intending to distribute them to 'the Speakers of both Houses, and as many of the Members as [400 copies] could furnish'.[5] On 9 June, however, Charles prorogued the parliament, as being unable to conduct its business properly, until 13 October. 'The Parliament rising just as the Book was delivering out and before it could be presented', wrote Marvell in the opening pages of his defence, Croft ordered the printer to suppress it until the next session. 'Some covetous Printer in the mean time getting a Copy, surreptitiously Reprinted it, and so it flew abroad without the Authors knowledge, and against his direction' (4:20). It also flew abroad without his name. Croft therefore published an authorized edition, with a new, very humble and apologetic preface to the parliament, but still retaining his ostensible anonymity. I call it ostensible because, as we shall see, Croft's authorship was one of those open secrets that living under censorship spawned.

These events caused a sensation, in a political climate already overheated by the increasingly bad relations between King and parliament, and particularly by the publication in late 1675 of the *Letter from a Person of Quality to his Friend in the Country*, now taken to be the joint work of John Locke and his patron the Earl of Shaftesbury. On 8 November 1675, the *Letter* was ordered by the Lords to be burned by the common hangman, and L'Estrange was in search of those responsible.[6] Marvell himself reported these facts to his constituents in Hull on 9 November: 'There being a late printed book containing a narrative of the Test carryed on in the Lords house last session, they yesterday voted it a Libell: and to be burnt by the hands of the Hangman & to inquire out the Printer and Author'.[7] By focusing on the 'Test' as the cause of the *Letter*, Marvell was explaining to Hull the significance of Chancellor Danby's sinister project to further cut off all criticism of the regime: the Non-Resisting Act, which Danby had proposed early in the session of April 1675, requiring a test oath for all members of parliament that they would 'not at any time indeavour the alteration of the government either in Church or State'. This passed the Lords despite the resistance of Shaftesbury, Buckingham and Wharton, and was only finally avoided by the distractions of the Shirley–Fagg case of privilege. The *Letter* had told the country the story of the Test as it was fought on the floor of the Lords, and so breached not only the licensing act but also the rule that parliamentary debates might not be published.

Unquestionably, the heat generated by the *Letter* was still swirling in London when Croft's *Naked Truth* hit the streets at the end of 1675. John Evelyn reported in his *Diary* for 18 February 1676 the first semi-official response – a sermon by 'Dr. Gunning Bish: of Elie . . . Chiefly against an Anonymous Booke called *Naked Truth*, a famous & popular Treatise against the Corruption in the Cleargie, but not sound as to its quotations; supposed to have been the Bish; Herefords.' He also mentioned an answer by Turner, whose *Animadversions upon a Late Pamphlet*, also published anonymously, had its imprimatur (by Henry Compton, newly appointed Bishop of London) dated 23 February. Although *Mr. Smirke* also mentions Gunning's sermon, as well as another anonymous answer that Marvell suspected to be by Gunning,[8] it was written exclusively to confute Turner, whose attack on Croft was quite differently focused than the sermon, and whose authorship, as Evelyn's letter shows, was the same kind of open secret as was Croft's. Self-advertised as *Animadversions*, Turner's pamphlet tore its victim apart phrase by phrase. It was also personally contemptuous in its tone, and this, along with the fact that Turner, like Samuel Parker, was a royal chaplain, brought Marvell into the argument. Marvell must have begun it, then, after 23 February, and another incentive or inspiration was provided on 11 March, when George Etherege's new play, *The Man of Mode; or, Sir Fopling Flutter* was first produced at Dorset Garden, providing Marvell with his subtitle and a new dramatic subtext.

For reasons to be explained below, Marvell must have finished his response before the end of April. In less than two months, therefore, he had put together not only his own refutation of Turner and defence of Croft, on the model of his extremely successful public disputes with Parker, but also the *Essay*, for which he had mastered the ecclesiastical history of Christianity from its origins. Marvell was now, of course, comparatively at leisure, since the short session of 1675, convened on 13 October, was prorogued by the king on 22 November 1675, not to return to work until 15 February 1677; the notorious Long Prorogation.

If the two pamphlets went to press at the end of April, it did not take long for the government to take cognizance of them. In early May the Wardens' Accounts of the Stationers' Company show evidence of intensive searches for them:

> May 8 Paid and spent with our master Mr. Norton &c. on a Search, & coach hire to mr. Secrty Coventry &c about Darby & Ponders Pamphlet being part of mr Smirk.
> May 9 Paid & laid out in another search for the residue of mr Ponders Pamphlet with our master & others.
> May 10 Paid for going to Whitehall to ye Councell about Ponders business in Coach hire & other expenses.

May 18 Paid & spent upon a Search at Ratcliffe & Ponders by my Lord of Londons order.[9]

These entries tell us several interesting things: first, that both William Coventry, the other Secretary of State, and Henry Compton, Bishop of London (who had licensed Turner's *Animadversions* and been politely rebuked for it in *Mr. Smirke*) were now trying to track down and suppress Marvell's pamphlets; second, that there was a 'part of mr Smirk' in which the authorities were particularly interested, almost certainly the *Essay*; and third, that at least three printers were involved in their production: Nathaniel Ponder, the non-conformist publisher of the *Rehearsal Transpros'd* and the works of John Owen, who would later become John Bunyan's publisher;[10] Thomas Ratcliffe, whose father had published much of the work of Edward Reynolds, the moderate divine to whose reconciling sermon at the opening of the 1660 parliament Marvell refers in *Mr. Smirke* as having itself been suppressed;[11] and John Darby Sr., who would later publish the 1698 editions of Milton's prose and Algernon Sidney's *Discourses*. The practice of dividing texts up between different printing houses not only made printing more efficient, but blurred the question of responsibility for an illegal publication.

On 1 July 1676, Marvell wrote to Sir Edward Harley about another phase of his pamphlet's reception, regaling his friend and fellow tolerationist with very first-hand gossip:

The book said to be Marvels make what shift it can in the world but the Author walks negligently up & down as unconcerned. The Divines of our Church say it is not in the merry part as good as the Rehearsall Transpros'd, that it runs dreggs; the Essay they confesse is writ well enough to the purpose he intended it but that was a very ill purpose … Dr. Turner first met it at Broom's went into a Chamber & though he were to have dined which he seldome omits nor approves of Fasting yet would not come down but read it all over in consequence. The Bishop of London has carryed it in his hand at Councill severall days, showing his friends the passages he has noted but none takes notice of them … I know not what to say: Marvell, if it be he, has much staggerd me in the busnesse of the Nicene & all Councills, but had better have taken a rich Presbyterians mony that before the book came out would have bought the whole Impression to burne it.[12]

This marvellously nonchalant account of his new success, told in the prudential third person, nevertheless indicates Marvell's confidence that he was not in serious danger from this new adventure in polemic. The vignettes of Turner getting hold of a copy of *Mr. Smirke* at Broome's eating house and forgoing his dinner in order to find out how effective was Marvell's counter-attack, and of Compton carrying his copy around trying to get the attention of his colleagues on the Privy Council, are delightful instances of thick description of London Restoration culture; but the final detail, of a rich Presbyterian attempting to stop dispersal of the pamphlets by buying up the entire stock, alerts us as well to the material life of books and booksellers.

Nathaniel Ponder, however, did pay a price for his commitment to this project. On 10 May Williamson recorded the indictment of Ponder 'for printing Marvells book':

> Owned to have had those papers from Mr. Marvell with directions from him to print them. That he, Ponder, gave them out to be printed, that he had no license for the book. Ordered to be committed. Lord Privy Seal opposed it, because the cause is bailable by statute. Lord Chancellor. That for contempt of the order of the Board made against printing without license, for the seditiousness of the matter of it &c he may be committed for it.[13]

To the high-ranking officials interesting themselves in this affair, therefore, we can now add Sir Heneage Finch, the Lord Chancellor, and the Earl of Anglesey, who had become Lord Privy Seal in 1672. Despite, or perhaps because of, his successful intervention in that year between Ponder and Sir Roger L'Estrange to prevent the suppression of the *Rehearsal Transpros'd*, Anglesey was on this occasion overruled. The other striking fact that emerges from this document is that Marvell's authorship was known virtually from the beginning, and not only to government officials. On 23 May Sir Christopher Hatton had written to his brother, 'I hope Andrew Marvel will likewise be made an example for his insolence in calling Dr Turner, Chaplain to His Royal Highnesse, Chaplaine to Sr Fobling Busy, as he terms him in his scurrilous satyrical answer to his Animadversions on Naked Truth.'[14] Yet no action was taken against him.

Indeed, there is evidence that the government was being blatantly thwarted in its efforts to shut off supplies of the pamphlets. On 6 June 1676, the Catholic antiquary Thomas Blount recorded that *Mr. Smirke* was selling 'for half crowns a peece and 15 non conformists took off the whole Impression to disperse'.[15] This entry is remarkable, not only for the high price it records for the now notorious Marvell pamphlets (Turner's

Animadversions was listed in the Term Catalogue at sixpence), but also for its evidence of an organization created to protect and disseminate them – the converse of the rich Presbyterian who had offered to buy the whole impression in order to suppress it.

The jokey tone in which Marvell wrote to Harley about the reception of his book and the frustration of his major opponents has its counterpart in *Mr. Smirke* itself, which begins with a sustained, yet elusive, attack on the system of licensing and its by-products. This is introduced by way of a defence of Croft from the specific charge applied to him by Turner that his book came out without a licence. Indeed, Turner has taken it upon himself to speak on behalf of parliament, thereby once again entrenching upon matters of state: 'not content with having passed his own ecclesiastical censure upon the Author, he forgoes too in his own mind a sentence of the Lords and Commons assembled in Parliament; who *he believes* and *'tis probable*, would have doomed the book to be burnt by the hangman' (4:15). We can see the shadow of the burned *Letter* at the back of Marvell's mind. And he thereupon proceeds to challenge, with heavy irony, Turner's appeal to the secular laws of the land:

> The Crimes indeed are hainous, and if the Man and Book be guilty, may, when time comes, furnish special matter for an Impeachment. That *he has made a breach upon their Glorious Act of Uniformity, Violated their Act, their most necessary Act* (the Animadverter hath reason by this time to say so) *against Printing without a License:*[16] And I suppose he reserves another for aggravation in due time; the Act against seditious Conventicles.[17] For these three are all of a piece, and yet are the several Pieces of the Animadverter's Armour:

It was a brilliant stroke to associate Turner with the punitive Clarendon Code, and even more brilliant to attack the Code for *its* blurring of the necessary boundaries between church and state. The two attacked are conjoined; for, writes Marvell:

> considering how empty of late the Church-Magazines have been of that Spiritual Armour, which the Apostle found sufficient against the assaults of whatsoever enemy, even of Satan; what could men in all humane reason do less, then to furnish such of the Clergy as wanted, with these Weapons of another Warfare (4:18)

The other warfare in question is, evidently, that of the unholy league of reactionaries in both church and state against their opponents. In a letter to his nephew William Popple, Marvell described with considerable venom the rise of a new 'Episcopal-Cavalier Party', one of whose first weapons was to have been the 'politic Test' referred to above.[18] In *Mr. Smirke*, however, he relies on indirection, circumlocution and a false hesitancy to make his case:

> But, although these Acts were the true effects of the Prudence and Piety of that season, yet it is possible (but who can provide for all cases?) that, if there have not already, there may arise thereby in a short time some notable inconvenience. For suppose that Truth should one day or other come to be Truth and every man a Lyar, (I mean [every man] of the humour of this *parliamentum indoctum*, this single representativer ...) you see there is no more to be said, as the case stands at present, but Executioner do your Office. (4:18)

If we are to appreciate the peculiarly Marvellian, as distinct from the Miltonic, attack on censorship, this passage requires close reading. First, Marvell refers to the various pieces of legislation that made up the Clarendon Code as the 'true effects of Prudence and Piety *of that season*', quietly undermining the absoluteness of the abstractions by the charge of time-serving. Second, he introduces, in the most hesitant syntax possible, the possibility that those legislators may have been wrong: 'yet', 'it is possible', 'but who can provide for all cases', 'if they have not already', 'there may arise in a short time some notable inconvenience'. That notable inconvenience must be the arrival of a better truth than that of the need for uniformity in religion. 'For suppose that Truth should one day come to be Truth...'

It is instructive to compare this formulation with Milton's in *Areopagitica*, where the same consciousness of epistemological uncertainty struggling with polemical conviction prevails, but the effect is entirely different:

> For who knows not that Truth is strong next to the Almighty; she needs no policies, nor stratagems, nor licencings to make her victorious, those are the shifts and the defences that error uses against her power: give her but room, & do not bind her when she sleeps, for then she speaks not true, as the old Proteus did, who spake oracles only when he was caught & bound, but then rather she turns herself into all shapes, except her own, and perhaps tunes her voice according to the time ... Yet is it not impossible that she may have more shapes than one.[19]

Milton begins in certainty, and creates an entire allegorical narrative, which eventually ends in constructive doubt. Marvell begins with a false compliment to the Cavalier parliament, and ends by slipping in the charge that it is a *parliamentum indoctum*, at least as represented by its would-be spokesman and instructor Francis Turner. The baffling formulation, 'suppose that Truth should one day come to be Truth', has the same function as Milton's acknowledgement of competing truths in the world we are forced to live in; but Marvell's irony, resting on tautology, runs deeper.

Then, and only then, does he challenge the heart of Turner's phrase, 'their most necessary Act ... against printing without a license'. Why is it necessary? What are its real motives? Is the law fairly and equally administered? The answer to the last, with Turner's pamphlet having been licensed by the Bishop of London, is emphatically no:

> Nor therefore can it ever enter into my mind, as to that Act particularly of Printing, that the Law-givers could thereby intend to allow any man a promiscuous Licentiousness, and Monopoly of Printing Pernicious Discourses intending to sow and increase dissension thorow the Land (of which there is but too large a crop already;) as neither of Prohibiting Books dictated by Christian meekness and charity of the promoting of Truth and Peace among us, and reconciling our Differences; no, nor even of such as are writ to take out the Blots of Printing-Ink, and wipe off the Aspersions which divers of the Licensed Clergy cast upon mens private Reputations: and yet this is the use to which the Law is sometimes applied. (4:18–19).

'It is something strange,' Marvell continued:

> that to publish a good Book is a sin, and an ill one a vertue; and that while one comes out with Authority; the other may not have a Dispensation. So that we seem to have got an Expurgatory Press, though not an Index; and the most Religious Truth must be expung'd and suppressed in order to the false and secular interest of some of the Clergy. So much wiser are they grown by process of time than the Obsolete Apostle, that said, *We can do nothing against the Truth.* (4:20).

The 'Obsolete Apostle' in this case is St Paul (2 Corinthians 13:8), and Marvell is using the strategy that will be central to his *Historical Essay*, of showing that the contemporary Restoration church has forgotten the lessons of the Gospel.

Indeed, Marvell now develops that charge to the effect that the Restoration clergy are steadily rebuilding the laws of the state so as to render sins against God insignificant, but attacks upon themselves 'hainous and unpardonable':

Insomuch that if we of the Laity would but study our Self-preservation, and learn of the them to be as true to our separate interest, as these men are to theirs, we ought not to wish them any new Power for the future, but after very mature deliberation. Forasmuch as every such act does but serve, as some of them use it, to make the good people of England walk in peril of their Souls, to multiply sin and abomination thorow the Land, and by ingaging men's minds under spiritual Bondage, to lead them canonically on into Temporal slavery. Whereas the Laity are commonly more temperate and merciful (I might say more discreet) in the exercising of any Authority they are intrusted with; and what power they have, they will not wear it thred-bare: so that if I were to commit a fault for my life, (as suppose by Printing this without a License) I would chuse to sin against good Mr. Oldenburg. (4:21)

This is a brilliant conclusion to Marvell's modest, half-hidden yet trenchant version of *Areopagitica*, trenchant because it does not depend, as did Milton, on the sharing of high ideals. Instead, it depends on a Lockean recognition of the universal role of self-interest. And tucked into the end of the paragraph are two remarkable moves: the first, a teasing defiance of the licensing laws: 'if I were to commit a fault for my life (as suppose by Printing this without a License)', a supposition that by now had been notoriously fulfilled; the second, a reference to a particular licenser, which also serves to date, for us, Marvell's completion of his pamphlet.

Henry Oldenberg, the distinguished Secretary of the Royal Society and friend of Milton, would not on the face of it seem to be connected to licensing; unless, that is, one knew that for barely three months, in February, March and April 1676, Oldenberg had held a license from Secretary of State Joseph Williamson to license political texts, presumably to enhance his always insufficient income.[20] However, on 29 April Oldenberg returned his license to Williamson 'because persons have been busy to impress on Williamson's mind disquieting suspicions concerning his affection to the Government, and also because of the tenderness of the employment and the vast expense of time it requires'.[21] In other words, the seat of the licenser had become too hot. In letters that preceded this one, Oldenberg, had been in trouble over 'one unhappy amorous romance' he had been asked to license; but conceivably another event that increased the heat was the appearance of Marvell's unlicensed pamphlet, with his own name teasingly highlighted. The disadvantages of the licensing system cut both ways.

As he teased his audience with his own scofflaw status, so Marvell plays with the device of anonymity, which he shares with Croft and his adversaries:

> But this is not only a Trick of the Animadverters, but ordinary with many others of them; who, while we write at our own peril, and perhaps set our names to it, (for I am not yet resolved whether I [will]) they that rail for the Church of England, and under the Publick License and Protection, yet leave men as if it were at Hot-Cockles, to guess blind fold who it is that hit them ... What should be the reason of it? sure there is not *so Vile a Cause* too that they dare not abide by it ... Or is it their own sorry performance that makes them ashamed to avow their own Books? ... Or would they reserve a Latitude to themselves to turn Non-conformists again upon occasion? Or do they in pure honesty abstain from putting a single Name to a Book, which hath been the workmanship of the whole Diocess? (4:26)

But tease or not, Marvell was undoubtedly aware that anonymous publication, even if one's authorship were an open secret, was not the bravest activity. In fact, it was not really action at all. In the same letter to Sir Edward Harley in which Marvell had described, with amusement, the reception of *Mr. Smirke* and the *Essay*, he described the investigation by the Privy Council of Francis Jenks for having made a motion in the Guildhall on 24 June 1676 calling on the Lord Mayor, Sir Joseph Sheldon (who happened to be the nephew of Gilbert Sheldon, Archbishop of Canterbury) to summon the Common Council so that it could petition the King to call a new parliament.[22] The Long prorogation, for over a year, having been illegal, the Cavalier parliament was in principle, so Jenks argued, dissolved. Jenks was placed in gaol. On 17 July Marvell wrote to Popple that Jenks refused to petition the King for his release: '[He] might so come out but keeps his prison as his fort & molests all judicatures wth requireing habeas corpus & offring bale, yet in vaine & perhaps may be prisoner till michaelmas terme, noe matter he is a single brave fellow (II:348)'. In the same letter Marvell described how 'Ratford for propagating the Libell was indited of Treason, tried & acquitted by the Jury and the rude People clappd their hands for joy and made a great acclamation at the Verdict' (II:344).

The Jenks affair being fully described in the press, Joseph Williamson ordered L'Estrange to confiscate *Jenkes His Case*, and John Marlow went to prison for printing his speech. A search was also instigated for *An Account of the Proceedings at Guild-Hall, London, ... Held 14th of June 1676.*[23] On 2 December Marvell wrote to Sir Edward Thompson in York: 'Freak of the Temple was try'd to day for misdemeanor in publishing a scandalous Libell ... Freaks Counsell spared all defense and the Jury ... forthwith acquitted him' (II:349). This flurry of news bulletins from Marvell to his friends elsewhere shows not only how nervous was the government at this time, but also how his own attention had been focused on the different spheres in which censorship operated, not always to its own advantage.

But the story of Marvell and censorship would not be complete without returning to his *Account of the Growth of Popery and Arbitrary Government*, in which, as I have elsewhere indicated, Marvell took upon himself the bolder task of confronting the Restoration government directly, and accusing it to its face of attempting to subvert the constitution; or, in his own words, attempting 'to change the lawful Government of England into an absolute Tyranny, and to convert the established Protestant Religion into downright Popery.'[24] If this sounds more like Milton's trumpet than Marvell's stage whisper, the explanation is that Marvell has reached the conclusion that the forces ranged against his principles are too large, too many and too well organized to be tackled by humour and innuendo; or even by quoting the scriptures.

The face of the government, strictly speaking, was the face of Charles II; but the one evasion Marvell used in this work was to claim for the King the fictional immunity that only his ministers were responsible; 'for so far is the relator himself from any sinister surmise of his Majesty, or from suggesting it to others, that he acknowledges, if it were fit for Caesar's wife to be free, much more is Caesar himself from all crime and suspicion.' Nevertheless, some of the charges he makes can scarcely be attributed to the undoubtedly powerful Danby; most notably the charge that Charles has engaged in a secret liaison with Louis XIV of France, whose ambitions towards a universal (and Catholic) monarchy were already widely feared in Europe.

It is all the more telling, therefore, given the scale of the concerns with which Marvell is now operating, that he returns over and over to the theme of censorship, now far more broadly interpreted than the application, fair or unfair, of the Licensing Act. One of his first strategies, to illustrate the 'work of darkness' of Anglo-French relations, was to publish the text of the Chancellor's speech on 24 October 1670, using the bait of the Triple Alliance between England, Sweden and the United Provinces as a means to persuade parliament that the French threat was under control, and to persuade them to grant a generous Supply. 'It is not without much labour,' wrote Marvell, 'that I have been able to recover a written copy of the Lord Bridgeman's speech, none being printed, but forbidden, doubtless lest so notorious practice as certainly was never before, ... might remain publick' (4:266–7). But forbidding the publication of parliamentary proceedings was only a minor trick compared to the suppression of parliamentary meetings – by the time-honoured device of prorogation after prorogation. Thus when the Commons protested the proxy marriage of James, Duke of York, to the Catholic Mary Beatrice, Duchess of Modena, 'it seemed an easier thing, and more decent, to prorogue the Parliament, than to dissolve the marriage' (4:297).

A major section of the *Account* is devoted to retelling the story already told in the banned and burned *Letter from a Person of Quality*; the story of the debates in the Lords concerning Danby's Non-Resisting Bill. Marvell's allusion to the *Letter* is interestingly vague: 'The particular relation in this debate, which lasted many days with great eagerness on both sides, and the reasons but one, was in the next Session burnt by order of the Lords, but the sparks of it will eternally fly in their adversaries faces' (4:809–10). And equally revealing, for those who have followed his previous views on anonymous and unlicensed printing, is his account of what the press contributed to the state of public knowledge of these events:

> There was another book likewise that came out by authority, ... intitled, *A Paquet of Advice to the Men of Shaftsbury, &c.* But the name of the author was concealed, not out of any spark of modesty, but that he might with the more security exercise his impudence, not so much against those noble lords [who had opposed the Test], as against all publick truth and honesty ... And on the other side, some scattering papers straggled out in print, as is usual, for the information of Parliament-men, in the matter of law concerning prorogation. (4:317)

In later pages of the *Account*, Marvell himself flouted the law against printing parliamentary debates, a law not successfully challenged for another hundred years, when John Wilkes led the move for reform, more or less against George III himself, in what was known as the 'Printer's Case'.[25] Marvell knew exactly what he was doing. For, on Monday 28 May 1677, he reported, the Commons was rebuked by Charles II for interfering in his business, and the Speaker unceremoniously pronounced the House adjourned, 'all the House being astonished at so unheard of a violation of their inherent privilege and constitution':

> And that which more amazed them afterwards was, that while none of their own transactions or addresses for the public good are suffered to be printed, but even all written copies of them with the same care as libels suppressed; yet they found this severe speech published in the next day's news book, ... the Parliament being grown to that height of contempt, as to be gazetted among run-away servants, lost dogs, strayed horses, and highway robbers. (4:405–6)

Marvell had come a long way from his gentlemanly complaints in *To his Noble Friend Mr. Richard Lovelace, upon his Poems*, that 'our wits have drawne th'infection of our times', and the civilized virtues have vanished. He now saw the connection between such comparatively minor hindrances as the Licensing Act and the lack of any independent news media (the *Gazette* was a government organ) and such fundamental aspects of the regime as the arbitrary royal control over the timing of parliamentary sessions, the appointment of judges (Charles had appointed five new judges of dubious character during a prorogation) and the functioning of the London Exchequer (to avoid paying his own debts to the banks, Charles had closed the Exchequer on 1 January 1672, throwing the country's system of credit into chaos). It would be going too far to include all these structural features of government under the heading of censorship; and yet it is clear that freedom of political speech and the people's right to know were only the most easily defensible of the other rights these wrongs had thrown into relief.

And if living censorship had shown him the bigger and darker picture, what would he have thought of what happened to writings after his death; specifically, first of the publication of his *Miscellaneous Poems* in 1681, by his landlady claiming to be his wife, in an attempt to retrieve some value from his estate; and second, of the suppression from the volume of his three major poems honouring Oliver Cromwell? The *Horatian Ode*, the *First Anniversary* and the elegy for Cromwell, only one of which had been published during the revolutionary era, were now cancelled while the volume was actually in press, surviving only in two known copies. Marvell's name now once more firmly on a title page, and his status defined as 'Late Member of the Honourable House of Commons', was, we can now assume, something of which he would have approved. Whether it should have been the title page of *this* volume is another question. It was almost certainly the defeat of the Whigs over the second Exclusion Bill, and the dissolution of parliament on 18 January 1681, that led Robert Boulter, the printer of the miscellany, to lose his nerve and cancel the Cromwell poems. But would Marvell himself ever have published them during the Restoration? The readers of this essay will have to decide for themselves.

Notes

1. *Poems and Letters*, ed. H. M. Margoliouth, rev. Pierre Legouis, 2 vols (Oxford: Oxford University Press, 1971), II, p. 357. The letter is dated 10 June 1678. Marvell died in August.
2. See *The Rehearsal Transpros'd: The Second Part*, ed. D. I. B. Smith (Oxford: Oxford University Press, 1971), pp. xx–xxv. Smith cites the documents showing Anglesey's intervention, and describes the extremely minor censorship L'Estrange applied to the text of the second impression before releasing it.
3. See Walter G. Simon, *The Restoration Episcopate* (New York: Columbia University Press, 1965), pp. 158–62.
4. Simon, *The Restoration Episcopate*, p. 172; see also Newton Key, 'Comprehension and the Breakdown of Consensus in Restoration Herefordshire', in T. Harris, P. Seaward and M. Goldie, eds, *Religion and Politics in Restoration England* (Oxford: Oxford University Press, 1990), pp. 191–215.
5. Pending the publication of the Yale edition of Marvell's *Prose Works*, most of his pamphlets must still be cited form *Complete Works*, ed. A. B. Grosart, 4 vols (Blackburn, 1875). See vol. 4, pp. 19–20, hereafter cited in the text. I have, however, adjusted the capitalization to reflect the 1676 editions.
6. See Richard Ashcraft, *Revolutionary Politics and Locke's Two Treatises of Government* (Princeton: Princeton University Press, 1986), pp. 120–7.
7. *Poems and Letters*, II, p. 172.
8. *Lex Talionis: Or, The Author of Naked Truth Stript Naked* (London, 1676); also attributed to Philip Fell, fellow of Eton College.
9. Robin Myers, ed., *Warden's Accounts 1663–1728, Records of the Worshipful Company of Stationers* (Cambridge: Cambridge University Press, 1985), Chadwyck Healey microfilms, Film 8520, Part 7, Reel 76; I owe this reference to Beth Lynch.
10. F. M. Harrison, 'Nathaniel Ponder: the Publisher of *Pilgrim's Progress*', *The Library*, 4th series, 15 (1934), 257–94.
11. This was the sermon preached by Reynolds to the Commons on Wednesday, 25 April 1660, at St Margaret's, Westminster, for which the House officially thanked him and requested him 'to print the same', *Journal of the House of Commons*, 1660, p. 1. (hereafter, *JHC*). In *Mr. Smirke*, Marvell observes that Gunning's sermon may never appear: 'I rather expect that after all, it will incur the same fate with that memorable sermon preached before the House of Commons, at their receiving the sacrament upon the first opening of the Parliament; which for some dangerous opinions there vented, was so far from ever coming forth, that one might sooner have obtain'd his Majestie's special command against ever printing it' (4:62).
12. *Poems and Letters*, vol. II, pp. 345–46.
13. *CSPD* 1676, pp. 106–07.

14. *Poems and Letters*, vol. II, p. 394; citing *Hatton Correspondence*, vol. I, p. 128; Hatton had presumably neither seen the play nor read the pamphlet, since he misnames Sir Fopling Flutter.

15. See *The Correspondence of Thomas Blount* (1618–79); *Catholic Antiquary*, ed. Theo Bongaerts (Amsterdam, 1978), p. 166. I owe this reference to Nicholas von Maltzahn. Bongaerts was writing to Anthony Wood, in a provocative mood: 'but above all what say you to Mr. Smerk or the Divine in mode, if you Churchmen put up so great a Joque – it will be no hard thing to prophecy, what will become of –'.

16. In May 1662 parliament had voted in a new licensing act, which largely reinstated the procedures instigated by Star Chamber in 1637; printers were required to obtain licences from a secretary of state for books on history and politics, and from the Archbishop of Canterbury or Bishop of London for religion and philosophy. During the two sessions of 1675, the Commons were concerned about illegal publications, and just before the Long Prorogation they were about to give a second reading to a 'Bill for reviving and making perpetual the Act for preventing of frequent Abuses in printing seditious, treasonable and unlicensed Books and Pamphlets, and for regulating of Printers & Printing Presses' (*JHC*, 17 Nov. 1675). Had they done so, it would not have expired in 1697.

17. In the seventeenth century, 'conventicles' was a technical term for outlawed religious meetings, that is, meetings of more than five persons beyond the family in whose house the meeting occurred. In 1670 the Commons passed a second act against conventicles (22 Car. II. c. 1) revising and strengthening that of 1664. Marvell refers frequently to this new act as a matter of concern. See *Poems and Letters*, vol. II, pp. 89, 91, 99, 101, 316, 318 ('There is like to be a terrible Act of Conventicles'). The text of the act is given in full in Marvell's letter to Mayor Tripp of 10 March 1670 (II, p. 101).

18. *Poems and Letters*, vol. II, p. 341.

19. Milton, *Complete Prose Works*, eds. D. M. Wolfe et al., 8 vols (New Haven: Yale University Press, 1953–86), II, pp. 562–3.

20. See *The Correspondence of Henry Oldenberg*, eds and trans. A. Rupert Hall and Marie Boas Hall, 13 vols (Madison, 1965–86), XII, pp. 254–5, 263–5; Adrian Johns, *The Nature of the Book: Print and Knowledge in the Making* (Chicago: University of Chicago Press, 1998), pp. 242–4.

21. *CSPD* 1676, p. 92.

22. *Poems and Letters*, vol. II, p. 345.

23. See Richard Greaves, *Enemies under his Feet: Radicals and Nonconformists in Britain, 1664–1677* (Stanford: Stanford University Press, 1990), pp. 231–2. See also Greaves' list of other warrants, indictments and punishments for printing or dispersing seditious material, p. 234.

24. *Complete Works*, vol. 4, p. 248. See Annabel Patterson, *Marvell: the Writer in Public Life* (London and New York: Routledge, 1999), pp. 142–55.

25. See Peter Thomas, *John Wilkes: a Friend to Liberty* (Oxford: Oxford University Press, 1996), pp. 125–40.

Afterword

12
Doing the Queen: Gender, Sexuality and the Censorship of Elizabeth I's Royal Image from Renaissance Portraiture to Twentieth-century Mass Media

Richard Burt

No study of the censorship of Elizabeth's royal image can be complete, it is becoming clear, without a consideration of her afterlives as a cultural icon. Recent work on English and Scottish monarchs has examined the long histories in the construction and performance of royal images.[1] If history is metahistory, as Hayden White has argued, then metahistory is also the product of mass media(tions), particularly film and television. The production of 'history' by mass media in turn has its own rather long history. Nineteenth- and twentieth-century non-academic accounts of monarchs like Elizabeth I, for example, are mediated by, among other things, post-French Revolutionary norms of realism. An understanding of the assumptions that govern our own narratives about historical figures like Elizabeth must take into consideration, I submit, the history of performances that go back from the present to their progenitors in nineteenth-century Romanticism and Victorian culture: operas like Gaetano Donizetti's *Roberto Devereaux* and *Maria Stuarda*; historical novels and plays such as Sir Walter Scott's *Kenilworth: a Romance*, Mary Shelley's *The Fortunes of Perkin Warbeck: a Romance*, Percy Bysshe Shelley's *The Cenci*, and Friedrich Schiller's *Maria Stuart*. (Madame de Lafayette's *The Princess of Cleves* is perhaps the earliest, post-Revolutionary progenitor.) Twentieth-century films and romance novels tend to rewrite and recycle these nineteenth-century versions.[2]

By examining the relations between gender, sexuality and censorship both in sixteenth- and seventeenth-century documents about Elizabeth and in some mass media performances of her image, I want to put into question some uncritically held assumptions that govern both our understanding of censorship and the practices of feminist and historicist criticism. Elizabeth herself censored the production and reception of her image (she both destroyed images of herself she did not like and sought to prevent the destruction of images she did like; additionally, she occasionally sought to regulate the circulation of images of powerful aristocrats like the Earl of Essex). Her role as agent of censorship rather than victim of censorship calls into question any attempt to provide a supposedly 'uncensored' account of our construction of Elizabeth, as if Elizabeth were the victim of patriarchal censorship practices, as if the corrective were simply to expand the data base of images to include those produced in mass media. I am not interested, then, in adjudicating how repressive Elizabeth's censorship of her image either was or was not, whether it was more or less enlightened than the censorship practised by male monarchs of their images. By conceiving the history of Elizabeth's royal image as a series of cultural performances, I want not only to expand and refine the range of what we might consider to be Elizabeth's censorship of her image but to explore how mass culture versions of Elizabeth intersect or conflict with academic feminist and historicist versions of Elizabeth. What might mass culture versions of Elizabeth tell us, I want to ask, that academic versions do not?

Historians and critics (feminist or not) tend to have conservative investments in the printed media and in literary performance histories. Recent work on Elizabeth and other monarchs, for example, pointedly excludes romance novels.[3] To be sure, some historians do make analogies between past historical moments and present mass media in their work. In her book on Marie-Antoinette entitled *The Wicked Queen*, Chantal Thomas writes, for example, of Marie-Antoinette's 'media image' (p. 87) refers to director 'Eric Von Stroheim' (p. 65) and explains her purpose via an analogy with horror films: 'I am trying to define what killed her, to trace the ever darker contours of her image (as a horror film might show the transformations of a young princess into a prostitute, a nymphomaniac, a vampire, a monster)' (p. 21). Even more directly, Natalie Davis writes in *The Return of Martin Guerre*: 'When I first read the judge's account [of Martin Guerre] I thought, "This must become a film." ' Davis went on to become a consultant in the film.

Yet the visual and non-literary mass culture performance history tends to be excluded, one presumes, for being unscholarly, tacky, trashy, trivial, lurid and prurient. This implicit denigration of mass media is, of course, in some ways quite understandable. After all, how seriously can one take a time-travel romance entitled *Queen of My Heart* (by Donna Valentino) that poses the question of whether the hero, one Dante, should return to sixteenth-century England to claim his bride Elizabeth Tudor or stay in 1887 Arizona with the 'queen of his heart', Gloriana Carlisle? I am happy to concede that twentieth-century mass media constructions of Elizabeth's image are not without their problems: they focus exclusively on heterosexual romance; aristocratic libertinism is pathologized; they can be historically anachronistic; they can often be deeply conservative in a number of ways; they are often sexist; they can be overly deferential to the authority of scholars, particularly historians; they are under-theorized, structured by humanist assumptions about the centred subject and by outdated biographical readings of literature; and, of course, they are generally very badly written.[4]

Despite their problems, mass media constructions of Elizabeth's image usefully link gender and sexuality to censorship, and thereby implicitly challenge both the way we tend to think about censorship exclusively in negative terms (as more or less brutally repressive) and the practices of feminist and historicist criticism (as politically progressive in the present). Mass media accounts may, among other things, clarify the 'professional unconscious' of a given critic or historian. A markedly deep conservatism (what, in another time and another place, might have been called 'counter-Revolutionary') often kicks in when the critic/historian turns her or his attention to a royal or aristocratic figure. The contemporary critical insight into the monarchy as a performance, a media image, coincides with a moment in which the English monarchy is in disarray: witness iconoclastic films like *The Madness of King George* (about a crazy king), *Mrs Brown* (about Queen Victoria's affair with her servant, John Brown); and *Elizabeth* (about her affair with Leicester). Yet critics and historians tend to engage conservatively in damage control when it comes to ruling élites. They nearly always argue, for example, that Elizabeth was a lifelong virgin, that she never had an affair with Thomas Seymour even though her stepmother Catherine Parr threw her out, never gave birth to a bastard son named Arthur Dudley; that Mary Stuart didn't really plot Elizabeth's assassination, nor was she involved in her husband Lord Darnley's murder, nor did she give birth to a daughter by Bothwell who was sent to court in France and survived her. Similarly, it took DNA evidence to convince scholars that Thomas Jefferson had an affair with his slave, Sally Hemmings, and fathered several children by her. And were it not for a stain on a dress subsequently sent to an FBI lab, scholars would no doubt have claimed that President William Jefferson Clinton never had sex with 'that woman', Monica Lewinsky. Mass media performances of Elizabeth may throw into relief similarly conservative investments in what counts as data worthy of study to make sure one's work will be recognized as academically respectable and legitimate.

Mass media performances of Elizabeth also entail, I think, rather major critical shifts in the how we define censorship. First, they demand that censorship be linked to iconoclasm, censorship of the word brought into conjunction with the censorship of the image. This in turn means thinking about the relation between word and image, whether one medium has priority over the other; that is, does the meaning of the image always outstrip and exceed any attempt to frame it verbally, or can the meaning of the image only be understood once it as been verbally framed? Second, censorship has to be thought of in terms of psychoanalysis, in terms of both the censor's and the critic of censorship's unconscious investments and fantasies.[6] (Even the political/feminist critic has a political unconscious which by definition she or he cannot access.) Third, consideration of gender, sexuality and censorship means rethinking work on the cinematic gaze (both male and female) in relation to Foucauldian work on spying and surveillance.

These shifts in turn raise a series of related questions that concern feminist and historicist criticism. Instead of asking how much autonomy a woman had, how subversive or proto-feminist she was, as if there were a consensus on what feminist subversion might mean in the present, I want to ask a different set of questions: How does a woman censoring men in the name of other women complicate feminist critiques about the marginalization and silencing of women's voices? And to what extent does Elizabeth's interest in unlocking secrets of her maid's of honour, an interest that could take the form of a demand for speech, complicate contemporary feminist notions that women's speech is a universal good, women's silence a universal evil? Is visibility necessarily desirable for women?

I raise these questions in order to expose and critique a model of censorship assumed by many feminist critics (patriarchy as censors, women as victims of censorship; contemporary critic/historian as engaged in the recovery of censored female voices) in order to displace and absorb it by a more dialectical and dialogical model, one which at the least throws into relief the conflicted, if not entirely censored areas of feminist discourses. In what follows, I focus first on the censorship of Elizabeth's image during her lifetime and turn to her afterlives in twentieth-century constructions of her role as censor. I take up four examples: the BBC television mini-series *Elizabeth R* (dir. Roderick Graham and Richard Martin, 1972) and the films *The Private Lives of*

Elizabeth and Essex (dir. Michael Curtiz, 1939), *Elizabeth* (dir. Shekar Kapur, 1998), and *Shakespeare in Love* (dir. John Madden, Jr., 1998).

I

Gender has perhaps not been taken into account by critics and historians working on early modern censorship, presumably because writing and painting were largely male activities; conversely, critics working on gender and Elizabeth's image have not taken censorship into account.[7] Censorship, it is assumed, was a practice of men censoring other men. Elizabeth may have been involved in cases of censorship such as John Stubbes' *The Discovery of a Gaping Gulf Whereby England is like to be swallowed by another French marriage, if the Lord forbid not the banns by letting her Majesty see the sin and punishment thereof,* Dr John Hayward's *The First Part of the Life and Reigne of King Henry the Fourth,* and Spenser's *Mother Hubberd's Tale,* and she may have regulated painting, but that was for reasons of state. It was the fact that she was a monarch that required such regulation. Her gender had no bearing on the matter. Yet censorship is always gendered in early modern commentary, if only in an explicitly male way. Writers refer to texts as being gelded or castrated.[8] If it is clear that censorship was often gendered male, however, whether it might be gendered female remains more difficult to determine. To be sure, Elizabeth was not alone among Renaissance monarchs in her desire to regulate the production of paintings of her, and the difficulties she had controlling the dissemination of her likeness had more to do with her failure to appoint a court painter with a monopoly, as the Valois monarchs did and Louis XIV after them, than it did with the fact that she was a woman. Nevertheless, her regulations of her portraits were specifically tied to her status as a woman, becoming acute, as Roy Strong notes, after she was no longer of marriageable age.[9] Hence most of the controls and regulations came into being in the 1590s. Though one may argue that the regulation was due to reasons of state and anxiety about the succession (no one wanted to remind the populace that Elizabeth was getting close to death and still had no successor in place), there is evidence she took these portraits to be personal insults. In his monumental *History of the World,* Sir Walter Raleigh writes, for example, of Queen Elizabeth's response to some portraits of her she disliked: 'pictures of Queen Elizabeth made by unskilful and common painters were, *by her own commandment,* knocked in pieces and cast into the fire' (my emphasis). Similarly, there existed to 'her great offence' similar portraits, for in 1596, on Elizabeth's orders, the Council seized and destroyed a number of pictures that showed her looking old, frail and ill.[10]

Critics working on Elizabethan censorship have recently argued that censorship was located in the politics of personality and patronage factions. Yet they remain fixated on a narrowly political notion of transgression, debating which censor did the censoring and which document and/or political event prompted the censorship. While such archival work may be quite valuable, however speculative it will necessarily remain, I suggest that locating censorship in patronage networks and personal conflicts means that censorship necessarily exceeds rational political calculations. The censor has an unconscious, after all, and any political calculation the censor makes is part of a fantasy of control. Elizabeth's stake in portraits of herself and of others is about her personal interest in the symbolic purity of her image, not only about a given discourse or narrowly political problem such as the succession.

Viewed in the light of patronage factions understood to be always already gendered, Elizabeth's desire to regulate her image may be seen to extend not only to paintings and miniatures but to the display of the image; similarly, what counts as an image extends from an oil painting or a miniature to live appearances at court (which were themselves, as New Historicists have reminded us, highly theatrical performances), to the circulation of books that metaphorically reflected (or were thought to reflect) on Elizabeth, to the performance of plays (Ben Jonson was criticized for bringing Elizabeth onstage at the end of *Every Man Out of His Humour*).

Consider, for example, Sir John Harington's translation of Arisoto's *Orlando Furioso*. Here Elizabeth's concern is for the morals of her ladies in waiting. 'To amuse the ladies of the court', Harington circulated the manuscript of his bawdy translation of the story of Giocondo from the twenty-eighth book of *Orlando Furioso* amongst the Queen's maids of honour. Elizabeth was, the tale goes, shocked when she read it, and she declared that it was an improper text for young maidens to read. The saucy poet was reprimanded and commanded not to come to court again until he had translated Ariosto's entire work – which took him another year.[11]

Elizabeth's intervention here, preventing the ladies from reading Harington's translation, and her mild and rather paradoxical punishment of Harington (paradoxical in that she demands he finish the offensive translation rather than amend it or stop writing it) is a function not only of Elizabeth's concern with her age and beauty but of her being at the centre of patronage factions in which access of courtiers to her maids of honour was a constant concern. Elizabeth regulated their bodies, how men might use them not only sexually but as spies and to construct their own masculine aristocratic images.

It is worth adding that Harington wrote to court ladies for their help. He asked Lady Russell, for example, to intercede on his behalf with Lord Burghley about the scandal over *The Metamorphosis of Ajax*.[12] Similarly, Harington used knowledge of Elizabeth's displeasure over the *Orlando Furioso* to give added spice to a copy he later sent to Lady Jane Rogers, a copy which made appealing by suggesting they were getting the uncensored version. This one had parts for their female eyes only: 'I have added a few others [passages] that were showd to our Soveraigne Lady, and some, that I durst never show any Ladie, but you two. And so wishing you to lock me up as safe in your love, as I know you will lay up this booke safe in your chest I commend me to you.'[13] Following up Patricia Fumerton's point that Elizabethan sonnets circulating in manuscripts were considered to be analogous to miniatures themselves considered to be secrets, we may see that Harington regards his manuscript in similar terms, with the Lady's chest as the locket containing Harington's secret manuscript, though perhaps not exactly a miniature one.

Elizabeth's regulation of her own image was inseparable from her regulation of other women's images. Elizabeth's rage at the secret marriages of maids of honor such as Elizabeth Throckmorton and Elizabeth Vernon is well known. Her banishment of her rival for Leicester, Lettice Knowlys, appears to have been based in part on Knowlys' ability to compete for male attention by constructing a royal image for herself. When Lettice dared to appear in court sumptuously attired, as befitted a countess, and attended by a large train of servants, the Queen advanced upon her like an avenging angel and boxed her ears, shouting, 'As but one sun lights the East, so I shall have but one queen in England'.[14] Elizabeth's refusal to allow Essex to publish a pamphlet describing his heroic exploits (p. 424) may in part be regarded as a function of her jealousy about his attention to other women, as may the destruction of prints of Essex by Thomas Cockson in August 1600 by order of the Privy Council. Richard Dutton speculates that the Privy Council was 'particularly anxious to keep [these] out of the people's hands', but 'the people' are of course gendered, and even if women were not then enfranchised, Elizabeth may have been galled at the thought of their popular support for her love, jealous that he should be getting affection and admiration that were rightly hers.[15]

Elizabeth's concern for her image in relation to those of other women might be put on a continuum with the censorship of images of other women who might compete with her such as the Virgin Mary. For example, on 10 August 1579, Elizabeth went on progress and visited

Thetford and stayed with a Catholic named Rockwood, owner of nearby Euston Hall in Suffolk. During the visit someone found a statue of the Virgin Mary in the house, which was brought into the hall and held up for Elizabeth to see. She ordered it to be burnt, which was done immediately, 'to the unspeakable joy of everyone'. After she had gone, Rockwood was arrested and imprisoned in Norwich gaol until his death 20 years later. His estates were declared forfeit to the crown.[16]

In maintaining that locating censorship in gender-inflected personal conflicts and patronage networks necessarily expands the range of censorship practices, I do not mean to suggest that there is a core personality, a private self we could identify as Elizabeth's that is doing the censoring. The display of images is caught up in a complex dynamic in which the personal and private are put on public display, a dynamic which complicates the possibility of Eizabeth ever being able to uncensor the meanings of images of her ladies even as it reveals Elizabeth to be engaged in the surveillance of these images, the circulation of which reflected upon her image of herself. Consider Elizabeth's response to a miniature worn by one of her ladies in waiting, Lady Darby. In a letter to the Earl of Shrewsbury, William Browne tells the following story about a locket in which Darby had a miniature of her uncle, Sir Robert Cecil:

> The occasion was, as I hear, that the young Lady of Darby wearing about her neck, in her bosom, a picture which was in a dainty tablet, the Queen, espying it, asked what fyne jewell that was. The Lady Darby was curious to excuse the shoewing of itt, butt the Queen would have itt, and fynding itt to be Mr. Secretarye's, snatcht itt away, and tyed it uppon her shoe, and walked long with itt there; then she toke it thence, and pinned itt on her elbow, and wore it som tyme there also; which Mr. Secretary being told of, made these verses, and had Hales to sing them in his chamber ... I do boldly send these things to your Lordship which I wold not do to any els, for I heare they are very secrett.

This is a case where Elizabeth engaged in the surveillance of another woman and her secret, and Elizabeth is on both sides of censorship: she is both the keeper of the secret and the picklock of the secret, one that is disclosed to us, but perhaps not to Elizabeth. As Patricia Fumerton comments on this letter, 'what exactly Browne means when he affirms "these things ... are very secrett" is itself secret' (p. 70). Elizabeth's adoption of the miniature is not only withdrawal into a private realm of her own but also a public pursuit of a personal secret and a display of her trophy. The public display of the miniature in a locket is also a site wherein a personal conflict between Elizabeth and one her ladies is also displayed. As if she assumed that the miniature of Cecil were Cecil himself, Elizabeth invites us to decode her display, implying by wearing the miniature that he is closer to Elizabeth – at her elbow, on, perhaps even under her foot – than he is to Darby.[17]

II

If introducing gender as a variable expands the meaning of censorship and brings in its relation to other related practices such as surveillance and iconoclasm, it also is perhaps becoming clear that linking gender and censorship does not simply confirm feminist accounts of censorship, since it does not simply put men on the side of patriarchal kinds of censorship and women, particularly, feminists, on the side of the censored. Ironically, addressing Elizabeth as censor might even be thought to produce a sexist account of her censorship. That is, her concerns as a censor arise out of what are stereotypically female concerns: age, fading beauty, vanity, the inability to bear children (especially sons), rivalry with other women, issuing in catfights; suspiciousness verging on, perhaps even crossing into paranoia, and so on. To see Elizabeth's censorship as being directed at other women, some critics might argue, is just another sexist way of delegitimating her as a woman ruler, one that harkens back to arguably misogynistic nineteenth-century operas like *Roberto Devereaux*, in which Elizabeth manages, too late to save Essex, to overcome her jealousy of her rival for his affections, or *Maria Stuarda*, the performance of which has historically always displaced the political conflict between the queens by the spectacle of the duelling divas playing them.[18] One could argue further that there is something of a double standard here: female patrons such as Catherine de Medici or female rulers such as Marie-Antoinette and Catherine the Great were similarly subject to misogynistic representations of their sexuality. (One wonders what *Penthouse* publisher Bob Guccione's projected film about Catherine the Great will look like. One assumes that horses will at some point make their way into the film.) Yet these female rulers are pathologized in ways that male rulers are not. The jealousy of Louis XIV, who exiled any courtier who dared to look at a woman Louis desired for himself, and the libertinism of Louis XV don't get the same attention. Similarly, Elizabeth's censorship, however severe, was arguably less severe than her father's, cutting off a hand once or imprisoning someone certainly being better than cutting off a head.

While I would agree that linking gender, sexuality and censorship does not necessarily reinforce feminist modes of criticism, I do not wish to shore up avowedly feminist moves to defend Elizabeth (or women rulers like her) since these will likely turn out to be counter-productive. For example, down-playing any censorship in which Elizabeth may have engaged tends to make her a victim, just like a sentimental, long-suffering heroine of a nineteenth-century novel or opera, and this redemptive move has quite reactionary implications considering that the suffering woman is a monarch.[19] Similarly, the charge that Elizabeth is unfairly singled out for certain kinds of criticism because she is a woman ignores the extent to which her sexuality, like Marie-Antoinette's after, could be a focus of political subversion. Although no one ever wrote a tract about Elizabeth like the scurrilous *Royal Dildo*, in which Marie-Antoinette complains about her husband, Louis XVI's impotence, Elizabeth was the subject of rumours and slanders about her involvement with Leicester, and certainly some people thought she was not a virgin at all. These iconoclastic attacks on her image were not simply misogynistic attacks on her as a *female* ruler. As Christopher Highley has shown in an essay on the circulation of Elizabeth's royal image in Ireland, the Old English Catholic community manipulated 'royal symbols to protest the acts of the queen and her representatives'. In July 1596, for example, William Lydon, the Bishop of Cork and Ross, complained to Lord Hunsdon that, during an annual inspection of school books, he had discovered 'Her majesty's style and title torn out of all the grammars, to the number of 74 in one school; the leaf in the grammar quite torn out, which containeth in it, Elizabeth, by the grace of God Queen of England, France, and Ireland, Defender of the Faith, &c., and in the end of the leaf, God save the Queen. Whereupon I caused search to be made in all the schools within my diocese, and found them all torn out, although they came new from the merchant's shop.'[20] Similarly, rebels hung the Queen's portrait behind a door rather than on it, and desecrated a statue of her. Attempts were made to harm the Queen by stabbing, burning or otherwise destroying her image, and obscene and blasphemous portraits of Elizabeth were displayed on the Continent. Destruction or denigration of her image by those she ruled was not necessarily anti-feminist, then.

It is worth pointing out that later attacks on portraits of women were also motivated in part for political and ostensibly feminist reasons. For example, in 1981, a young man ripped a hole in Bryan Organ's portrait of Princess Diana in the National Gallery. He wanted to draw attention to the deprivations in Northern Ireland caused by the English.[21] Similarly, the suffragette Mary Richardson slashed Velasquez's *Rokeby Venus* in

March 1914 for political motives. In an interview 40 years later, she said 'I wanted to show that the most beautiful woman on canvas was nothing compared with the death of one woman prisoner [Mrs Pankhurst]. I wanted to draw attention to the plight of Mrs. Pankhurst, our leader, who was then in an undergound cell green with mould in Holloway Prison. We believed she was dying.'[22] She also gave another motive that explained her particular choice of the Velasquez: 'I didn't like the way men visitors to the gallery gaped at her all day long'. Is this a feminist motive? Or evidence of her prudery? Hard to say, I think.

If these modern examples make possible a defence of iconoclastic attacks on Elizabeth and other female rulers, they also complicate that defence in so far as the attacks rather oddly conflate the image and the person represented by it. Elizabethans customarily doffed their hats at painted portraits of their superiors, and modern critics in some ways continue to pay images this homage: those who wish to honour images of Elizabeth as a powerful female ruler tend to share with her iconoclastic attackers a similar over-valuation of her image. The personal may well be political, but what some feminists take to be the political may turn out to be deeply unsettled by the personal.

III

It is not my intention, I hope it is clear, to defend criticisms of Elizabeth and her image by reading attacks on her sexuality as political attacks on the ruling elite, since that defence effectively forecloses an analysis of female sexuality. A too rapid sublimation of sexuality into a progressive, republican politics is the flipside of criticism that sees any attack on women in power (or women writers) as reactionary and anti-feminist. Mass culture constructions of Elizabeth can, I think, suggest a different way of thinking about the relation between her gender and sexuality and the censorship of her image. I want to turn specifically to portrayals of Elizabeth as a censor in the films *The Private Lives of Elizabeth and Essex*, the final episode of the BBC *Elizabeth R*, the end of *Elizabeth*, and *Shakespeare in Love*.

Both *The Private Lives of Elizabeth and Essex* and the episode 'Sweet England's Pride' of *Elizabeth R* contain scenes about censorship in relation to the Essex rebellion. Each takes a very different view of Elizabeth as censor. In the former, Elizabeth is against censorship, and her wisdom in this matter is an instance of her ability to keep in line male courtiers who think she is mad and about to lose her crown. After a shot of trumpets in silhouette announcing her entry in the middle of night at a court which resembles the palace of the Wizard of Oz more than it does Whitehall, we get a long shot of a regal Elizabeth, and, as upbeat music plays, the camera tracks backwards as Elizabeth nears her throne. After she sits down and complains about the gloomy facial expressions, she turns to Burleigh and addresses him:

> **Elizabeth**: Burleigh, you at least should be merry. I hear you've been attending the theatre.
> **Burleigh**: No madam.
> **Elizabeth**: But you did forbid the performance of *Richard II* by Master Shakespeare and his players. Why?
> **Burleigh**: The … the play is treason, your majesty. It shows the dethronement of a king.
> **Elizabeth**: What then? Are my people so easily led that they would run from the theatre to pull their Queen from out of her chair? Who is there here who fears a rebellion against me? Not myself, certainly.
> **Burleigh**: But there are mutterings, your grace.
> **Elizabeth**: Let them mutter. Let them cry out. When they've worn themselves out, they'll get drunk and go to bed, sleep soundly, and wake up the wiser.

Wiser than her anxious men at court who are concerned only about their own hides, Elizabeth dispenses with theatre censorship because she knows her people, including the rebellious Earl of Essex, pose no real threat to her.

In contrast to Bette Davis's Elizabeth, who has no need to close the theatres, *Elizabeth R*'s Glenda Jackson portrays Elizabeth as a jealous, censorious spinster. A scene involving the censorship of Hayward's *Life of Henry IV* intersects with a plot concerning one of her ladies in waiting, Elizabeth Vernon. At court, Essex tells Southampton he has been appointed Earl Marshal and will go to Ireland. After Essex leaves, Vernon catches up with the Earl of Southampton. He has been using her to gain intelligence about Elizabeth's view of Essex, who has been out of favour, and now Vernon tells him that she is pregnant. Southampton says he will marry her in secret, and says they can count on Elizabeth's sympathy as a woman. But Vernon rebuffs him, pointing out that Elizabeth has never had children and probably couldn't have had any even if she had married. Southampton manages to console her, but in an aside to the camera, the cad makes it clear that he intends to hire an actor to play a priest.

This conversation is followed by a scene between Sir Francis Bacon and Sir Robert Cecil about Elizabeth's concern over Hayward's book and her own translation of Horace's *Ars Poetica*. Bacon is called in as an expert, and his scepticism is juxtaposed with Elizabeth's paranoia.

> **Elizabeth:** This book (pause) History of Henry IV, printer John Hayward, dedication to my Lord Essex. This book contains a detailed description of the deposition of Richard II. Read the preface, bottom of the page.
> **Bacon:** (quoting) 'Most illustrious Earl, with your name adorning the front of our Henry, he may go forth to the public happier and safer.'
> **Elizabeth:** Meaning, Mr Bacon?
> **Bacon:** That the book may be well-received.
> **Elizabeth:** It could also mean that had Henry IV had the names and titles of my Lord Essex, his right to the throne would have been recognized. This book is treason.
> **Bacon:** It is history, madam. Richard II was deposed.
> **Elizabeth:** Of all the history in England, they choose this one incident? The idea behind it is treason.
> **Bacon:** T'would be hard to prove.
> **Elizabeth:** Then it must be forced from him.

Bacon counsels her to charge the writer with theft, as he plagiarized the works, and before Elizabeth can agree or disagree, Lady Vernon enters and Elizabeth becomes apopletic:

> **Vernon:** I'm sorry, your majesty, I thought.
> **Elizabeth:** Thought?! 'Damned' should be your word, milady tart.
> **Vernon:** Your majesty.
> **Elizabeth:** Get out. (To Bacon) She has used these rooms for a brothel. See how she swells from the profit of her fornication. God's death, get out! I wish that book suppressed. You will find me a legal cause.

Her desire to censor seems an irrational symptom of her questionable desire to punish the body of a lady-in-waiting whose desires she has failed to control.

Elizabeth and *Shakespeare in Love* replay this contrast between a censoring Elizabeth and a Elizabeth who has no need of it, with Cate Blanchett as a woman who has to censor her own body to rule as a Queen and Dame Judi Dench as a wise elder stateswoman who is above censorship (which is here only the product of the Master of the Revels base motives) and is a fine judge of romance and theatre. Breaking with traditional treatments of Elizabeth's virginity, *Elizabeth* gives us an 'uncensored' account of her early love life and ends with the story of her construction of a royal image: the film ends with the subtitle 'the Virgin Queen'. *Elizabeth* takes an iconoclastic turn, showing Elizabeth having sex with Robert Dudley, but it does so in order to show how Elizabeth becomes a national icon and at what personal cost. The film ends with a freeze frame, as if she had become an oil painting, and the credits begin with a frame first of the title Elizabeth, then the subtitle 'the Virgin Queen'. In a quite post- Diana way, the film makes us see her suffer, even die, Mozart's *Requiem* suggests, in order to become an icon capable of uniting the country. The religious imagery is pointed. In a discussion between Elizabeth and Walsingham, we see glimpses of a close-up shot of a statue of the Virgin Mary followed by a close-up shot of Elizabeth, and in the following sequence, we see Elizabeth made up in white to look like the statue. Furthermore, the scene of her ladies-in-waiting cutting her hair recalls the film's opening scene of a woman Protestant martyr having her hair brutally shaved off with a straight razor. Elizabeth too, we are to infer, is a martyr.

In *Shakespeare in Love*, Elizabeth is represented even more positively than in *The Private Lives of Elizabeth and Essex*. In the more recent film, Elizabeth is an enlightened, older monarch – she stands entirely outside of romance – who overrules the theatre censor. After the performance of *Romeo and Juliet*, Sir Edmond Tilney and his 'cops' enter the theatre and shut it down on the grounds that the actor playing Juliet is a woman. When Tilney makes his move to arrest the actors 'in the name of Elizabeth', Elizabeth interrupts him and rises from her seat: 'Have a care with my name, you will wear it out. The Queen of England does not attend exhibitions of public lewdness, so something is out of joint. Come here. Let me look at you.' 'Yes, the illusion is remarkable and your error, Mr. Tilney, is easily forgiven, but I know something of a woman in a man's profession, yes, by God, I do know about that.' She later tells Wessex he has lost his wager as to 'whether a play can show the very truth and nature of love'. As she leaves, she says 'And tell Mr. Shakespeare something more cheerful next time, for Twelfth Night.'

What do these clips of Elizabeth as censor tell us about gender, sexuality and censorship, then? Viewed from the standpoint of feminist criticism and historicist criticism, nothing much necessarily changes. One could always do standard feminist readings of these films, lamenting their various perceived failings and/or celebrating their strengths. Bette Davis's Elizabeth, while strong, twitches uncontrollably, is obsessed with her looks, and manages to unite with another woman in a bond of sisterliness only through their shared sufferings from the love of a man they both prize above each other; Glenda Jackson's Elizabeth is a vain, petty, tyrannical and paranoid bitch; Cate Blanchett's Elizabeth is a timid, suffering martyr (while the educated viewer may realize that many of her costumes are derived from actual paintings, the only portrait we actually see in the film is a massive one of her father, Henry VIII); and Dame Judi Dench's Elizabeth is less powerful, if more humane, than usual. In contrast to the Elizabeth in the earlier film *Fire Over England*, who makes decisions about sending men to war or executing princes and aristocrats, Elizabeth's power is narrowly domestic. The most difficult questions she decides in *Shakespeare in Love* are whether Viola can go to Virginia and who won a wager over whether a play can truly represent romantic love.[23]

Conversely, one could try to redeem these films as feminist. Bette Davis's and Glenda Jackson's performances could be regarded as precursors of the modern-day 'bitch' celebrated by twenty-something (post?) feminists such as Elizabeth Wurtzel. Cate Blanchett's Elizabeth could be seen as a case-study of what happens to women who assume power in patriarchal regimes; and in *Shakespeare in Love*, Elizabeth exerts an enormous power over the theatre and the genre of plays produced there.

Critics interested in the films for their accounts of censorship might find less to make use of, and may perhaps want to sniff their noses and simply turn away from them. To be sure, no one in her or his right mind would go to these examples to learn much about the censorship of *Richard II* or of Hayward's *Life of Henry IV*.[24] In *Elizabeth R*, the Hayward episode is loosely based on an anecdote recorded twice by Bacon, and the screenwriter gets the printer wrong (it was John Wolfe, not Hayward).[25]

I think it is worth asking, however, what these films (and other films and novels like them) can tell us about feminist criticism of Elizabeth and historicist criticism of censorship. Bringing media representations of Elizabeth to bear on feminist and historicist criticism enables us to ask what are their enabling and unconscious narrative assumptions, their cultural fantasies about women and censorship. And it may lead us to conclude that feminist critics and historians of censorship don't make very good novelists, librettists or screenwriters. As a rule, they do not allow much room, that is, for human complexity or for indeterminacy of meaning, relying instead, in the case of feminism, on pop-psych notions of feminism as female self-assertion, self-empowerment and self-esteem, and in the case of censorship criticism, a kind of paranoid assumption about meaning and communication.

Let us consider feminist criticism first. Feminist critics have often focused on Renaissance debates about the status and worth of women and on women patrons, and have tended to look for subversion of patriarchal authority.[26] The questions feminists tend to ask often mirror those asked by critics who look at censorship: how much autonomy did women have? How far could a woman go in opposing patriarchy? These questions rest on the assumption that women who are repressed by patriarchy may be empowered by having as role models 'strong', resisting women from the past, and that women's voices were effectively censored either by patriarchy or by a canonical tradition that excluded and/or marginalized women writers.

Yet it is not entirely clear that the goal of recovering repressed voices from the early modern past has much political purchase in the postmodern present. As Jayne Lewis writes at the close of her book attempting to account for the enduring interest in Mary, Queen of Scots: 'Since British women today can hardly be described as excluded from, unknown to, history, their consciousness of Mary Stuart seems to originate in something deeper, older, darker than political exclusion – in a matter, finally, of spilled blood, of a hole in the bottom of the historical mind' (*Mary Queen of Scots*, p. 227). Lewis goes on to conclude that it is the immaterial desire for the lost mother than drives the interest in Mary. Without necessarily agreeing with Lewis's conclusion, I think her point about the inadequacy of political exclusion as an explanation could usefully be broadened to ask what kinds of concerns beyond political emancipation produce such a wide interest across so many media in figures like Elizabeth I. One could still demur that the romantic fantasies about women and women rulers in the films of Elizabeth we have considered are in any case rather obviously sexist. But any critique of media-produced sexism seems rather weak when it comes to heterosexual relations and romance. Even if they do not transcend sexism, these films and other mass media constructions like them often take up a huge terrain which feminism of all kinds has unsuccessfully engaged, much less transformed, namely, conflicts between women as produced by hetero-sexual romance. The catfight, female masochism, beauty, age, paranoia and so on are all issues which have been effectively censored inside feminist discourses (except in so far as women who fight with other women in order to align themselves with men are said to have 'false consciousness'). As Cora Kaplan points out, female sexuality has historically been erased from feminist discourse since its inception in the nineteenth century.[27] Moreover, mass media accounts of Elizabeth implicitly challenge the model of censorship on which feminist critique rests. The notion that patriarchy is exclusively on the side of the censor, women exclusively on the side of the censored, has led many feminist critics (particularly those over 40) to regard any challenge to their views as so much anti-feminist 'backlash', and thus left them deaf to any questions posed by (especially) younger feminists (much less men) that might enable them to rethink their own accounts of what feminist liberation might now be.[28]

The four film clips about Elizabeth we have examined can also instructively be brought to bear on some uncritically-held assumptions implicit in much work on Renaissance theatrical and print censorship.[29] Critics and historians tend to make the following corollary assumptions: one, that there is a point at which one could say what happened, if there were enough documents; two, the meanings of language (especially writing) and History are transparent;[30] three, subjects are centred, fully conscious, and know exactly why they do what they do; four, subjects do one thing for one reason; five, a *cordon sanitaire* separates the grey archive from glittery mass media performances, History from fiction, scholarly seriousness from screen-writing silliness. These lead critics to ask the following questions: did censorship occur? If so, who did it? What kind of censorship was it, theatrical or press? How effective was censorship? Was it systematic or capricious? Was censorship benign or repressive? If a text we now take to be subversive went uncensored or was censored after being licensed, why?

At best, critics working on censorship produce accounts that remain speculative: maybe 'x' was the censor, maybe 'x' censored 'y' text for 'z' reason. But the more rigorous the critic, the more likely he or she is to conclude that nothing can be known about anything regarding censorship with certainty. The critic's commitment to a rational sphere of political discourse and conflict itself tends to become irrational, resembling more and more a paranoid delusion, what we might call *Elizabeth A(R)lington Road*. Although critics strive to arrive at a point where they could say with confidence 'this is what happened, this is why "x" censored "y"', it is in fact the impossibility of ever arriving at this point that makes this kind of inquiry possible; that is, the self-defeating nature of this mode of criticism enables it to continue. (I say it is self-defeating because writing is not transparent and because criticism of censorship is necessarily conflictual: no matter how many documents there were, those documents would still have to be interpreted, and no consensus about their meaning would ever arrive, anymore than it has thus far, since to have something publishable to say, a critic must disagree, however slightly, with critics who have researched the material before she or he has.)

Let me conclude by clarifying what I am and am not saying about what we might learn about feminist and historicist criticism and about censorship by studying mass media performances of Elizabeth's image. I am not saying that bringing these mass media constructions to bear on criticism will improve work in the archive or produce a superior account of Elizabeth, one fuller or somehow more historical or more true. I am saying that these constructions may at least open up new scenarios when answering long-standing questions, and lead us to ask new questions and explore new problems regarding what counts as knowledge of Elizabeth I.

Notes

1. See Barbara Hodgdon 'Romancing the Queen', in *The Shakespeare Trade* (Philadelphia: University of Pennsylvania Press, 1998); Nicola J. Watson, 'Victoria and the Cultural Memory of Elizabeth I', in Margaret Homans and Adrienne Munich, eds, *Remaking Victoria* (Cambridge: Cambridge University Press, 1997), pp. 79–104; Jayne Lewis, *Mary Queen of Scots* (London: Routledge, 1999); Adrienne Munich, *Queen Victoria's Secrets* (New York: Columbia University Press, 1996); and Margaret Homan, *Royal Representations: Queen Victoria and British Culture, 1837–1876* (Chicago: University of Chicago Press, 1997). Nicola J. Watson has a book forthcoming entitled *England's Elizabeth: National Fictions of Elizabeth I, 1603–1990*.

2. There is a vast array of historical novels and romance novels in which Elizabeth appears as a character, including Robin Maxwell's *The Secret Diary of Anne Boleyn* (New York: Scribner, 1998) and its sequel *The Queen's Bastard* (New York: Scribner, 2000), as well as Donna Valentino's *Queen of My Heart* (New York: Harper Paperbacks, 1996), a time-travel romance in which the main character, Dante, betrothed to Elizabeth Tudor, finds himself in Arizona in 1887, where he hooks up with 'a feisty redheaded ex-circus performer named Gloriana Carlisle.' Should he return to England to claim the Queen as his wife, the novel asks, or stay in Arizona with the queen of his heart? See also Susan Kay, *Legacy* (New York: Avon Books, 1985); Brenda Joyce, *The Game* (New York: Avon Books, 1994), Malia Martin, *Much Ado About Love* (New York: Avon Books, 2000); Michelle Jaffe, *The Water Nymph* (New York: Pocket Books, 2000); Rosalind Miles, *I, Elizabeth* (New York: Doubleday, 1994); Faye Kellerman, *The Quality of Mercy* (New York: Fawcett, 1989); Julie Beard, *The Romance of the Rose* (New York: Berkely, 1998); Elizabeth Byrd, *Immortal Queen: a Novel of Mary Queen of Scots* (New York: Ballantine Books, 1956); Reay Tannahill, *Fatal Majesty: a Novel of Mary Queen of Scots* (New York: St. Martin's Press, 1999) and Margaret George, *Mary Queen of Scotland and the Isles* (New York: St. Martins, 1992). See also Victoria Holt's *My Enemy, the Queen*, as well as romance novels in which Elizabeth appears as a character: George P. Garrett's *Death of the Fox: a Novel of Elizabeth and Raleigh* (1991), Patricia Finney's *Firedrake's Eye* (1992) and *Unicorn's Blood* (1998), Margaret George's *Mary, Queen of Scotland and the Isles* (1997). The mass-marketing of the Renaissance extends to biographies of monarchs such as Carrolly Erickson's studies of Henry VIII, Anne Boleyn, Mary Tudor, and Elizabeth I, Alison Weir's *Six Wives* (dir. Waris Hussein, 1973), *Elizabeth* (dir. Shekhar Kapur, 1998), *Black Adder, The Prince and the Pauper, Shakespeare in Love,* and a forthcoming film about

Mary Stuart (with Glenn Close). Since the first decade of this century, there have been films about the English Renaissance monarchy with courtship at their center. Films include *Young Bess* (dir. George Sidney II, 1953), *The Virgin Queen* (dir. Henry Koster, 1955), *Elizabeth R* (dir. Claude Watham, 1971), *Henry VIII and His Six Wives* (dir. Charles Jarrott, 1969), *Les Amours de la reine Elizabeth* (dir. Henri Desfontaines and Louis Mercanton, 1912), *Konigin Elizabeth's Doechter* (dir. Johan Gildmeijer, 1915), *Anna Boleyn* (dir. Ernest Lubitsch, 1923), *The Loves of Mary, Queen of Scots* (dir. Denison Clift, 1923), *Drake of England* (dir. Arthur B. Woods, 1935), *Mary of Scotland* (dir. John Ford, 1936), *Fire Over England* (dir. William K. Howard, 1937), *The Private Lives of Elizabeth and Essex* (dir. Michael Curtiz, 1939), *The Sea Hawk* (dir. Michael Curtiz, 1940), *Young Bess* (dir. George Sidney II, 1953), *The Virgin Queen* (dir. Henry Koster, 1955), *A Man for All Seasons* (dir. Fred Zinneman, 1966), *Anne of the Thousand Days* (dir. Charles Jarrott, 1969), *Mary, Queen of Scots* (dir. Charles Jarrott, 1971). Derek Jarman also represents Elizabeth I in *Jubilee* (1989), and Sally Potter's *Orlando* (1991) includes Quentin Crisp as a 'queen' Elizabeth in drag.

3. Barbara Hodgdon, for example, explicitly excludes romance novels, and Jayne Lewis simply ignores them, as she does film and opera.

4. Conversely, one could argue that mass media constructions of the Renaissance often have a progressive potential. See, for examples, Vicki Leon, *Outrageous Women of the Renaissance* (New York: John Wiley & Sons, 1999) and Vicki Leon, *Uppity Women of the Renaissance* (Berkeley, Calif.: Conari Press, 1999), as well as a novel about a thirteenth-century teenage aristocratic girl marketed to girls 'twelve and up' written by Karen Cushman entitled *Catherine, Called Birdy* (New York: Harper Trophy, 1994).

5. The private lives of Renaissance people has similarly been taken up as a legitimate object of historical inquiry. The success of Natalie Davis's *The Return of Martin Guerre* (1983) and Judith Brown's *Immodest Acts: the Life of a Lesbian Nun in Renaissance Italy* (1986) inspired a number of like-minded studies, including Gene Brucker's *Giovanni and Lusanna: Love and Marriage in Renaissance Florence* (1986), Richard Kagan's *Lucretia's Dream: Politics and Prophecy in Sixteenth-century Spain* (1990), Margaret F. Rosenthal's *The Honest Courtesan: Veronica Franco, Citizen and Writer in Sixteenth-Century Venice* (1991), Davis's own *Women on the Margins: Three Sixteenth-century Lives* (1995), and Stephen Ozment's *The Buergermeister's Daughter* (1996).

6. See, for example, Michael Levine, 'Freud and the Scene of Censorship', in Richard Burt, ed., *The Administration of Aesthetics: Censorship, Political Criticism, and the Public Sphere* (Minneapolis: University of Minnesota, 1994). Levine develops this essay in his book *Writing Through Repression: Literature, Censorship, Psychoanalysis* (Baltimore: Johns Hopkins University Press, 1994).

7. For a recent example see Louis A. Montrose, 'Idols of the Queen: Policy, Gender, and the Picturing of Elizabeth I', *Representations* 68 (Fall 1999), 108–61.

8. See Arnold Hunt's fine chapter in this collection, for example.

9. See *Gloriana: the Portraits of Queen Elizabeth I* (London: Thames and Hudson, 1987), p. 20.

10. While there was a misogynistic tradition of representing older women as grotesque, there were plenty of exceptions. Rembrandt painted an elderly

couple, for example, in separate portraits and another portrait of a woman who was 83. In a late self-portrait, he also complicated a misogynistic tradition by revising the painting of a pupil so that the old woman is barely visible, while his own face looks unusually feminine. Closer to Elizabeth I, elderly English Ladies had their portraits painted quite realistically without any disrespect. Elizabeth's vanity in her old age is documented by the French ambassador De Maisse. On 15 December 1597, he encountered an ageing Elizabeth all decked out like a porn star: 'She received him in a gown of silver gauze in the Italian style, edged with wide bands of gold lace.' It had 'slashed sleeves lined with red taffeta', and was open in the front to display a white damask kirtle, beneath which was a chemise, both open to the waist, exposing 'the whole of her bosom', which was somewhat wrinkled. As she talked 'she would open the front of this robe with her hands, as if she were too hot', so that he could see her stomach right down to her navel. De Maisse could only conclude that she was trying to bewitch him with her faded charms. 'So far as may be, she keeps her dignity,' but 'her face is very aged: it is long and thin, and her teeth are very yellow and irregular. Many of them are missing, so that one cannot understand her easily when she speaks.' Cited in Alison Weir, *The Life of Elizabeth I* (New York: Ballantine, 1998), p. 431.

11. The anecdote is recorded in John Harington, *Nugae Antiquae*, vol. 1 (New York: AMS Press, 1966), p. x.
12. He entreats her 'Honor, to send his Lordship the rest of it [his MS], which I have, before now, for the moste part of it read unto you'. See *The Letters and Epigrams of Sir John Harington together with The Prayse of Private Life*, ed. Norman Egbert McClure (Philadelphia: University of Pennsylvania Press, 1930), p. 65.
13. Ibid., pp. 86–7.
14. See Weir, *Elizabeth I*, p. 323.
15. Richard Dutton, *Mastering the Revels: the Regulation and Censorship of English Renaissance Drama* (Iowa City: University of Iowa Press, 1991), p. 311. Similarly, when Elizabeth caught Essex flirting with Katherine Bridges and Elizabeth Russell, two of her ladies, she shouted at him in disgust, slapped Bridges (who later became Essex's mistress), and banished the girls from court for three days. And William Fenton wrote to John Harington about how he might advise Lady Mary Howard to behave at court so as not to continue to suffer Elizabeth's wrath: 'she must not entertaine the earle [of Essex],' Fenton writes, 'in any conversation, but shunne his companye; and moreover be less careful in attiringe her own person, for this seemethe as done more to win the earl, than her mistresses good will.' Fenton adds that 'since the Irish affairs, [Elizabeth] seemeth more froward than commonlie she used to bear herself toward other women, nor dothe she holde them in discourse with such familiar matter but often chides for small neglects; in such wise, as to make these fair maids often cry and bewail in piteous sort.'
16. Weir, *Elizabeth I*, p. 315.
17. There is a portrait (artist unknown, 1590s) of Lord Burghley with a cameo portrait of Elizabeth pinned on his hat. See anonymous, *Tudor and Jacobean Portraits in the National Gallery Collection at Montacute House* (London: National Portrait Gallery, 1999), p. 15.
18. The opera was censored and the dress rehearsal ended with the two divas, Ronzi de Begnis and Del Sere, in fisticuffs on the stage. See the Earl of

Harewood and Anthony Peattie, eds, *The New Kobbe's Opera Book* (New York: G. P. Putnam's Sons, 1997), p. 196, and Antonia Fraser, 'Mary Queen of Scots in Fact and Fiction', in *Mary Stuart*, programme notes for the English National Opera Performance, 1998.

19. These are also the terms in which mass market fiction often frames these rulers. For example, in a brief afterword to her novel *Mary, Queen of Scotland and the Isles*, Margeret George asks: 'Was [Mary] the depraved Jezebel of [John] Knox's imagination, steeped in folly and lust? Or was she the long-suffering, tolerant goddess of her partisans?' (p. 867).

20. Christopher Highley, 'The Royal Image in Elizabethan Ireland', in Julia M. Walker, ed., *Dissing Elizabeth: Negative Representations of Gloriana* (Durham, NC: Duke University Press, 1998), pp. 60–76, p. 66.

21. See David Freedberg, *The Power of Images: Studies in the History and Theory of Response* (Chicago: University of Chicago Press, 1989), p. 414.

22. David Freedberg, 'Iconoclasts and their Motives', *Public* 8 (1993), 18–19.

23. The films could be seen to assimilate the Victorian tendency to represent Elizabeth as a woman whose domestic aberrance as a repressed spinster and whose personal suffering is the price she pays for political power and, arguably, makes her unfit for rule. See Nicola Watson's fine essay on this Victorian interpretation of Elizabeth, note 1 above.

24. On Hayward's case, see Dutton, *Mastering the Revels* and his essay 'Buggeswords: Samuel Harsnett and the Licensing, Suppression and Afterlife of Dr John Hayward's the first part of the life and reign of King Henry IV', *Criticism* 35 (1993), 305–39. See also Cyndia Susan Clegg, *Press Censorship in Elizabethan England* (Cambridge: Cambridge University Press, 1997), pp. 202–5. Clegg goes so far as to claim that there is such a thing as 'genuine "new history" free of preconceived ideology' in her essay ' "By the choise and inuitation of al the realme": *Richard II* and Elizabethan Press Censorship', *SQ* 46 (1995), 433.

25. It is retold in his *Apophthegms*. See James Spedding, ed., *Bacon's Works*, vol. 7 (1872, rpt. New York: Garret Press, 1968), p. 13.

26. See Barbara Kiefer Lewalski, 'Anne of Denmark and the Subversions of Masquing', *Criticism* 35 (1993), 341–55. A longer version of the essay may be found in her book *Writing Women in Jacobean England* (Cambridge, Mass: Harvard University Press, 1993), pp. 15–44. For other reassessments of Anne of Denmark, see also Leeds Barroll, 'Inventing the Stuart Masque', in David Bevington and Peter Holbrook, eds, *The Politics of the Stuart Masque* (Cambridge: Cambridge University Press, 1998), pp. 121–43, and, in the same volume, Stephen Orgel's very subtle and sophisticated essay 'Marginal Jonson', pp. 144–75.

27. See Cora Kaplan, 'Wild Nights', in *Sea Changes: Essays on Feminism* (London, Verso, 1989), pp. 31–56.

28. This was ironically true of many papers delivered at a conference entitled 'Gender Based Censorship' held at the University of Michigan, February 1999. The meaning of 'censorship' was broadened to include marginalization and spin-doctoring as well as outright repression. Any account of feminism the person delivering the paper had happened to dislike, especially those produced by television journalists, was regarded as an instance of patriarchal backlash.

29. See Dutton, *Mastering the Revels*. 'In short, we know virtually nothing for certain about this matter', p. 12. 'The plethora of possibilities ... make [sic] rational discussion of the subject almost impossible', p. 125.
30. Even Annabel Patterson's notion of 'functional ambiguity' isn't really polyphonic meaning but a rigid hierarchy of meanings in which one is the cover or official meaning, and the other is the true, deniable meaning, or subtext. Similarly, Richard Dutton argues in the case of Hayward's *History* that 'what the book meant (or, more correctly, how it was construed) changed radically, as a result of changing circumstances and the roles of those who actually read it. As modern reader-response theory so graphically demonstrates, hermeneutics are not static but dynamic, a fact of which censors are aware, but for practical purposes have to ignore' ('Buggeswords', p. 308). Yet Dutton faces no such problem as a critic of censorship. He confidently traces what he takes to be changes in the book's meaning by pointing to changes in the political landscape. The documents used to construct this historical background are, at least in practice, assumed to be transparent, not in need of interpretation.

Index